T0247967

A REFUGEE'S AMERICAN DREAM

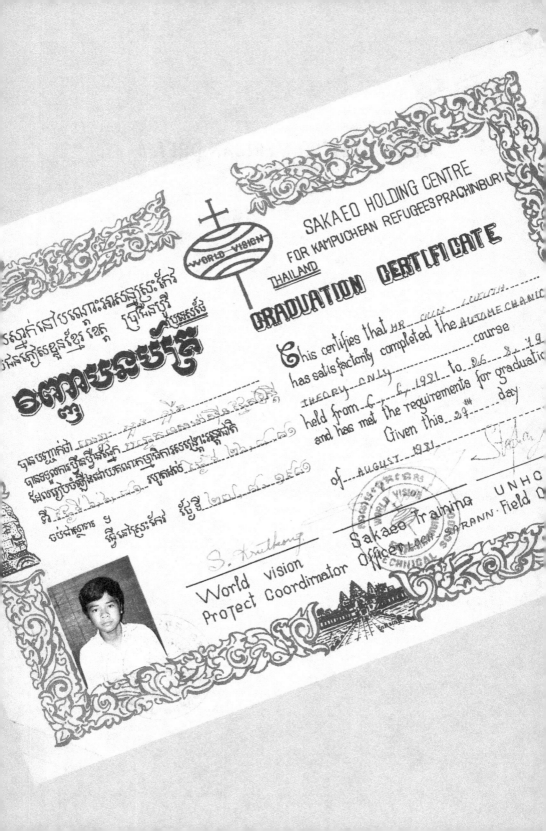

SAKAEO HOLDING CENTRE
FOR KAMPUCHEAN REFUGEES PRACHINBURI
THAILAND

GRADUATION CERTIFICATE

This certifies that MR. OUN LUCITH
has satisfactorily completed the AUTOMECHANIC course
THEORY ONLY
held from 6 - 6 - 1981 to 26 - 8 - 19
and has met the requirements for graduation
Given this 29th day
of AUGUST 1981

ឯកសារបញ្ជាក់

S. Krutkong
World vision
Project Coordinator

Sakaeo Training
Officer ____ SCARANN · Field O

UNHC

A REFUGEE'S AMERICAN DREAM

From the Killing Fields of Cambodia
to the U.S. Secret Service

LETH OUN
WITH JOE SAMUEL STARNES

TEMPLE UNIVERSITY PRESS
Philadelphia • Rome • Tokyo

TEMPLE UNIVERSITY PRESS
Philadelphia, Pennsylvania 19122
tupress.temple.edu

Design by Kate Nichols

Library of Congress Cataloging-in-Publication Data

Names: Oun, Leth, 1966– author. | Starnes, Joe Samuel, author.
Title: A refugee's American dream : from the Killing Fields of Cambodia to
  the U.S. Secret Service / Leth Oun with Joe Samuel Starnes.
Description: Philadelphia : Temple University Press, 2023. | Summary:
  "After barely surviving the horrors of the Killing Fields of Cambodia as
  a child, Leth Oun spent almost four years in refugee camps before
  immigrating to America, where he persevered to become an officer in the
  United States Secret Service"—Provided by publisher.
Identifiers: LCCN 2022029455 (print) | LCCN 2022029456 (ebook) |
  ISBN 9781439923368 (cloth) | ISBN 9781439923382 (pdf)
Subjects: LCSH: United States. Secret Service—Biography. |
  Refugees—Cambodia—Biography. | Refugees—Maryland—Biography. |
  Genocide survivors—Cambodia—Biography. | Cambodian
  Americans—Biography. | LCGFT: Personal narratives. | Autobiographies.
Classification: LCC E184.K45 O96 2023 (print) | LCC E184.K45 (ebook) |
  DDC 325/.21095960750092 [B]—dc23/eng/20220912
LC record available at https://lccn.loc.gov/2022029455
LC ebook record available at https://lccn.loc.gov/2022029456

Printed in the United States of America

9 8 7 6 5 4 3 2 1

———————

This book is dedicated to

my mother, Sin Chhoeum, and my father, Oun Seuth,

who loved me and were willing to do anything for me.

I miss them dearly, but they are with me always in my heart.

I know that every day they still look after me.

———————

Contents

PART IV: AMERICA

A REFUGEE'S AMERICAN DREAM

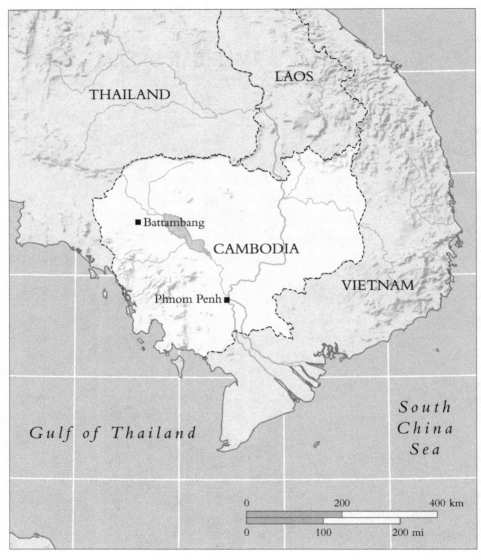

Map of Cambodia. (Nat Case, © INCase, LLC.)

Prologue

[2012]

I COULD RECOGNIZE MY PA from far away simply by watching him take a single step. He stood about five feet, seven inches tall and had short, thick black hair. He walked with his fists clenched and his elbows bent sharply as he brought his powerful arms up in time. His strides were rigid and purposeful, a gait he had learned when he was a soldier in his teens. He held his back ramrod straight and his shoulders high and kept his head very still, his dark eyes looking ahead. He had been in the army for so long that he marched everywhere. Even when not wearing his green officer's uniform, he marched. He marched when he could have relaxed.

That's what a lifetime of war does to a man.

I think of him while returning to Cambodia for the first time in thirty-two years. I have not been back to my native land since I crossed the border into a Thai refugee camp in 1980, fortunate to have survived a torturous three years, eight months, and ten days in the Khmer Rouge's Killing Fields and a year of homelessness that followed. So much has changed in my life since: I'm an American citizen, a college graduate, a father, and an officer in the U.S. Secret Service Uniformed Division.

I'm traveling to Cambodia with a contingent of fellow Secret Service officers and agents on a C-17 military cargo plane. We are going to protect President Barack Obama, the first American president to visit Cambodia. As the enormous plane, which is as big as a warehouse, carries us toward Phnom Penh, my mind is not on the history of this moment but on the memories of my heart.

My pa had enlisted in the army during World War II, when he was only sixteen, a decision that ended his school days. A French colony since 1863, Cambodia was under the control of the French Vichy government that led the nation after the Nazi invasion of France. This new wartime leadership sought to enlist as many of Cambodia's young men as possible into an expanding military. My pa was poor, like most of Cambodia's people, and needed work. When World War II ended, the French government reasserted its rule over the colony. My pa continued to serve. He had no other option.

A few years into his service, my pa was forced to take on a new assignment. French officers marched him and a group of his fellow Cambodian soldiers to a transport plane and flew them above the countryside near Phnom Penh. They sat along each side of the windowless fuselage, unable to see outside. It was the first time he had ever flown.

The Cambodian soldiers had not been told the purpose of the flight. Once in the air, the French sergeants handed out parachutes and ordered the Cambodians to strap them onto their backs. My pa and the other men put on the parachutes, watching the officers' instructions. Once they were outfitted, a tall sergeant shouted, "Count to five—then pull the cord." He gestured to the parachute strap. "That's all there is to do. Count to five and then pull."

When the sergeant opened the airplane's side hatch, humid, warm air rushed in as they flew through thick, rolling clouds. The green of the land loomed far below, and the wind roared into their faces. My pa resumed his seat and gripped the side, deciding that under no circumstances was he going to jump. He would wait until the plane touched back on the ground, and hopefully he would never have to fly again.

"Allez!" yelled the sergeant, who weighed at least fifty pounds more and stood six inches taller than most of the Cambodian infantrymen. "Allez. Line up!" The soldiers formed a line, but my pa did not move from his seat. He clenched his teeth and hung on as the French sergeant shoved the first young Cambodian soldier in line out of the open hatch and into the sky. "Allez!" the tall officer screamed, his brow furrowed and his brown mustache trembling with anger. "Allez!" The young soldier disappeared, plummeting toward the earth. My pa shivered with fear despite the warm air.

He watched as the French sergeant shoved the Cambodian soldiers, one after the other, from the airplane. Soon my pa was the last one. The sergeant looked to him and gestured to his fellow officer. They grabbed my pa by his arms and yanked him to his feet. "Allez! Allez!"

He tried to resist, but he had no chance against these much larger men. He knew that they liked to throw punches and slam rifle butts into soldiers. He had no way to escape, but fear had overtaken him. He couldn't make himself leap from the plane.

The French officers walked my pa to the open hatch and threw him out into the Cambodian sky. He fell headlong, but fortunately, although he didn't count to five, he remembered to pull the cord. (I would not be here to tell you his story if he hadn't.) His parachute unfurled, and he righted himself and drifted down feet first, his heart racing as he took in the lush landscape bisected by the Mekong River. Cambodia from the air was breathtaking, green as far as the eye could see.

It was the most beautiful sight he had ever seen.

He landed safely in a field not too far from a road. He lay there on the ground for a while and caught his breath. He took inventory of his body and realized he was not hurt. After a while, he stood, gathered up the parachute, and found his way back to the army base in Phnom Penh, walking many miles to get there by sunset. The aerial view remained vivid in his mind with every step.

I think of my pa now as I'm flying in this huge American military transport plane. What must it have been like to be forced into the sky? It strikes me that I am wearing a uniform, as he did, and I am carrying a weapon, as he did. He had wanted me to get an education, not arm myself for battle. I have gotten the education, but I am armed.

After arriving in America at the age of seventeen, I learned English, earned high school and college degrees, and completed thousands of hours of training to become an excellent marksman, explosives expert, master of self-defense, and trainer of protection dogs. I worked hard to develop and still strive to maintain and enhance my skills for the Secret Service, one of the world's most elite and highly trained law enforcement agencies. I am on the front lines of protecting America, my new home, and I am proud to do so. Although my pa did not want me to be a fighter, I believe that he would be proud of me.

After the French officers forced my pa to jump, he could have run away from the army, but instead, he embraced it. He would make many more jumps, training as a paratrooper with the expanding airborne battalion schooled by the French. In the late 1940s, he fought with French forces against the Khmer Issarak, a group of guerrillas backed by Thailand who attempted to overthrow French rule. He jumped from planes with his rifle and engaged in many gun battles.

I know his story and Cambodia's history well, as the small nation's harrowing fate has set my life's trajectory. After the country became a kingdom independent of the French in 1953, rebel groups thrived in the mountain jungles, growing their organizations and often attacking Cambodian troops. My pa fought for the Royal Cambodian Armed Forces in those battles. While Cambodia in the 1950s and 1960s was more peaceful than neighboring Vietnam, there was always some fighting, as much of the conflict spilled over the border. He rose to the rank of lieutenant, leading many platoons in battles long forgotten.

When I was born in 1966, he had more than two decades of service behind him. While the escalating battles between Cambodian troops and the growing Khmer Rouge forces hadn't reached Battambang City in northwestern Cambodia—where he lived with me, my mom, and my older sister—my pa was deployed frequently all over the country to fight. He was regularly gone for long periods of time, sometimes for weeks, other times for many months, leaving my mom to take care of us. He would go away and we never knew when he might return. We had no telephone and there was no nationwide postal service for him to send us a letter. All we could hope for was that he would show up at our door. I always looked for him, his rigid walk, hoping he would come down the dirt road that led to our simple home.

My mom, who worked as a seamstress and a roller of cigarettes, told me that one time before I was born he was away fighting in the jungles for so long she thought he was dead. She had given up hope and had resigned herself to being a widow. But then one day, he came home. Normally clean-cut, he had a long beard, shaggy hair, and a uniform covered in mud. She said he looked like a wizard. When he walked up to the door, my mom did not recognize him until he spoke. She cried, and then my pa cried. After the crying, she cooked for him. Other men in his platoon joined them to celebrate. They pooled what little money they had to buy beer, and several of his men slept on the floor of our house that night.

She was glad to have him back, but she knew, as always, he would be deployed again.

One reason for his long absences was that traveling to and from the battle sites was difficult. Being a poor country, the military had very few personnel carriers, airplanes, or helicopters to move troops. Many times when he returned home, he would have walked all or part of the journey, often hundreds of miles, journeys that took as long as a week. He would hitch rides if he could, sometimes in a farmer's cart pulled by an ox. He often would show up in the middle of the night. I would wake up and give him a hug, and my mom would light candles and fix him something to eat. We always were so relieved and glad to see him.

Once he showed up with a treat. His troops had been surrounded for weeks on the top of a mountain. When they ran out of food, a U.S. airplane in support of the Cambodian military dropped rations of beef stew. He carried those cans hundreds of miles for us. It was delicious, unlike anything I had ever eaten.

I cherished my pa's time at home, but it was always fleeting. The platoons he led were very successful, and the army needed him back at the front. He was awarded many medals for his bravery in battle over the years, including a paratrooper award. He often would show me that medal and say, "I got this one for jumping from airplanes."

To the detriment of his career, he was strong-headed and not good at internal politics. He was a man who was never afraid to say what he thought was right, even if his superiors disagreed. Many of his friends who had enlisted when he did rose to higher ranks, including some who became generals, but he never moved above the rank of lieutenant. They played politics and climbed up the ladder. He never did because of his outspokenness.

His low rank meant that he never made much money. It wasn't worth it to him if it meant pretending to be someone he wasn't. "Be who you are," he told me. "Don't be afraid to stand up for what you think is right. What's right is right. People might not like it, but be yourself."

IN 1974, when the Khmer Rouge was gaining ground across much of rural Cambodia but had not yet conquered the cities, my pa was transferred home to the army base in Battambang City to work in a managerial capacity. It was nice to have him at home and see him more often, although I sensed the war was going badly.

I enjoyed riding my bicycle to visit my pa at the army base. It was a long ride, about seven or eight miles through heavy city traffic. I was only eight, but I had been riding the small, one-speed bike for several years. The base was next to a Buddhist temple and not far from a large market. It consisted of a three-story office building where the clerks and officers worked, and four long and very old dormitory buildings that housed soldiers. When I finally arrived at the base, often coated in dust from the ride through the city, he would smile and pat me on the head and take me around the compound and introduce me to his friends. "I fought many a battle with this soldier," he would say. He also would point out soldiers he hadn't fought with, whispering about who could or could not be trusted. It was a time of much suspicion in the army, as the Khmer Rouge had spies infiltrating the Cambodian troops. My mom later said one of the soldiers in my pa's platoon turned out to be a spy for the Khmer Rouge.

ON APRIL 16, 1975, the first day after the Cambodian New Year had ended, my mom heard rumors of an invasion. We had no electricity and no radio, but she heard news by word of mouth. My pa had been at the army base for six days, and we had not heard from him. We knew he was deeply involved in the war.

As we often had been, we were on our own.

My mom didn't tell me what she knew, and I didn't ask. Much later she told me of an argument my pa had gotten into with his superior officer and the governor of Battambang province regarding the defense of the city. The governor and a higher-ranking officer had ordered him to bring a fleet of six tanks from the edge of the city into downtown and station the tanks around Battambang's city hall. They wanted to defend the government offices. My pa, however, was insistent that the tanks were needed in the peripheral areas to keep the rebel guerillas out of the city. He said if they penetrated the city, there would be no point in trying to protect only one building.

He argued with them and won. The tanks remained on the outskirts, but ultimately, it didn't matter. The Khmer Rouge troops were winning the war and had worn down the weak army supporting the troubled Cambodian government. Six tanks were not enough to hold off hordes of rebel soldiers.

Soon Khmer Rouge soldiers crowded city streets and took control of our community, banging on every door in the circle of seven small houses around a common area. It was the first time I saw the ominous uniform that became the Khmer Rouge trademark—black pajama-like outfits with red-and-white checkered scarves, known as *kramas*, and sandals made of cut rubber tires. They rode down our street in trucks and jeeps and a few tanks, hanging from the sides and back, often ten to a jeep meant to seat four passengers. Most carried AK-47s, supplied by the Chinese, and some fired machine-gun bursts into the air. Others carried rocket-propelled grenade launchers. They swarmed in packs around our house and the houses of our neighbors. My mom, my older sister Dy, and I hovered inside, our curtains pulled over the windows and door. I also had a dog, Dino, a little French bulldog, whom I held and petted as we waited. "Be very quiet," my mom said.

The Khmer Rouge soldiers were young, many of them teenagers, and a few as young as twelve. We could tell by their posture and the way they talked that they were illiterate farm boys. They were thin, their faces gaunt, as though they had been starved. Their skin was very dark from long exposure to the sun. All had a look of hatred in their eyes. Some had been fighting in the jungles for years and had endured many battles. We listened as these rebel soldiers shouted at our neighbors. Our homes were close, and we could hear everything. They were very rude, screaming at even the elderly, forgoing the traditional respect Cambodians paid to seniors.

We were frozen with fear as we heard them climb up our steps. They pulled open the curtain that served as our door. Five rifle-wielding soldiers stepped inside, looking around, crowding our one-room home. My mom had taken down a black-and-white photo of my pa in his army uniform and hidden it under her clothes. She knew they were looking for anyone who had been in the army or the police. I wrapped my arms around my dog Dino, pulling him against me.

The soldiers' faces and eyes were expressionless. One soldier, rifle hanging from his shoulder with the barrel pointing at us, stared angrily at my mom. He stepped toward her. "Are there any men here?"

"No," she said.

"Are you sure?"

"Yes. You can see. This is all we have."

"Where is your husband?"

"He went to work."

They looked around a little more, tracking dirt on our floor, glaring at me and my dog and my sister, but they didn't ask us anything else. They left to go interrogate more neighbors and search for men.

We breathed a sigh of relief, but we knew that trouble was far from over. Thoughts raced through my mind about where my pa might be and what these young rebels would do to him. I slept very little that night.

The next morning, I set out on my bicycle in search of my pa. Mom didn't want me to leave the house, but I lied and told her I would be right back, leaving Dino behind with her. He was not happy, but as always, he obeyed when I told him to stay. "Come back quickly," my mom said.

I rode my bike into the heart of the city. The streets were bustling with the rebel soldiers, their trucks, and a few tanks. The usual traffic was gone, and the market and all other businesses were closed. Many cars and trucks had been abandoned in the streets. I saw businesses that had been ransacked. Smoke rose from homes around town, and I saw the smoldering remains of a car that had exploded and burned. The smell of gasoline hung heavily in the air.

I continued through the city, making the long ride to the army base. I passed many Khmer Rouge soldiers along the way. They were going door to door in packs, brandishing their AK-47s. They didn't pay attention to me, a boy furiously riding a small bicycle.

I arrived at the army base and stood across the street from the cluster of buildings. No one was there except for a few Khmer Rouge soldiers. I was afraid to speak to the rebels, but some women and children who had come to the base to look for fathers and husbands and sons were gathered on the street. I overheard a woman say that all of the Cambodian government's soldiers were being held prisoner in the city's schools.

I immediately started riding toward the schools I knew in Battambang City, hoping I could find my pa. I had roamed with friends all over the city, scavenging for plastic and aluminum that we sold for pennies. I knew the streets well.

I began stopping at schools closest to the army base. One school was locked up and vacant, but at others I saw many men in army uniforms on the school grounds and big groups of Khmer Rouge soldiers guarding them. I could see through the windows that there was much commotion inside. I looked hard at the faces I could see, but I didn't find my pa or any of his friends. I was careful to avoid attracting the attention of the Khmer Rouge soldiers who patrolled with their AK-47s.

I rode my bike as fast as I could from school to school, hoping to find him, hoping that he was OK. I must have covered at least fifteen or twenty miles that day, driven by worry about my pa. It was hot, nearly 100 degrees Fahrenheit, but it didn't deter me. Sweaty and covered in dust, I was determined to find him.

I searched all day. By late afternoon, I was losing hope. I knew of more schools, however, and continued my trek.

Near the end of the day, I visited Salar Sor Huer, the school where I had attended first grade. My pa had made special arrangements for me to start my education early there. I had very fond memories of the place where I had started to learn, but it was no longer a school when I got there.

My old school had become a prison.

Khmer Rouge soldiers were everywhere, all in matching black uniforms and checkered red-and-white scarves and rubber sandals, each with an AK-47. I also saw many soldiers from the Cambodian government's army, sitting outside in front of the school. They were unarmed and held their heads down. I scanned the faces in the crowd, desperately searching each one until *finally*, I recognized some men from my pa's army base. They were not tied up, but the armed Khmer Rouge soldiers stood close by.

I walked up to Sreang, one of my pa's best friends, who was sitting on the ground outside. Sreang had been to our house many times. He recognized me. I had never seen anyone look so hopeless. "Have you seen my pa?" I asked.

He moved as though it pained him to raise his head. He glanced over to see if any Khmer Rouge soldiers were watching him. When he saw they weren't, he pointed toward the main door. "Inside," he said. "I think he's near the first classroom."

I knew the building's layout well. I went in the front door, walking past the Khmer Rouge soldiers who were there. They were arguing with each other, yelling and gesturing angrily with their rifles. They didn't see me—or at least they acted like they didn't see me.

I went down the hallway, stunned at what was happening to what had once been my school. This was where I had started to read and learned that two plus two equals four. I had loved my first-grade teacher, Teacher Peo, as we called him, who had instilled in me a passion for learning. But there were no teachers and students. Instead, I saw men from my pa's army base sitting dejectedly on the floor.

At the end of the hallway, across from the classroom that had been Teacher Peo's room, I found my pa.

He was in a doorway that led to the back of the schoolyard. He sat on a step, wearing green shorts and no shirt. He was leaning forward, a green handkerchief tied around his head. He held his head in his hands and was looking down at his feet.

"Pa!" I said and started to run to him.

He raised his head. As soon as he saw me, he started to cry. I had never seen him cry before.

He put his arms around me. "Sokomasath," he said, using my full birth name. "My son."

He got control of his tears. "How did you find me?"

"I heard they took all the soldiers to the schools."

"Where's your mom? Is she here?"

"No. Mom is home."

"Tell your mom not to worry. I'm OK."

I nodded. He said he was OK, but he was not convincing.

I asked, "Have you had anything to eat?"

"No. They haven't fed us anything. I do not think they will."

"Do you want me to bring you something to eat?"

"Yes, but wait until the morning," he said. "I want you to be careful and not stay too long. Do not draw the attention of these rebels."

He looked around to see if the Khmer Rouge soldiers were watching us. He said, "Remember, tell your mom I will be OK. Tell her not to worry."

I rode my bike home, arriving in the twilight. I had been gone all day and my mom was very upset. I told her I had found Pa and where he was and what he had said.

She cried but didn't say much more.

As soon as the sun rose the next day, my mom made rice soup and fried fish for him to eat. She tightly wrapped the fish and a bowl with a lid in a cloth. I carried it under one arm while steering my bike with the other.

The Khmer Rouge soldiers at the school seemed unorganized, arguing with one another. Again they ignored me. I went inside. I found him sitting in the same spot. He hugged me and thanked me for the food. He gave me a 500-riel bill. It seemed like a fortune because I had never handled paper money, but it was worth no more than an American dollar, and although we didn't yet know it, under the Khmer Rouge it would be worthless. He said to bring him something else to eat later in the day.

Again he encouraged me not to stay too long. He spoke softly. "Stay away from these young rebels. They are dangerous." He gave me a hug, patting me on the back of the head as he pulled me tight. "You should go. Be careful, my son."

I walked slowly out of the school, turning to look back at him several times as I went down the hall. He leaned forward a little, his eyes watering, and smiled warmly at me. I didn't want to leave him, but I knew I had to go.

I rode my bicycle back home, the streets not as busy in the early morning.

I gave my mom the money he had given me and told her about seeing him. She said she would make more fish and rice for him at lunchtime. I waited inside the house with my dog Dino, petting him and counting the minutes until I could go see my pa again. We could hear increasing traffic going past our house and the voices and footsteps of Khmer Rouge soldiers on the road. Occasional gunshots rang out, and we could sometimes hear distant screams. My mother forbade me from going out-side until it was time for me to deliver the food.

Shortly after noon, I returned with his meal.

I was shocked to find the school abandoned. The Khmer Rouge reb-els and the soldiers whom they had held captive were all gone.

I walked the hallway of my old school, tears pouring from my eyes. There wasn't a soul inside.

I went to the spot where my pa had been sitting.

His green army uniform and some of his clothes were laying on the floor. I considered picking them up, but I did not. Maybe he would be back. I was petrified with fear and didn't know what to do.

I lingered for a bit, crying quietly, before I got control of myself. I went outside where I saw a woman who lived across the street from the school standing in her doorway, watching me. I didn't know her name, but I had seen her before. I approached her house, walking my bike over slowly. "Excuse me," I said. "Where did the soldiers go who were here? The Cambodian soldiers?"

"The rebels took them all away in trucks."

"Where?"

"I do not know. I heard they were going to be taken to work on farms."

"Do you know where?"

"No. They said nothing."

I rode my bike home, pedaling more slowly this time.

The Khmer Rouge soldiers were everywhere that afternoon, even more than had been there the day before. I could see them with their rifles in doorways, yelling at people inside their homes.

All the residents I saw were cowering, peeking out of windows and doors. More abandoned cars and trucks were on the streets. Some homes and businesses had been trashed. I heard gunshots and people inside houses and businesses screaming and crying. It sounded like some were being shot. I kept my head down and tried to hurry on my way when I heard the rifles firing. I could hear the thump of what must have been bullets hitting flesh and bone. The smoke around the city had increased.

Many children were out wandering alone, much as I was, looking for their parents. I saw a little girl, not more than five or six, walking by herself and crying. I wanted to help her, but I had nothing to offer.

This is not right, I said to myself. *This is not right*.

I kept pedaling toward our home.

My mom saw me coming and ran out the door and down the steps to meet me when I arrived. "How is he?"

"Pa's gone," I said.

"Get inside," she said and started to cry.

I told her and my sister what the woman had said about soldiers being taken to the farms.

My mom lay down on her mat on the floor and cried for a long time.

I was upset my pa was gone, but working on a farm didn't sound so bad to me. It meant he was still alive. I thought they would keep him for a while and then they would let him come home.

But I was wrong. I didn't yet understand the murderous ways of the Khmer Rouge. I didn't know the horrors they held in store for me, my mother, and my sister.

I had seen my pa for the last time.

I DON'T SAY ANYTHING about these memories of my pa to the other Secret Service officers who are traveling to Cambodia on the C-17 with me. The Secret Service Uniformed Division has about 1,300 officers, most of whom I don't know very well. I am the only native Cambodian. We are focused on our jobs and rarely learn each other's personal details.

I have an easygoing attitude and spend many idle moments casually chatting and making small talk with my fellow officers. I often joke a lot and make my coworkers laugh, so they are surprised when they learn about this side of me. When a fellow officer learns my background, he says, "Did you live through the Killing Fields?"

"Yes," I say. "I lived through it."

"What was that like?"

"I saw many killed. I almost starved. But I escaped to refugee camps in Thailand and eventually made it to the U.S."

I tell him about washing dishes in a Chinese restaurant for $3.15 an hour in Maryland, learning English, and going to college before finding my way to the Secret Service.

He nods. "That's an amazing story." He shakes my hand.

It's not easy—no, perhaps impossible—to describe the holocaust I endured. I don't point out that approximately two million people, about a quarter of Cambodia's population at the time, were killed or died of starvation and disease under the Khmer Rouge's reign.

And I could never bring myself to tell him about seeing my pa for the last time. Nor could I tell him about the time I saw decaying bodies stacked in an open mass grave and how I searched among them for my pa's dog tags.

MY APPREHENSION BUILDS as the plane's altitude drops and we prepare to land. I have no windows, but I can picture the lush landscape, the broad and muddy rivers, the vast rice paddies, and the red dirt roads of the countryside. I can see the productive coconut tree behind our house that my grandmother had planted years before I was born. I am really going back home. The trip, including stops, has taken almost twenty-four hours. I've had much time to reflect. I hide my emotions, not showing or saying that I have anxiety about returning. I am an officer of the U.S. Secret Service. I have an important job to do. I cannot let others know my fear.

One traveling with me, however, can sense my anxiety. I cannot hide it from him behind jokes or my serious business face. He knows me too well. He is the only one who can read my mind.

My dog Reik.

He is a highly trained Belgian Malinois, a breed some mistake for a German shepherd, although the Belgian Malinois are smaller. An expert in the detection of explosives, Reik's sense of smell is a hundred thousand times stronger than a human's. I've gone through extensive training with him and give him commands in Khmer and English, making him the only protection dog in the Secret Service that is bilingual. On the C-17, he flies in a kennel, sleeping for much of the flight. When he wakes, I pet him on the head. *"Angkouy.* Sit," I say. *"Chhke da la-or.* Good dog."

Reik and I have traveled to forty-nine states and more than a dozen countries. Once when we were traveling overseas with a vice president, Reik and I alerted the local police to a suspicious backpack. I can't give you more details due to the top-secret nature of my position, but we might have helped avert a terrorist bombing that could have had global implications. It could have been a worldwide news story, but we prevented the possibility. We are good at what we do.

Reik knows me as well as anyone and can sense that I have much on my mind as the C-17 descends. He looks in my eyes, and he *knows.*

He can smell my emotions, the memories I have, and my fear about returning.

I pet Reik on the head and I think about my first dog, Dino. I remember seeing Dino open his eyes for the first time and look at me when I was seven years old. A French bulldog with an expressive black-and-white face, he always looked at me with love and warmth. When Dino was killed a few years later, I was struggling to stay alive in the Killing Fields.

I clung to Dino and cherished his love. He was the last strand of my normal life before the Khmer Rouge took everything away.

I thought I would never recover from Dino's death.

But I did recover.

I've recovered from so much it is hard even for me to imagine.

Although I don't discuss my past with my coworkers, I have tried to tell some of my American friends and my American-born children about what I went through in the Killing Fields, but it feels impossible to convey the agony through which we lived, the fear and the hunger and pain and terror. I didn't have a stable home for eight years, from the age of nine until I was seventeen. When we were on the run in the jungle, I sometimes slept standing up because of monsoon flooding. I was always hungry and resorted to hunting and eating rats to survive, much at the risk of being shot and killed for doing so. I ate bugs and leaves and almost anything I could find that was digestible, and some things that weren't, which made me very sick. I almost starved to death. At my first physical examination after coming to the United States in 1983, I weighed eighty-nine pounds. Today, I weigh 175 pounds and can bench-press almost three hundred pounds.

This life I live now in the Washington, D.C., suburbs and working for the Secret Service includes walking the floors and patrolling the grounds of the White House, protecting the president and all the office stands for. I am living my American dream.

I have not, however, forgotten the misery of the Killing Fields. It happened not that long ago in a country many Americans cannot find on a map. I want to share these hard memories that I have carried with me all my life, but I also want to tell of the new life I have found. I am not writing this book to make money, but if it does, all proceeds will go to help families in Cambodia. I have established a fund to help those in need in my native land. I am where I am because people helped me. I want to give back.

I also want to tell you of my return home. Although I work hard while I am in Cambodia with President Obama, I find time after my shifts to reunite with long-lost family, including some of whom I thought had been dead for decades. And I remember those who are gone.

There are so many.

THE C-17 TOUCHES DOWN shortly after noon in Phnom Penh. My heart is thumping as I take Reik from his kennel and the hatch on the plane opens and we begin to disembark. I'm stepping out under a Cambodian sky for the first time in more than three decades. The sunlight is bright and it's hot, as it almost always is in Cambodia. I look out and see palm trees and the skyline of the city. It's dusty and humid, and it smells.

I smile. *This is Cambodia!*

I look around, and for a moment I forget what year it is. I don't move, but a wave of fear sweeps over me. *Is anybody going to shoot at me now?*

The memory is overwhelming: I am a child shortly before the Khmer Rouge wins the civil war, before they take my pa away. I am playing with other kids, all of us without shirts and shoes. There is a war going on, but we enjoy ourselves in spite of it. We swim gleefully in the warm Sangke River and run in the fields and make up games of hockey in the mud with bamboo sticks. We stop when we hear bombs and gunshots. When the fighting is nearby, we lie face-down on the ground until the explosions and gunfire fade. We always resume our games, until the Khmer Rouge takes over in April 1975 and all games stop.

This memory is so strong for me, it's as if I have gone back in time. After a moment, I realize that this is not the seventies. The war is over. The Killing Fields are just a memory. My pa is long gone, yet he is with me on every step of this trip.

My eyes begin to water, but I don't have time to cry. I have to make sure the president and his staff will be safe when they arrive.

Duty always comes first. It did for my pa, and it does for me now.

I make eye contact with Reik. He knows that we have a job to do, and we will do it well. Failure, as we often say in the Secret Service, is not an option.

We are here to protect the president.

PART I

CHILDHOOD IN CAMBODIA

Happy Hearts

[1966–1973]

I WAS BORN IN THE RAIN. The day of my birth was a Friday in October 1966, the heart of monsoon season. Our one-room house where a midwife delivered me sat four feet off the ground, a traditional Cambodian construction designed to stay above the frequent floodwaters. It was built from cheap wood and the roof was sheet metal. When the sun beat down, the roof generated even more heat. We did not have electricity or running water. Sometimes the roof leaked, as it did on the day I was born.

In the Cambodian tradition of basing one's name on the day and month when you were born, my parents named me Sokomasath: *Sok* in Khmer means "Friday," *Koma* means "child," and *Sath* indicates a rainy month. My name Leth would not come until many years later.

Our house did not have a door but simply a curtain, and we didn't have glass in the windows. My mom cooked on a wood-fired, clay stove on a side porch of the house. My parents and my older sister slept on the floor, using blankets and pieces of cloth my mom stitched together for padding. When I was big enough to move from my mom's side, they put me to sleep in a hammock hung from the rafters.

My pa, Oun Seuth, who was ten years younger than my mother, often was away on deployments with the army, as he was when I was born. My mother, Sin Chhoeum, was a seamstress who worked on a sewing machine she kept in our home. My mom also rolled tobacco when there wasn't enough work as a seamstress. I remember regular pickups of clothes and cigarettes at our house. Although both of my parents were employed and had basic educations, we were still very poor.

My mom, who had suffered many miscarriages over the years, was in her late forties when I came along. Although I arrived later in her life, I filled a place of honor in our family: the first boy. I had only one sibling before me, my sister Dy, who was nine years old when I was born.

Our town, Battambang City, the capital of the province of the same name in northwestern Cambodia, was about seventy miles east of Thailand and north of the Cardamom Mountains. Although it is the country's second-largest city, it had only about one hundred thousand people, much smaller than Phnom Penh, about 180 miles to the south.

Our home was one of seven built in a circle, all simple constructions like our house. We knew our neighbors well and in many cases were related. We socialized in the common space between the houses, and the men built fires during the dry season when the weather cooled. I remember my parents sitting and talking with friends late into the night. On special occasions, such as the Cambodian New Year, much food would be shared and many traditional folk songs would be sung.

We also stuck together when it flooded. During the monsoon season, water stayed under the houses for months. There was no drainage system and there were no sidewalks. Everywhere you walked was mud.

None of the homes had an outhouse. To relieve yourself, you had to walk a short distance down the road to a spot behind dense trees. You always had to watch closely where you stepped. Because they wanted privacy, most girls and women waited until after dark to go.

Everyone looked out for each other. When one family had an abundance of food or a special fruit, they shared it. I often climbed the tall coconut tree behind our house to knock loose coconuts that we gave to our neighbors. My mom would often remind me, "Your late grandmother Proeung planted this tree."

Although we were poor, we had something valuable in this close-knit community: We had much love for one another. We didn't have many material possessions, but we had happy hearts.

WITHOUT A LOT OF LOVE AROUND ME, I might not have survived my first few years on this Earth. At ages two and three, I was often sick and was very skinny, almost wasting away. There were many times when I could not sit up or eat. There is a Khmer phrase that I do not know how to easily translate—the best I can interpret the sound into English is *Koun ar rerse*, which means "a child is finding it hard to be alive." Many nights my family didn't think I would to live to see the morning.

They didn't know what ailed me. Our home had mosquito nets, but I could have had malaria. I was fortunate my mother had two neighbors who helped her care for me. I call them "my other mothers."

One was my mother's friend Ath Yonn. Yonn came to our house daily to help my mom feed, bathe, and take care of me while I was sick, and my mother worked to earn what little living she could eke out on her sewing machine or by rolling cigarettes. If my mom didn't work, we wouldn't eat. So she worked and Yonn helped out.

Day and night, when I cried, Yonn would come. She fed me, cleaned me, and carried me around until I fell asleep. Then she would lay me in my homemade hammock and watch me to make sure I slept well.

When Yonn was not home, Oum Sakum would step in to help. Sakum was my mother's aunt who lived next door, and she loved me just as much as she loved her own children. Sometimes she gave my mother money when we needed it, and often she did not want my mom to pay it back.

My three mothers often sold belongings to raise money for my medical visits and medicine. They also listened to anyone who would offer advice to heal whatever ailed me. When someone told them that a bath in beer would help me heal, that's what they did. They pooled all of their resources and spent everything they had to buy several bottles. They poured the beer over me in a tub and washed me and let me soak in the golden bubbles of Cambodian lager.

It was just one of many folk myths that they believed. Anything that might save me, they would try. Although I am doubtful that a bath in beer helped me, I know for sure that my three mothers working together with love and care saved my life. They are why I am here today.

AS I GREW OLDER, my health grew stronger. By the age of four, I was out and about, playing and running around with other children. All the running around I did, I did barefoot. Shoes and boots were not practical, as the water was too high and would get inside and soak your feet. Most families could not afford sneakers or boots anyway. We were too poor even for flip-flops, which would just get stuck in the mud. The skin on our feet toughened up and was immune to the dry heat and the moisture. We walked many miles barefoot and thought nothing of it.

One place we walked to every day was the Sangke River. Our lives revolved around it. My mother washed everything by hand there. The muddy water was neither clear nor clean, but there was no other way.

The river is also where we bathed. After the sun set, my mother and sister and I would join people in the community who gathered to go to the river. We waited until darkness because there was no shelter for privacy where women could change their clothes.

Even though the river was home to pythons and king cobras and sometimes crocodiles, we were not afraid, although we were always watchful. I didn't worry too much about the deadly creatures, but instead always enjoyed the happy sounds of the children and adults chatting and laughing. I spent many hours of my childhood swimming and splashing with other little boys.

In many ways, the river gave us life. In fact, if it wasn't for the river, I might not have been born. It is where my mother and father saw each other for the first time. It was sometime in the late forties or early fifties. My pa was in his early twenties, and my mom a decade older.

They hadn't known each other when they were younger. My mom was born in Battambang City, where she grew up, but my pa was born in Phnom Penh. The army brought him to Battambang City.

They crossed paths when my mom went to the river one evening with her friends and family while my pa was there with his friends. My mom went far upstream to get away from the men. My pa, who was downstream, looked upstream and saw her. "Who is that who bathes above me?" he said to one of his friends. "I'm going to marry her."

He followed her home to see where she lived and find out who she was. He eventually asked my mom's mother for permission to marry her daughter. My grandmother said yes, so my mom had no choice in the matter. She couldn't refuse.

Less than a year after my pa first saw my mom, they married. All they could afford was a small ceremony with just a few family and friends. At first, my mom said, she didn't like my pa, but after they lived together a while, they grew to love one another.

I'm glad they did. More than fifteen years later, they made me.

WHEN I WAS ABOUT FIVE YEARS OLD, my world changed. My pa gave me a bicycle!

He put me up on the seat, but I was so small that my feet didn't reach the pedals. I stood on the pedals and he gave me a push down the dirt road by our house. I fell, but I got up. He put me back on it again. I fell again and again, but I kept getting back up. Pretty soon I got the hang of it and was riding everywhere.

I thought having a bicycle was the greatest thing a boy could have. It seemed to me as if I owned a fancy car.

THAT SAME YEAR my pa took me on a very exciting trip. We flew from Battambang City to Phnom Penh on a commercial flight, and he showed me the big city where he had grown up. Flying was amazing to my young eyes, and Phnom Penh was enormous and glamorous compared to my hometown. It was definitely worthy of its nickname "the Pearl of Asia."

When we returned home, we flew in a small military plane, a French T-28. It was a model built for combat dating back to World War II, a propeller plane that seated only five people in a cramped space. The army plane was very noisy, with an almost deafening roar from the engines. We flew low and I could see everything on the ground. It was like a movie to my young eyes.

OUR HOME IN BATTAMBANG CITY was near the big Psar Krom market, only about a quarter of a mile away. My mom often took me with her on daily shopping trips. Everyone rubbed shoulders there. There were endless stalls with food and clothes and jewelry. I loved the thrill of walking through the bustling crowd.

My favorite thing when we could afford it was a *teak ka lok*. The vendor mixed crushed ice and condensed milk and every kind of fruit you can imagine: bananas, papaya, and mango, but also lychee fruit, purple mangosteens, custard apples, and rambutans. I loved coconut in mine too. When the temperature was hot, as it was most of the year, I relished the refreshing cold and the calm feeling a *teak ka lok* gave me.

I also loved seeing the stalls that were run by people who grew fruit and vegetables in their backyard and picked it that day to sell. I remember broccoli, watercress, and banana blossoms. Of course, you could buy rice at the market, being that it was the biggest agricultural product in Cambodia and the main staple of our diet. Battambang Province is known as the "rice bowl" because its land is so well suited for growing rice. It also was the cheapest food we could buy and what we ate the most often. Seafood was plentiful, and catfish were common, and there were also many snakehead fish, monkfish, and eels. I remember watching wide-eyed as fish in huge tanks thrashed about. When we could afford it, my mom would buy pork or beef for dinner. When she cooked it, she'd catch all the grease in a jar under the stove and save it. When we couldn't afford meat, she would get out the jar and mix the grease with rice so we'd at least get a taste of it.

When I grew older and went to school, I often walked through the market by myself. I usually did not stop to look closely because I rarely had any money. I didn't want to get too excited about something I could not afford. Occasionally, my mother would give me a coin—the equivalent of a penny in Cambodian money, even though its value was worth much less than one American cent. When I had one, I would stop at one of the vendors to buy the only dessert I could afford: the syrupy mixture of black beans, coconut milk, and sugar called *sgnor sarn dek khmao*. I would buy a very small cup to take home. "Mom, I brought some *sgnor sarn dek khmao* for us," I'd say.

She would take a small bite and give it back. "Thank you for sharing with me," she'd say. "But I want you to have it."

BECAUSE MY MOM had suffered many miscarriages, my sister Dy and I were the only two kids. My other mother Sakum, in comparison, had given birth to six, which was common for most neighboring families. Perhaps this dynamic is why Dy and I developed a rivalry and childhood jealousy of one another. We were not close. I also think much of our distance from one another is due to Cambodia's patriarchal culture. Boys were celebrated because we would carry on the family name, while girls would be married off and move away to live with their new husbands. Dy spent much time in the house cooking and cleaning and helping my mom with other chores. As she grew into her teenage years, my parents worried that she would attract men. They strictly limited how much she could go out on her own. While I could go play in the river anytime I wanted, my parents made Dy wait until it was dark. They required her to keep herself covered in a long-sleeved shirt. She had a bicycle of her own, but my mom kept close tabs on her and didn't let her ride it far away.

EVERY SEVEN DAYS, my mom would take me to the Buddhist temple. I hated it. I couldn't just sit there and listen to monks chanting the whole time. We would give food to the monks and listen to them preach. I was always fidgeting. I would ask my mom if I could go outside and play with other kids. "No. You should listen to this," she said. "They are telling you about what you should do. How you should be nice to other people."

After a while, my mom usually would let me go outside and play. My sister Dy, however, didn't go to the temple with us very often, probably because she was not allowed to go outside and play as I was.

My grandfather on my mother's side, Sin Soeuth, was a leader in Wat Kampong Sey Mar, a Buddhist temple outside Battambang City, about two hours away by bicycle. I often would ride my bike to see him. He was an *achar*, a lay person in charge at the temple, second to the chief monk.

Although I didn't pay close attention to its teachings, Buddhism was always in my life as a child. Many of the lessons sank in over time in spite of my restlessness. I realize now that it had a major influence on me, and I still practice my Buddhist faith. I learned young that if you do something to somebody, either good or bad, you will get those same results in return. That is karma. That belief has stuck with me throughout my life. If you always do good to people, and even if a particular person isn't good to you in return, someone will be good to you.

OFTEN CHILDREN in my neighborhood would stay home and help their families make money any way they could, forgoing learning how to read and write and do mathematics. Some went through only the first few grades before they started helping their families in shops, fixing bicycles, or selling fruit and vegetables in the market. They were destined for lives of hard, physical work just to survive. But in my family, education was important to both of my parents, especially my pa, who had left high school to join the army. He always regretted not being able to continue his education. "Don't be like me," he said. "You don't have to put your life on the line. You don't have to carry a gun. Get an education. You can do better by being a doctor or somebody who uses your brain."

He insisted I go to school. He knew a teacher, whom everyone called Teacher Peo, in the school for girls, Salar Sor Huer. Boys and girls were sent to separate schools, but each school had a few students of the opposite gender. The girls' school and the boys' school, Much Chhim Salar, were next to each other, near the river.

My pa got permission from Teacher Peo to send me to the girls' school because I was only six years old, and the schools normally would not accept anyone under seven. A few other boys were there, but it was mostly girls.

On my first day my mother walked with me, about half an hour from our house. She had dressed me in the requisite school uniform of a white shirt and khaki pants. We found Teacher Peo outside the school where students were lining up. She presented me to him. "This is my son, Sokomasath."

"Yes," he said. "His father has told me about him."

I didn't say anything.

"Thank you for educating him," my mom said. "He is in your charge. Just leave me the bones."

More than fifty years later, I can still hear her say, "Just leave me the bones." It was her warning to me that I must behave. That was no problem. I was terrified to do otherwise.

I began the routine of going to school six days a week, Monday through Saturday. Classes started at seven in the morning and stopped for lunch at 11:30. School resumed at two and continued until 5:30. Teacher Peo taught every subject. I learned much from him, including the Khmer alphabet, how to read and write, and math. He was a big influence on me. "Education is your life," he said. "Work hard on it. Put time to it. You'll go somewhere."

Once I got used to going, I walked to school by myself. After my first year, I began attending the boys' school. The amount of homework I was given increased and included memorizing lessons of mathematics, science, and literature. I learned much in my first few years of school, thanks in large part because of the great start that Teacher Peo gave to me.

IT WAS ALWAYS A RACE for me to get to school on time in the morning before the national anthem started playing in the streets of Battambang City. Most in the city were very patriotic, as was my family, especially because my pa was in the army. The rule was that when the anthem was broadcast, everyone had to stop and stand where they were while the Cambodian flag was raised. Even the traffic in the streets had to stop until the song ended.

The anthem played precisely at seven, the same time that school began. I was running late one day when I heard the opening notes blasting from a loudspeaker near the market. I knew the students were lined up outside the school and that my teacher was looking for me, so I picked up my pace.

A police officer saw me running. He stepped into my path. "What are you doing?" he yelled at me, raising his black baton.

"I'm trying to get to school."

He gave me a hard smack on my back with his baton. It hurt. "You can't do that. You have to stay still until it's done."

"I'll be late."

He gave me another smack with the baton. It hurt more than the first. "Don't move," he said. "Get started earlier next time."

I waited until the anthem ended and the last notes faded out. Then I took off.

My teacher was ready for me at the front of the classroom. "You are late!" he said. "Five minutes late. Five lashes!" He made me lean over a table in the front of the room, and with my classmates looking on, he gave me five whacks with a bamboo stick. Those also hurt, especially the ones that landed where the police officer had hit me with his baton.

I made sure to be on time after that.

WHEN I CAME HOME from school, sometimes I helped my mother cook rice, but most of the time my sister Dy did the cooking. I dropped my books and ran outside to play with other children. One of our favorite things to do was to play hockey with a bamboo stick and a hard piece of bamboo for the puck. We dug a hole in the ground that served as the goal. The game was very similar to ice hockey, but there was no protection for our bodies. If the bamboo stick hit us, that was part of the game. Many times I came home covered with bruises. My mother thought I had been fighting, but I assured her that was not the case.

Other times we played soccer. All we had was a ragged old soccer ball. There were no shin guards and no soccer shoes. We played barefoot and we played hard.

I also enjoyed martial arts. It was very popular with boys in Cambodia—similar to how baseball is in America. A distant relative on my mother's side of the family, whom we considered an uncle, taught boys in my school the techniques. We practiced Bokator, the traditional Cambodian martial art that is very similar to Muay Thai. He often would take us to citywide competitions to earn belts. I started at the age of five and became very good at the moves, which I practiced regularly. We didn't have any equipment, so I used a banana tree for a punching bag.

Another pastime I loved was to go with my friends to catch the brilliantly colored fighting fish. The fish were small, about finger-sized, and multicolored. I would see these tropical fish in the market for sale and watched them fight in glass bottles. I thought they were beautiful with their intense mixes of red, pink, blue, and purple. We caught them in the rice paddy ponds not far from our house. It was a great competition among the boys to see who could catch the most and the best fish. It wasn't easy catching those little fish by hand, but we often did. The only tool we had was a handheld fish trap made of bamboo in the shape of a tray.

I often waded in the shallow, muddy water, looking intently for little bubbles that indicated a fish's presence. When I would see a bubble, I'd take the tray and scoop underneath it. You had to be fast to catch the fish, and I was. I caught lots of beautiful little fish and took them home in a plastic bag or a bottle to show off to my friends. My mom didn't like me catching fighting fish because she said it was dangerous. We heard about kids who drowned. And there were the pythons and crocodiles and king cobras to worry about. But I did it anyway.

I was hardheaded as a child, and occasionally I would disobey my mom. One day I came home from school and she told me not to go anywhere. Only a few minutes went by before I snuck out with my friends to catch fighting fish. She looked for me, but I was nowhere to be seen. Sometimes she sent my sister Dy to look for me. Other times she looked for me herself.

She always found me, and that's when I got my punishment, which was a hard spanking with a bamboo stick. Looking back, I know I deserved it. Of course, I would go on to do it again and get punished again. Was I afraid of being hit by my mother? Yes, but I was a boy who couldn't resist the urge to play, especially the thrill of catching the best fighting fish.

WHEN I WAS SEVEN YEARS OLD, I tried to help my family by scavenging. Anything plastic or aluminum had some value. My friends and I went everywhere in the city, often crawling into muddy filth under houses when we saw discarded trash. Many times we raced one another to get it. My mother didn't like it. She worried it distracted me from school, and she knew my pa would not approve. But I continued doing it. I enjoyed the chase, just like catching the fighting fish. I sold what I found to an old Chinese man who came around with a wagon. He didn't pay much, but it was something. I always gave the coins to my mom, and she appreciated the extra money. We needed it just to survive.

One day my mom splurged at the market and bought me a gold ring that she said was a reward for bringing home money and for doing well in school. "Here," she said, handing me the ring. "I want you to have this. You have been a very good boy. You work hard and you deserve it."

I was amazed. I put it on my left hand. It was small, but I had never owned any jewelry before. "Are you sure?" I said.

"Yes, I want you to have it."

I smiled, holding my hand up to admire the ring's design. It featured a dragon, a Cambodian symbol of toughness and power. It made me feel strong. I loved it.

The next day I went to the river to play with my friends. After swimming and splashing for a while, I looked down at my finger.

The ring was gone.

I felt terrible. I asked my friends to help me search for it. We looked everywhere, but in the broad, muddy river, there was almost no chance of finding it. I dug around on the riverbank but had no luck.

I was afraid to go home. I felt so bad for my mom, losing this gift she had given me with pride. It was rare that we could afford such a thing, and here I had lost it after only two days. I felt sick.

I walked home with my head hanging low. I did not tell my mother the bad news right away. I wanted to hide the truth, but I knew it would come out. I waited several hours before I got the courage to tell her what had happened. "I lost your ring," I said, looking at my feet.

"*What?*"

I told her again, and she promptly gave me a spanking with bamboo. It was always bamboo back then.

It hurt, and I cried. I did not blame her. She grounded me. Each day after school I asked her if I could go to the river, but the answer was a simple "No." It was many weeks before she let me play with my friends again.

ONE AFTERNOON about a month or two later, I arrived home covered in mud from scavenging to find that my pa had returned from the battle-fields. He asked my mom what had happened to me. Before she could answer, I said I had been trash picking. I told him Mom didn't allow me to, but that it was something I could do to help. He was very upset with both of us. He told my mom not to let me do it again. He said it was unsafe and disgraceful to our family if any of his friends saw me.

My mom agreed and forbade me from scavenging.

After my pa left again, I did it a few more times, but when my mom caught me, she got angrier than I had ever seen her before. She hit me with a bamboo stick the hardest I had ever felt. I decided then that my scavenging days were over.

I SOON HAD ONE of the best surprises of my life. A distant relative of my mother came by with a basket of puppies and asked my mom if I could have one. This relative owned a French bulldog that had given birth to a litter, but the mother dog had died and they couldn't care for all the puppies.

"Do you want one?" my mom asked.

I peered into the basket with the little black-and-white pups curled up together sleeping. "Yes!" I said.

I was lucky, as few in our community kept dogs. Most of us had a hard time feeding ourselves, so another mouth to feed was something many families could not afford.

I chose a tiny pup, only a few weeks old. He had a cute black-and-white pattern on his face and a mostly black body. His eyes were just beginning to open. I picked him up and held him. He had little ears, like a bat, and a pug nose and wrinkly flat face. I fed him condensed milk and hot water and cared for him like he was my baby.

I named him Dino. I had learned the name from old movies that I had seen at a wealthier neighbor's house. That family lived about ten minutes from us and occasionally would set up a movie projector outside to show old films for the neighborhood kids. We loved Charlie Chaplin, and we laughed uproariously, even though we couldn't read the subtitles that were in French. Because we didn't have a TV, it was a treat to see moving pictures of any kind, even if it was silent films. I don't remember in which movie I learned the name Dino, but when I saw my little dog for the first time, I knew the name fit.

When Dino was about six weeks old and his eyes were fully open, I began feeding him human food. Every time we ate, he ate what we ate. I put his food—usually rice mixed with fish or pork, condensed milk, and hot water—on a small plate for him. He always slept in the house, curled up next to me on the floor.

As he grew older, he went almost everywhere I went, running by my side if I was on my bicycle. He was like my little brother, but he was better behaved than a human child. I never needed a leash for him—not in his entire life.

I even took him to the movies with me. The theater in Battambang City was enormous, with hundreds of seats in the old-style movie palace. It was cheap, only two coins to get in, but I still couldn't afford to go very often, maybe only about once every two months. The theater played Cambodian and Chinese movies, including westerns, romances, and martial arts films. My favorites were the martial arts movies. I was amazed by the fantastic fight scenes, the action, and the heroes who did incredible things.

Fortunately, the theater staff did not mind my dog. Dino, who stood about a foot tall at his shoulder and weighed only about twenty pounds, would sit on the seat next to me. He knew better than to bark. He watched the movie as though he could understand the story and follow what was happening. He was not only a sweet, loving dog, but he was very smart. He understood some of what he saw. After we left the theater, we would walk home and I would talk to him about the movie, telling him my favorite parts. He would look up at me, nodding in agreement.

About the only time Dino and I were apart was when I went to school. Every day when I came home, he was waiting for me in front of our house. He knew when I would arrive and never missed a day. He would be so happy to see me that he would jump up and down and bark happily. I would pick him up and hug him, and he would lick my face. I loved that dog as much as anything, and I know he felt the same about me.

We had a good thing, Dino and I, with our happy hearts and love for one another. It would not, however, last much longer.

Before the Darkness

[1974–APRIL 1975]

I WAS A TODDLER and too young to remember it, but my mother told me about a time when she and my father took me to Angkor Wat, the towering architectural wonder that is the largest religious temple in the world. Our home in Battambang City was about one hundred miles from the temple that was the center of the ancient Angkorean empire, also known as the Khmer empire, which included all of present-day Cambodia and much of Thailand and Vietnam. Built in the twelfth century, first as a Hindu temple, Angkor Wat eventually became a Buddhist temple. Although the Khmer empire faded in the fifteenth century, the vast beauty of Angkor Wat and its lost empire remains a national symbol and source of pride for me and my family, as it does for many Cambodians. While my mom was admiring the temple and paying her respects, I snuck away and found a hole with bat poop and smeared it in my eyes. I started crying, and she worried that I had hurt myself. I was OK, but I had distracted her and made it hard for her to enjoy the visit to this landmark that had so much meaning for us.

My native country, sandwiched as it is between two larger and more powerful nations, often has been at risk. Thailand, known as Siam until 1939, lies to the west, and Vietnam lies to the east. Both have long been combative rivals. Battambang Province was under the rule of Siam and later Thailand for various periods. In 1863, the French occupied Cambodia, much as they had Vietnam, and stayed for ninety years.

My parents had greatly admired Prince Norodom Sihanouk, the most powerful figure in Cambodian politics from the early 1950s through 1970. He was a member of the royal family and served at different times as king, prince, and prime minister. When King Monivong, his grandfather, died in 1941, the French chose Sihanouk to be king when he was only eighteen years old. They selected the young prince over older royal family members, including his own father, because they wanted a puppet. They thought he would be easier to manage than a more experienced ruler.

Many Cambodians, my parents included, believed he had been sent down by the gods to save the country. His divinity was a myth the French encouraged as a way of controlling the population, most of whom were uneducated. My mom told me that when Sihanouk went to China, he learned how to speak Chinese while he was on the airplane. I didn't challenge what my parents told me about him, but I was suspicious. I had respect for Prince Sihanouk's power, but I didn't believe he was all that they said.

He definitely was a smart and wily politician. He was instrumental as king in negotiating independence from France in 1953. Once free of French control, in 1955 Sihanouk abdicated his throne and appointed his father king. He ran for head of state as Prince Sihanouk under the People's Socialist Community, a political party he founded. He won the election and ran the country with one-party rule for the next fifteen years.

For years he tried to position Cambodia internationally as a neutral state, loyal to neither the communist powers of China, which he visited often, or the Soviet Union, which backed the North Vietnamese. He also tried to keep at arm's length the United States and Western powers, which were trying to stop the spread of communism. This worked for a while. While Cambodia in the 1950s and 1960s was not as war-torn as Vietnam, much of the conflict between North Vietnam and South Vietnam spilled over the border into the eastern part of our country.

The Khmer Rouge had its origins in the 1960s as the militarized wing of the Communist Party of Kampuchea. In 1962, Pol Pot became the party's leader. Based in mountainous jungles in the northeast of the country, the group had little impact at first.

In 1970, General Lon Nol, Sihanouk's cousin, led a coup while Sihanouk was in China. He believed his cousin Sihanouk eventually would
turn the country toward communism. Lon Nol took control of the
government, assumed the position of prime minister, and changed the
country's name from the Kingdom of Cambodia to the Khmer Republic. This prompted the Khmer Rouge, which had the support of China,
to escalate its civil war against Lon Nol's government, which had gained
the backing of the United States.

In its failed efforts to win the Vietnam War and to support Lon Nol's
government, the United States added fuel to the fire that unintention-
ally aided the Khmer Rouge. During an eight-year period starting in
1965 under President Lyndon Johnson and escalated by President Richard
Nixon, American B-52 planes heavily bombed the Cambodian countryside, hoping to destroy hideouts and supply lines used by the North
Vietnamese army and the Viet Cong, but also in support of Lon Nol's
government's defense against the Khmer Rouge. Reports are that more
than 2.7 million tons of bombs were dropped. Conservative estimates are
that between 50,000 and 150,000 Cambodian civilians were killed before
Congress halted the bombing in 1973. Those air attacks emboldened the
Khmer Rouge, helping them recruit peasant villagers who were victims
of the bombs.

The U.S. military campaign was limited and ineffective, as the
Americans didn't send ground troops into Cambodia to back up the air
attacks. This was a time when the United States was losing the war in
Vietnam and was looking to extricate itself from a conflict in Southeast
Asia that had become very unpopular at home.

After he was ousted in 1970, Sihanouk threw his support to the
Khmer Rouge in an attempt to regain power. He was, however, out-
smarted by Pol Pot. Even though he was the leader, Pol Pot was un-
known to us and most Cambodians at that time. He stayed in the background and used the prince's name to get people to support the Khmer
Rouge. Many Cambodians were on the side of the prince and joined
the Communist Party because they thought he supported it. They wor-
shiped Sihanouk and believed he was the person they should trust.

The long-suffering plight of the peasants was a major factor in the
rise of the Khmer Rouge. The Khmer Rouge focused their recruiting
efforts on the rural villagers, spreading their propaganda to peasants

who were very poor and uneducated and believed that the country was hopelessly corrupt. When the Khmer Rouge told them the government was oppressing them, they believed it. Many of the villagers also had been subjected to years of bombing by U.S. warplanes that were targeting Cambodia. They were desperate and fed up. They had nowhere else to turn, and no one else was reaching out to them. The Khmer Rouge's communist promises of a perfect society, combined with Prince Sihanouk's stamp of approval, was not only appealing—it was their only option.

Although many in the rural areas turned against Lon Nol's Khmer Republic and supported the Khmer Rouge rebels, my father and mother, as most did in the cities, remained loyal to the recognized Cambodian government. The civil war shaped up as a conflict between educated people in the cities who supported the government and uneducated peasants in the villages who sided with the Khmer Rouge. My father stood with Lon Nol's administration and fought many battles against the Khmer Rouge soldiers. Most of the battles of the early years of the civil war were fought in eastern Cambodia, near the Vietnamese border, and far away from our home. About the time I turned seven in late 1973, however, the war began to become more audible and visible to me.

The fighting hadn't penetrated Battambang City, but those who lived in the rural areas surrounding the city were facing bombardment from both sides. Sometimes in the middle of the night, we would hear distant explosions and feel the ground shaking. We occasionally would see distant fire in the night sky. In spite of this, my family's routines did not change. I continued attending school and going to the river and playing with my friends.

By 1974, the war had intensified and started to have more impact on the city. I saw Cambodian soldiers in the streets, carrying rifles and grenade launchers, and I remember seeing special forces units in black uniforms emblazoned with a skull and crossbones. They had hard faces and were known for brutal fighting, the looks in their eyes saying, *I don't know if I'm going to die tomorrow, and I don't care.*

In addition to more soldiers in the streets, Battambang City swelled with many refugees from rural areas who came to the city to seek shelter from battles and bombings. I saw more beggars and people living in the streets than I had in the past. Estimates are that the city's population more than doubled, growing to as many as 250,000.

As THESE CHANGES were happening in the city, I realized that my mom, even though she was in her fifties, was pregnant. She didn't say anything about the pregnancy to me, but I could see that she was as the delivery date became close. With the war looming and the uncertainty of the future, it was not a good time. Many women died during childbirth in Cambodia, and I know my mom worried about the medical complications of having a baby at that age. She had suffered through many miscarriages, and I'm sure she worried about another one. She said nothing to me, as pregnancy wasn't something that was discussed with a child. In those difficult circumstances, it was not something to celebrate. She continued to work at home while she was pregnant, making dresses and rolling cigarettes all while looking after me and my older sister Dy, who was well into her teens.

On a rainy day, late one afternoon in the spring of 1974, she went into labor. She had enlisted the help of a local midwife who arrived and made me leave the house. "Close this," the midwife said, gesturing to the curtain that covered our door. "And wait outside. Don't come inside until you hear the baby crying. And then, ask permission."

I waited on the steps under the eaves so I would stay dry. I didn't hear anything from my mom. She was not the kind to scream during labor, even though she had no medicine to soften the pain of childbirth. I waited. After a while, I heard the baby's cries.

I walked up to the curtain. "Can I come in?"

"Not yet. I have to clean your mother up," the midwife said, raising her voice to be heard over the baby crying.

Soon, though, I met my baby sister. My mom named her Poch. She was in good health, as was my mother.

Like babies do, Poch kept us awake with her crying in our small house many nights, but my mom held her and comforted her. I had Dino by my side. I petted him and tried to shut out my little sister's crying.

I helped out with Poch's care, mainly running to get milk for her at the market or taking her dirty cloth diapers to the river to wash. Washing the diapers was always an unpleasant task. I hated doing it. Sometimes I thought, *Why does it always have to be me?* But I didn't complain. My mother, with help from my other mothers, had raised me. I owed it to my little sister Poch and my family to help take care of her.

About a month after my sister Poch was born, my father was transferred to work on the army base in Battambang City in a managerial capacity. He had been away at the front for many of the previous years, so it was a blessing to have him home. He was very busy though, as the Cambodian government's army was losing the war, and he worked long hours.

THE KHMER ROUGE REBELS were not visible to us in the city in 1974, but they were there in disguise. About one week after Dino and I had been to see a popular Cambodian movie, a Khmer Rouge terrorist threw a grenade into the crowded theater. The explosion killed a number of people and wounded many more. The theater was closed for more than a month before it reopened.

Other attacks on the movie theater and places in the city followed. It happened so many times that it became routine. These terrorists were heartless. Their sole purpose was to kill people, and they didn't care if they killed young or old, men or women.

People were afraid to go to the movies because of the explosions. Dino and I, however, were not deterred. We went to the movies several times after the attacks had begun. When we got inside, we would sit in the very back row of seats. I believed that if anyone threw a grenade, they would throw it to the front.

Some said the theaters were haunted by those who had died in the explosions. They believed that the spirits of those who had died while watching movies pulled the legs of living moviegoers. Others said the spirits scratched their backs, talked to them, and walked the aisles.

I did not see or feel the spirits, but sometimes in the theater I felt goosebumps and cold air on my neck. I was a child, and those stories bothered me, but I believed that Dino would protect me from the ghosts.

As the war continued to escalate, we could hear gunfights every night. Sometimes rockets were launched into the city, killing innocent people. But most of the fighting remained in the rural areas and away from Battambang City. Our home was not affected by the bombs and gunfire.

The closest I came to the battles was when I would visit my grandfather, my mother's father, who lived near Wat Kampong Sey Mar, the temple where he worked outside the city. When we did not have school, my older sister Dy and I would ride our bicycles to visit him. The rough dirt-and-gravel road was very bumpy and cut through thick stands of bamboo trees. Cars and trucks shared the road. They did not slow down for us, but usually the traffic was light.

Often when I went to my grandfather's house, which was near the river, I would see the fighting firsthand. I would witness helicopters shooting fireballs from the sky, trees burning and exploding, and branches flying into the air and crashing to the ground.

I would always go to the river to bathe when I went to see him. That's when I would be closest to the gunfights. From about a mile or two away, I would see helicopters flying overhead, shooting at Khmer Rouge soldiers in hiding.

Back at his house, we would sit on the front porch and watch. The fireballs and the sound of the gunfights were very scary. Sometimes, it seemed like a movie, but this was real. His house was not in the line of fire, so it was safe to watch, even as the ground shook from miles away. I did not know anything to do other than to enjoy the sight. My grandfather warned me many times of the danger. "Come in," he would say after a while. "Don't stay outside too long." But I often would stay on the porch for hours.

The worst part of being near these battles was when the gunfire and the bombs tapered off. That's when we would hear the victims' cries for help, often children and the elderly, caught in the middle. They had nowhere to go. The sounds of agony can carry a long way. I remember hearing children and their parents cry for their missing and killed family members.

I would sit on the porch of my grandfather's house, thinking of children the same age as me who were hiding and crying for help. Some children lost limbs and suffered other injuries. Some were dead at a young age. I would listen and picture dead bodies on top of other dead bodies.

I would thank God for where I was, on my grandfather's porch and not in the middle of the nearby gunfights.

After the visits to my grandfather's house, I would ride my bicycle home along the river. It was a mostly quiet road, but sometimes I would see taxis loaded with people driving very fast. I would watch out and move to the side to make sure they didn't run over me.

With each trip, the speed of the cars and trucks passing by seemed to increase, and the faces of the people in the vehicles looked more and more upset. These vehicles churned up dirt as they flew by. My hair sometimes was colored red with the dust, as were my clothes. I could sense in these dusty red clouds that change loomed for Cambodia, but nothing could have prepared me for what was to come.

MY MOM had a better understanding of how dangerous life was becoming in the city. In early April 1975, before the Cambodian New Year celebration, she decided to take my baby sister Poch, who was about one year old, to stay at my grandmother's house. My father's mother, Oun Som, lived about fifteen miles outside the city in a farm area that, unlike my grandfather's home, was not near the fighting. My mom and I took Poch there on a motorcycle taxi, the kind that pulled a trailer behind it and held five or six people. It was a bumpy ride and took about an hour.

We left my little sister there for my grandmother to take care of. It would prove to be a fateful decision.

Back at home, my mom and I celebrated the Cambodian New Year. My pa was busy at the army base, and my older sister Dy did not like to go to the temple, so it was just the two of us fulfilling the traditional rituals. The holiday is an ancient custom, based on the Buddhist calendar, which lasts three full days. In Cambodia, this is also the time when children become one year older. Unlike America, where birthdays are celebrated on the anniversary of one's birth, we all become older with the New Year. Although I was born in October 1966, in April 1975 I became a nine-year-old.

The first day of the New Year celebration, which fell on April 13, is when the angels come down from heaven. My mom cleaned the house very thoroughly in preparation for the angels' visit, and we dressed up in our best clothes. Many in our country wore colorful clothes and jewelry, including diamonds if they owned them, but we didn't have anything fancy to show off. My mom wore a white blouse and a loose, blue silk skirt called a *kben*. I wore my white shirt and khakis, my school clothes.

At home I knelt down and offered food to my mother and gave her thanks for all she had done for me. I asked for her forgiveness for bad things I had done, such as not obeying her. We offered the small Buddha statue we kept in our home a selection of cakes, fresh fruit, soda, and water.

The temple we regularly attended, Wat Dom Rey Sor, which means "temple of the white elephant," was in the city, but an hour's walk from our home. We walked there and offered bouquets and garlands to the large Buddha statue as well as gifts of fruit and aromatic water to the monks. The monks offered many blessings to the living and the dead.

The second day is devoted to the spirit of charity and giving. We took food to the temple to share with the monks, as well as our friends and family members. Again there was more praying, and we asked for blessings. We ate well on this day and celebrated at home with our friends in the community.

The third and final day is the one I enjoyed the most because there were many games for children at the temple. We played tug of war, hide and seek, and other games I loved.

In the evening, we gathered with the temple community to bathe the Buddha statues and the monks. At home, in the traditional last act of the celebration, I gave a ceremonial bath to my mother. We prepared a jar of water with perfume, and I poured it on her and used a cloth to wash her feet and her arms. The bath is intended to wash away sins—not just for my mom but for my father too—and grant them forgiveness.

The next day, April 17, 1975, the Khmer Rouge rebels, clad in black and carrying AK-47s, were standing in our doorway.

The day after that, I saw my pa for the very last time.

On the Road to the Killing Fields

[APRIL 1975]

THE DAY AFTER MY PA WAS TAKEN AWAY, a swarm of Khmer Rouge soldiers came to our circle of homes around noon. Each carried an AK-47. It was their second visit in three days. They fired bursts into the sky to make sure they had our attention.

Four of them stepped into our house. They were different soldiers from the ones who had come looking for my father, but they looked and acted the same. It was as though thousands of rebels had been cloned and dressed in black. "You must leave the city," one said. "We will come back here in an hour. You'd better be gone. If not, we will kill you."

We believed what they said. The word spread quickly that those who refused to leave had been shot and killed on the spot. Old people, children, women—it didn't matter. Many were executed because they did not want to give up the belongings they had worked all their lives to obtain.

My mom, my sister Dy, and I were terrified and confused. We did not know what to do or say. We couldn't understand why this was happening.

We could hear some neighbors resisting. "Why do I have to leave my house?" a woman who lived near us asked.

"You have to leave," a Khmer Rouge soldier said. "You must go."

"Why is this happening to our family?"

"Angkar—the new government—insists you leave," he said. "Because you live in the city, you are a merchant. You are corrupted. You need to go outside the city to become a farmer."

That was the first time we had heard of the Angkar, what the Khmer Rouge called the new government. Literally it translates to "the organization," but it also contains a reference to the ancient Khmer dynasty that had built the temples of Angkor Wat. Its followers never referred to themselves as the Khmer Rouge.

We would hear much about the Angkar in the years to come. Its plan was to clear out the cities and to turn everyone into farm laborers. Its followers dreamed of utopia—an agrarian, communist society where everyone was equal.

The exodus would turn Battambang City, just as it did Phnom Penh to the south, into a ghost town.

AFTER THE SOLDIERS left our house, we started packing. My mother pulled me and my sister close to her. "Do not say your father was in the army," she whispered. "Do not tell them his name."

We scrambled around, putting everything we could carry into three small packs my mom made out of cloth and quickly stitched together. We didn't take much—mainly clothes, rice, and essential cooking pots and pans. My mother packed a small collection of jewelry and a black-and-white photo of my father in his uniform that she hid in her clothes. She took the photo out of its frame to lighten her load.

I took a few of my favorite comic books, including one about the tortoise and the hare, and a coloring book and a few crayons. My sister Dy and I strapped these packs on our backs and got onto our bikes. My mother walked and carried her bag.

Dino, watching attentively, stayed by my side. I would never leave him. He was coming with us.

We joined five other families from our community, about twenty people in all. This group included Oum Sakum, my mother's aunt and one of my "other mothers," and her husband, Ho Kim Ban, who had been a commando and a mechanic in the army. Their daughter's family also joined us.

We set out as a group on the dirt road, falling in with the mass of humanity leaving the city. Just as our six families had stuck together in

The only surviving photo of my father, Lieutenant Oun Seuth.

support of one another in our community, we stuck together on the road. The road we took leading out of Battambang City was crowded with dazed residents, people walking like zombies, no destination in mind, leaving only because they had been told to evacuate.

It was very hot, and it started raining hard. We marched on, getting soaked. Many, especially the oldest on the road, struggled to keep up.

We heard gunshots echoing over the city. Everywhere we looked, we saw Khmer Rouge soldiers gesturing angrily with their AK-47s. "Keep moving!" they shouted. "Hurry! Keep moving!"

We kept our heads down and did as we were told.

OUR SIX FAMILIES marched together out of Battambang City, leaving behind the only home I had ever known. My mom decided that we should try to seek refuge at the home of my father's cousin and his family outside the city, which was in the direction we were being forced to walk. They lived about eight miles away on a farm. We hoped and prayed that with our connection they would let us stay there, and that it wouldn't be too long before we could return to our home.

We walked among the throngs of people, the rain continuing to pour down. The farther we walked from the city, the more the crowds spread out. We got far enough away that we did not see Khmer Rouge soldiers every step of the journey. We knew we would encounter them again, but it was a relief to be free of their menacing presence, if only briefly.

Eventually, we left the road and trudged through rice paddies and fields to reach my father's cousin's home. We walked across many narrow dirt dams built to hold water in the rice paddies. It was fraught with mud and not an easy trip, especially while pushing a bicycle. It took us six hours to reach our destination.

We were exhausted, scared, and hungry when we arrived.

The day was late, and the sun was beginning to set. My mom told our group to wait on a rice paddy dam while she and I walked the few hundred yards up to the house. She didn't want to overwhelm my father's cousin with our large group.

I leaned my bicycle over on its side. I scratched Dino on the back of his head and under his ears and told him he was a good boy. I knew he was hungry, as I was, but I wouldn't feed him until my mother said I could. My mother had warned me that we needed to preserve the food and water we had. We didn't know how long we would be on the road.

I left Dino with my sister Dy while I went with my mom. "*Angkouy,*" I told him. "*Chhke da la-or.*"

My mother and I approached the house. It was a big home that they had built high off the ground. I waited in the yard while my mom climbed the tall stairs and approached the door with her hands together and bowed, the traditional Cambodian greeting of respect.

My father's cousin opened the door, but he did not invite her inside.

I could hear voices, but I could not make out what was said. It was a short conversation. My mom turned and came down the stairs.

She was crying.

She took my hand and we walked back to our group, waiting in the rain on the rice paddy dam. "We cannot stay," she told the group. "We can sleep here tonight, but we have to leave tomorrow. They do not acknowledge us as family. They say, 'If I let you stay, we will all get killed. You have to leave.' They are afraid because Seuth was in the army. They said everyone from the army is being killed, families and all."

She paused and turned to look at the house and then at us. "Tomorrow, we have to move on. We should leave soon, because they might turn us in. We cannot trust them."

WE BEDDED DOWN on the rice paddy dam, sleeping on pieces of plastic on the packed dirt. It rained that night, as the dry season was giving way to the spring rains that would be followed by monsoon season. There was nothing that we could do but get wet and wait in the mud for the dawn.

At least I had my dog lying next to me. I rubbed Dino on the head and belly, and he licked my face in happiness.

Early the next morning, before we departed, four Khmer Rouge soldiers arrived. They approached with their AK-47s. We worried that my father's cousin had turned us in and these soldiers knew our connections to the army, but all they did was tell us to move. "Go! You can't stay here! Keep moving! Into the country! You are farmers now!"

They told us to leave, but they didn't tell us where to go. We walked with no destination in mind. We dared not ask them any questions. We knew they were ignorant and would have no answers.

We walked all day under a bright sun, but we could feel another rainstorm building on the horizon. It was so humid that the soaking wet clothes we started out in that day would not completely dry out. Dy and I pushed our bicycles along muddy roads. The wheels often sank in the thick mud, and sometimes we had to stop to scrape off our tires. Dino got filthy, trotting along beside me, but he didn't seem to mind. As the evening approached, mosquitoes started to feed on all of us.

We covered about eight or ten miles, walking until it was almost so dark we couldn't see. We came upon a rice field and the home of a farmer. My mother asked him if we could stay for a day or two, and even though he did not know us, he was kind enough to agree.

The adults cooked rice by wrapping it in a cloth and wetting it and burying it shallowly in the ground, then building a fire over the top of it. When the ground began to get dry, they dug it up and mixed in a little salt. They passed it around, and each of us ate a little bit.

Again we slept without cover, six families sprawled on the ground.

WE WERE ALREADY STARTING to run out of rice. One of the men in our group, Po Ke, who was in his thirties, decided to go back to Battambang City to get more food. (*Po* means "uncle," and I called him this out of respect even though he and I weren't related.) I convinced my mother to let me go with him. I could help him carry the food, and I also could get a few more belongings that we had left behind in the rush to leave. She did not like the idea, but we needed food and I was insistent.

Po Ke and I left before sunrise. The trip was long, about fifteen miles. Po Ke traveled on foot, alternating running and walking fast, and I rode my bike. Sometimes when the road was very muddy, I stopped to push the bike, but most of the time I was able to ride. The dirt had been packed hard by thousands of evacuating footsteps. We were fortunate that it did not rain on this day.

We saw many Khmer Rouge soldiers on the road. Trucks and jeeps were speeding about. A few times they stopped and asked us where we were going. Po Ke and I were very polite and said we were just going to get food from our home and that we would be on our way. Po Ke, who did most of the talking, called them "comrade," which they seemed to appreciate.

When we reached the city, we could see the terrible havoc the Khmer Rouge invasion had wreaked. The streets smelled of smoke and gasoline and death. Cars and trucks were abandoned with broken windshields, doors open, tires shot flat. Some of the vehicles had been burned. Houses were ransacked with their doors and curtains left wide open. Other houses had been burned to the ground. Animals, everything from stray dogs and cats to pigs and chickens, were running loose. Many dogs had been shot and left to lie where they fell.

Even worse were the human corpses left to rot in the streets or in their businesses and homes, the doors wide open. We saw bodies of people who had been killed along the side of the road, sometimes entire families it appeared—fathers and mothers and children lying every which way. Flies buzzed on remains both human and animal. The smell of the dead bodies in the heat was unbearable. I was afraid to stop moving, and I didn't have the stomach to look at them closely. We wanted to get in and out as quickly as we could.

When we arrived at our circle of homes, there was not a soul in sight. I had never seen the place that had been so full of life and love look so desolate and lonesome.

Our house had been trashed. I dug through the mess and grabbed some clothes I'd left behind—a hat and shirt that had belonged to my dad and an antique ceramic teapot that my grandmother had given to my mom as a wedding gift many years ago. I found some dried fish we had not taken. I bundled it all in a piece of cloth and headed back out to meet up with Po Ke.

We traveled as fast as we could back toward where our group had stopped. It was a long trip in the heat, but we never slowed down. At one point when I was very tired, Po Ke tied a long, thick string around my waist and pulled me on the bicycle.

I couldn't wait to return to the company of what family I had left. The closer we got, the harder I pedaled.

I was so relieved when we arrived that evening and they were still in the same spot. I felt lucky to see my mom again. I told her what I had witnessed, and she put her arms around me and cried. "My son," she said, "I should not have let you go."

THE NEXT DAY, knowing we might be in danger if we overstayed our welcome, we resumed walking. We had no destination. We were afraid and confused and didn't know what to do or where to go. We were just walking. It felt like we were going to keep walking until we reached the end of the Earth.

We walked for two or three days—I can't remember how many. It seemed like forever with the heat, the rain, the mud, the mosquitos, the hopelessness.

After several days on the road, Ho Kim Ban declared that we could not continue. He had decided to go to the Khmer Rouge and offer to be a mechanic, which he believed might provide protection for us. "We can't keep going like this," he said. "I don't know where we are going to go. They need mechanics for the farm tractors. I will tell them that I can help them, and maybe they will help us. I will come back for you."

Kim Ban was older than my father, well into his fifties or maybe even his sixties, and he looked older than that. He'd led a hard life, suffering many burns and injuries from years of fighting in the army and from working as a mechanic. He was a small, slight man, and he had scars all over his face, his arms, his chest.

Offering to help the Khmer Rouge was an excruciating decision. He had fought them for years. "I don't like it, but I don't know what else to do," he said. "We might all die out here if we don't do something. If I die, if they kill me, what will be will be. You can go ahead. We don't have any other chance that I can see. If you don't see us back in three days, keep moving."

He and his son-in-law, Jak, who was part Vietnamese, started back toward Battambang City. They were taking a chance, and they knew it. We watched them go.

Kim Ban's decision caused our group to splinter. Three of the families—my family, Kim Ban and Sakum's family, and their daughter Lin Ban's family—would await Kim Ban and Jak's return.

The other three families from our community, however, did not agree with Kim Ban's plan. They did not trust the Khmer Rouge and opted to keep going. Where they were going, they did not know, but they did not want to try to join the communists who had taken over our country. They also worried that without a man in their family who had the skill of being a mechanic, they had nothing to offer. "We only know how to fix bicycles," Po Ke said. "They don't need anyone to fix bicycles."

I also wonder if Kim Ban's past in the army made them afraid to stay with us. They didn't say it, but perhaps they worried that being connected to him would be perilous for them.

The splitting up was friendly. Neither group's choice had any guarantees. We were just trying to survive. We hugged them goodbye and cried and wished them good luck.

The three families moved on ahead of us, eventually disappearing like specks in the distance.

After we'd sat by the roadside for several hours, a cadre of Khmer Rouge soldiers came along. They told us we couldn't stay, that we had to keep going away from the city. We were already a long way, but they said we must keep moving, gesturing with their AK-47s. "Go!" they screamed at us. "Keep going!"

We did as they said and started walking.

IT WAS VERY HOT, as the days always are in April in Cambodia. We walked along an open road that ran through the middle of treeless fields. There was no shade, only the sun beating down. We were worn out, miserable, morose. We worried that Kim Ban and Jak, if they came back, would never be able to find us. We trudged along, not speaking.

Dino had moved in front of me for a while and started trotting about one hundred yards ahead. About two hours into the walk, Dino ran back to me and began to bark. I did not know what he wanted. We were passing a lone sawtooth oak tree, the first tree we had passed in a long time. It was in a barren area and stood very tall, about thirty to forty feet. Its leaves offered a welcoming patch of shade. Dino ran to get into the shade, waiting for me, but I kept going.

After I went past him, he ran behind me and began to bark as loudly as he could, something he almost never did. I realized that he wanted my mother and me to rest for a few minutes. He was telling us to get in the shade, that it was too hot. When we turned and followed Dino, his tail wagged with happiness. I sat down under the tree and gave him some water. He drank it and rested his head on my legs, looking up at me with love in his eyes.

We all rested there for about fifteen minutes before starting our journey to nowhere again.

We walked and walked. Hours passed. We kept walking.

As the afternoon grew late, we reached a small hill in the middle of a rice field. No one was nearby.

It seemed safe, so we decided to stop there for the night. We gathered leaves and branches from all around and fashioned them into a small tepee that we could use for shade. A few hours after the sun went down, heavy rain started to pour. We tried to use the tepee to stay dry, but it was no use.

We got soaked.

After a night of pouring rain, the sun began to rise and the weather cleared. We decided to stay on the small hill along the road until Kim Ban sent us some news. We were hopeful he would find us and that he had found somewhere safe for our families to go.

We didn't know if we would ever see him again, but we waited.

A FULL DAY PASSED on the hill with no news. We decided to wait another day. Kim Ban had told us three days. No rebel soldiers had been by to make us move, so we stayed put.

On the second day, Kim Ban's son-in-law, Jak, appeared on foot. We stood and cheered, we were so happy to see him.

He was smiling. He said Kim Ban had made arrangements to become a mechanic for the Angkar and found a place where they would let us stay. He would take us there. "Follow me," Jak said.

We walked about four miles to a tractor, which had a flatbed trailer behind it. We piled onto the trailer, all ten of us from the three families who had waited for Kim Ban. I put my bike on it and brought Dino too.

Jak drove the tractor pulling the trailer toward Chroy Sdao, a very small town north of Battambang City that was a rice-farming hub. Even though riding on the trailer was a bumpy journey, it was an improvement over walking.

I held onto Dino as the tractor pulled us along.

We arrived about an hour later to see our new home: an abandoned rice-processing factory and warehouse. The huge, rusting structure had been a functioning factory and rice-storage facility until the Khmer Rouge invaded.

The area had been a stronghold of the Cambodian government, and many battles had been fought there. The Khmer Rouge had vowed that once they took Chroy Sdao, they would kill everyone there. As the communists had advanced, everyone in the area had fled.

We reconnected with Kim Ban, who was waiting for us. The Angkar had established its local headquarters in a brick building across the street from the factory. Area leaders there told Kim Ban that we could stay inside the factory.

We went inside. It was an open space with no windows and a ceiling that rose about forty feet high, similar in size to a basketball gymnasium in America. Bags of rice were stacked high along the walls. I could see rats with long tails darting in and out of the bags.

Our three families took up residence in the abandoned factory. We had no beds, no bathrooms, no running water—nothing but a concrete floor.

Each of us placed a plastic sheet on the floor to stake out the spot where we would sleep. Others were coming into the warehouse and doing the same. By the end of the day, about twenty-five other families consisting of roughly one hundred people in total would stay there.

When it got dark, we lay down to sleep. We had no pillows or blankets, but at least we had a roof over our heads for the first time in a week. As always, my beloved dog Dino was near me. He slept by my side.

I lay awake that night and listened to the sounds of the people surrounding us. I heard an old woman repeatedly asking for help. "Help me," she said, her voice weak. "Help me."

I also could hear adults crying softly and a baby crying loudly. The baby screamed much of the night. I could hear the mother singing to the baby, trying to soothe her infant with a sweet Cambodian lullaby.

The mother's voice was beautiful and very peaceful, but it did not quiet the baby. The baby cried and cried and cried, giving voice to the way we all felt.

PART II

THE KILLING FIELDS

Shades of Black

[April 1975–September 1975]

"WAKE UP," MY MOM WHISPERED, shaking my arm. "Wake up." I opened my eyes to see her crouching over me. My sister and Dino were sitting next to her. My back hurt from the rough concrete floor where we had spent the night. At least it was dry, unlike the previous nights when we had slept in the mud. I had not slept much, but sometime before dawn, the baby who had kept me awake finally stopped crying, and I had fallen into a deep sleep. When my mom woke me, it took me a minute to get my bearings, to remember where we were and what had happened to us.

"Come with me," my mom said. She gestured to my sister Dy and said, "You too." I petted Dino and told him to stay with Kim Ban and Sakum and their family. My mom, my sister, and I stepped between the other families who had staked out spots on the floor, tiptoeing to avoid waking anyone up. Those who were not asleep were lying on the floor on pieces of plastic or old sheets and blankets, staring up at the ceiling, their faces forlorn. Mom led us out the door of the factory, which was guarded by a young man dressed in black and holding an AK-47. He looked like a farm boy, dark-skinned from the sun, the most obvious trait that distinguished the rural people from the city people. We had lighter complexions because we had not spent our days in the fields. Unlike most of the soldiers who scowled at us, he had a friendly face.

He stared at us but not in a threatening way.

"I'm taking my children to pee," my mom said.

He nodded that it was OK.

We followed my mom, who walked behind the factory and across a field. She kept her eyes down but snuck glances to see if we were followed or there was anyone around. It was still early, no later than eight o'clock, but the sun was already very hot and the temperature more than 90 degrees Fahrenheit. The small town—with an abandoned row of small businesses, a market, and a few homes and buildings scattered around—was quiet.

Once we were about one hundred yards away from the factory, my mom turned and looked behind us. No one was in sight. "Sit down," she said. She sat, folding her legs under her in the same way she did when she prayed at the wat. My sister and I obeyed, forming a triangle with my mom.

She put her hands on our shoulders and leaned forward, her face inches from ours. "What I am about to tell you is *very* important," she whispered, her voice on edge. "Very important. Be sure to listen closely: Never tell anyone that your pa was in the army. *Never.* That will get us all killed right away. Kim Ban said they are murdering soldiers and their families. You have to say you never met your pa. He was a taxi driver. He drove a tricycle. Do not say his real name. You should use my father's family name, Sin, and say his name was Rith. Sin Rith. You must say he left after you were born."

I did not understand. I was only nine years old. My pa's name was Oun Seuth. I had hoped my pa would join us. He could make everything right. "Where is Pa?" I asked.

"He is gone. I do not know."

My sister, who was seventeen by then and much taller than me, spoke up. "Do you think they killed him?"

"I do not know," my mom said, her eyes filling with tears for a second. "I do not know. We cannot know for sure. Kim Ban thinks they did, but we don't know. We can pray that he survived. But for now, we must deny he was in the army. If you don't, we all will be killed."

She wiped her eyes and the momentary unsteadiness of her voice faded away. "Listen to me. We must be strong. You can tell no one the truth.

His name was Sin Rith, and he was a taxi driver. He drove a taxi, a tri-cycle in Battambang City. He didn't live with us. You didn't know him."

She turned to me, putting her hand on my shoulder, gripping it hard. "Imagine I am a Khmer Rouge soldier," she said. She put on an angry voice. "Who is your pa?"

I paused, having a hard time putting words together. She gripped harder. "*Who is your pa?*"

I couldn't get the words out, tears forming in my eyes. It tore me up inside to deny my father, the man whom I'd looked up to like a god.

"*Who is your pa?*" she said again, even more intense.

"His name was Sin Rith, and he was a taxi driver," I said, sputtering out barely intelligible words. "He drove a tricycle. In Battambang City."

"Again," she said. "Imagine my finger is a rifle." She poked me hard in the chest. "I will find some bamboo and whip you if you don't do this right. *Who is your pa?*"

I took a deep breath, and this time I was able to get the words out without crying too much. "His name was Sin Rith, and he was a taxi driver. He drove a tricycle. I never knew him."

"That's better, but do it again. You must be strong."

I said it once more, this time without crying.

She looked at me. "Much better. You must remember that. Your name is not Sokomasath. It is Prou. And your family name is not Oun. It is Sin."

She checked around to see if anyone was coming. "What is your name?"

"My name is Prou."

"What is your name? Your full name?"

"My name is Sin Prou."

"Repeat it back to me."

"My name is Sin Prou."

"Again," she said. I repeated it once more.

"Good. Remember that. It could save all our lives. Never tell them your real name. Never tell them that your father was in the army."

She turned to my sister and made her go through the same exercise, giving her a new name as well. Then she told us the new name she had for herself, as well as the new names Kim Ban and Sakum would use.

We repeated the names back to her, and then she made us do it three more times.

"You also must not ever tell them you went to school," she said. "They hate those with educations and the ones who can read. Act like you are an idiot. You should become stupid. It might save your life."

She paused and then took on the angry face again. "Where did you go to school?"

My first thought was to answer, but then I said, "I didn't."

"Can you read?"

"No."

"Did you work?"

I didn't know what to say, then an idea came to me. "Yes. I collected plastic and aluminum trash to resell, to help my family eat."

My mom nodded and smiled. "Yes, that's good," she said. "Very good. Use that story."

But then she put on her angry face and went through the same questions with my sister, and then again with me, asking about my father, asking if I went to school. Each time she poked me and squeezed my shoulder. Her whispers were intense, her eyes sharp and menacing. We practiced that way for I don't know how long. It was only ten or fifteen minutes, but it seemed like forever. My mother was angrier than I had ever seen her, but after a last round of repeating the names and answering her practice questions, she relented. Her shoulders slumped and her eyes softened and she reached out to hug both of us. My sister and I leaned forward and she kissed our faces. "I'm sorry, my children," she said. "I'm sorry. But this is the only way. I do not know what the future holds for us. I'm sorry, but this is all I know to do. All I want is for us to survive."

IN THE FIRST DAY in the abandoned rice-processing factory in Chroy Sdao, after my mom had assigned us our new names, we waited and worried about what our fate would be. Others who had been forced out of their homes in Battambang City and Phnom Penh arrived and crowded into the factory, filling up every inch of floor and making the second night even noisier with babies crying and worried adults whispering.

On the second day, in the morning, the guards with AK-47s called us outside. "Angkar wants to talk to you. You must come to a meeting."

We gathered in the open area in the wide street outside the factory. The late April sun was very hot. More guards appeared, all in black with AK-47s, surrounding our group of about one hundred people. I stood close to my mom and kept Dino by my side.

A dark-skinned man in a crisp black uniform with a cap on his head and a red-and-white *krama* around his neck stepped out of the brick office building that was next to the factory. He walked with an upright posture, his shoulders high and his neck very straight. He inspected us as though we were troops. He reminded me of high-ranking officers I had seen on my father's army base, except that he was dressed in black and not green. After he looked us over, he spoke. "You are all workers for Angkar now. There are no more personal possessions. You must turn in everything but your clothes. You can keep three sets of clothes. You will have to dye those black. Everything else you must share. All is property of Angkar. Go get your possessions and return with them and put them over there." He pointed to a small building across from the factory beyond the brick building. Two guards waited there beside a pile of odds and ends.

I owned only two things other than my clothes: my bicycle and my dog Dino. My bicycle, which my father had given to me when I was five, was where I'd left it in the factory. Dino was by my side. I looked down at him, and he looked up at me with questioning eyes. "Good boy," I said and reached down to pet him. If I had to part with one, I thought, I could give up my bike.

A few of the others in our group raised their hands to ask questions and began to speak, but the Angkar leader cut them off. "*Silence!* No questions! You heard me. You keep nothing but your clothes. Go get everything else and turn it over to Angkar! You should not have jewelry or dishes or anything. We will do an inspection later. We will discuss dyeing your clothes black on another day. For now, turn in everything you have."

We all filed back into the factory. Standing in the line that moved slowly through the door, I looked up at my mom and spoke to her softly. "Mom, do I have to give up my bicycle?"

"Yes," she said, whispering. "They are serious."

"What about Dino?"

She looked down at Dino by my side and pursed her lips. "We will see," she said.

I rolled my bike out, and my mom carried our pots and pans. We joined the procession turning in meager belongings by simply dumping them in the pile where the guards stood with their rifles.

Mom dropped her pots and pans into the pile with a clang, including the teapot that had been a wedding gift many years before. I rolled my bike up to the edge of the growing pile and let it fall. It was a very simple vehicle, only one speed, and the tires were worn and the chain rusty. I was nine years old and too big for this bike, which had been perfect when I was five. But I had ridden many miles on it and loved it. My pa had given it to me. I did not want to give it up, but I did.

I turned and walked away, tears building in my eyes, my mom on one side of me and Dino on the other. I thought about the day when my father had given me that bike and how happy I had been. I reached down to pet Dino. He licked my hand. We walked back into the factory, and I worried that I would have to give him up too.

AT MIDDAY, the guards called us out to the common area. There was a woman in all black with a bob haircut standing beside a big pot. "Get a bowl and a spoon and eat," she said. Her voice was angry, and she stared at us with hatred.

I heard my mom sigh behind me. She had thrown all our dishes into the pile that morning. She crossed back to the pile, as others in the factory did, and dug through it looking for our bowls and spoons. She found bowls and spoons for me and my sister and herself and then returned and handed them to us.

I looked at mine. "This is not my bowl," I said.

"Be quiet," she said. "It is now."

We lined up, and the woman with the bob haircut and angry eyes dished out small servings of a very watery rice soup. I looked up at my mom and started to ask if this was all we would get, but she shook her head to say, *Don't ask any questions.*

I was very hungry, as we hadn't eaten in more than a day. This watery mix of rice was far from satisfying.

We returned to our spot on the factory floor to get out of the sun and wait for whatever happened next. They did an inspection of our belongings later that afternoon—two guards with their rifles looking over everyone's spots on the floor of the abandoned factory.

I tensed up when they came to us, pulling Dino close to me and petting him. One of the guards who was poking through our clothes and blankets looked right at Dino, but he said nothing. There was even a hint of a smile on the guard's face. I think because Dino was so cute and such a good dog, they let me keep him.

WE WHILED AWAY THE HOURS, stretched out on the floor of the factory. There was always at least one man in all black with an AK-47 guarding the door, watching us day and night. I sensed that we were not allowed to leave, but if we left, we had no place to go because we couldn't go back to the cities. I spent these days petting Dino. I was able to take him out to walk around the old factory and the surrounding fields, but it seemed somebody was always keeping an eye on me. Other children were around, but we were too scared to talk to each other and play.

On our third day at Chroy Sdao, Kim Ban approached the guard at the door. "Comrade," he said, "when might we get jobs? We would like to work."

The guard, this one a very gaunt, dark-tanned Khmer Rouge with an angry face, answered harshly. "You must wait," the guard said. "Angkar will send you instructions when we are ready."

"Yes, thank you, comrade," he said, bowing and putting his hands together in the traditional thankful gesture.

From the guard's ragged grammar and poor pronunciation, I could sense even at my young age that this young farm boy had never been to school a day in his life. He was enjoying bossing around people from the city, his shoulders thrust high. The tables had turned, and for the first time in his life he had power and was not just a peasant digging in the mud of a rice paddy.

I knew it pained Kim Ban deeply to cower before this ignorant young man with the gun, but he had no choice.

AFTER ANOTHER DAY OF WAITING, Kim Ban gathered our family group and led us outside. The guards were letting those who had settled in the warehouse move about more. Perhaps they were bored of watching us in there too. We were very hungry, as the watery bowls of rice soup they served us had very few calories and practically no vitamins.

Kim Ban began walking through the fields behind the factory, looking for old piles of straw and brown grass that had been cut to feed the oxen that farmers often used to plow fields. He came to a pile of straw and lifted it up and pointed to white mushrooms growing under it. "We can eat the hay mushrooms," Kim Ban said.

He picked one up and handed it to me. "Eat," he said.

I took it from him. I had eaten very little in several days, and as hungry as I was, the mushroom tasted great. A hay mushroom in your stomach is better than nothing. Kim Ban had lived many years and knew about survival, including the longtime custom of the very poor in Cambodia to seek out the hay mushrooms when nothing else was available. It turns out that hay mushrooms have many proteins, carbohydrates, and vitamins. We all munched on the mushrooms, glad to have something to satiate the hunger burning inside us.

THE NEXT DAY, a group of about ten Angkar, several of them with AK-47s, appeared in the factory. "Come outside for a meeting," one shouted. "Bring all your clothes outside."

We gathered up what few clothes we had and went out to where everyone living in the factory had gathered. "You must dye all your clothes black," one of the leaders said. "If you have clothes you don't dye, you must throw them away. Black is the color of Angkar."

I didn't know how we would do this, but my mom knew. She and Sakum and other women went to the river on the edge of Chroy Sdao. From low ebony trees, they picked tiny hard fruits that were about the size of grapes. They scavenged around Chroy Sdao and found a few buckets. They filled the buckets about half full of water, and they began squeezing the fruits, which had a dark juice inside. "Do not eat these," my mom said to me as I watched her. "They will make you very sick."

After the water turned black, my mom carried the bucket back to the factory where we had left our clothes. She put a bundle of our clothes in the bucket, submerging it and pressing it down. "We leave these for a day," she said.

The next day she pulled out the bundle of clothes and then put the rest of our clothes in a second bundle in the bucket. This bundle included my mom's blue *kben*, a skirt that was her nicest piece of clothing and that she had worn only about two weeks before during the Cambodian New Year. I could see she was not happy about dyeing it black, but she said nothing.

The clothes we pulled from the bucket were dripping wet and black with the dye. My mom carried the bundle back to the river and lay them on the muddy ground. "Help me cover them with mud," she said. She cupped her hand in the edge of the river and pulled up mud from the bank and tossed it on the clothes. My sister and I did the same. I didn't understand why we were doing this, but I did as I was told. I learned later that curing the dye in mud was an ancient Khmer method.

We carried the muddy clothes back to the factory and let them dry for a day. The next day we washed the mud from the clothes in the river.

Our simple clothes had gone in white and khaki and blue and other light colors. They came out black—black as night, black as the Angkar's hearts, black as our future appeared to be.

IT WAS A STRANGE SIGHT, all of us dressed in black. I could not get used to it, and I never would. But we had no choice.

A few days after we dyed our clothes, Kim Ban was called to the office building by the warehouse, where the local Angkar leaders had set up shop to oversee the district. He was gone a long time, several hours at least, and we all sat nervously waiting for him, hoping he would return. We had seen a few other men be called out and never come back. Nothing was said about what had happened to them.

Fortunately, Kim Ban came back at the end of the day and told us about the Angkar's plans for us. He had told them about his skills as a mechanic, so they assigned him, his son-in-law Jak, and me to work on tractors used by the surrounding rice farms. He said my mother, my sister Dy, Sakum, and her daughter Lin Ban were assigned to plant and harvest rice in the paddies.

Kim Ban had denied that he had ever been in the army, but claimed he had been a mechanic all his life. The truth was that he had served many years in the military and seen many battles against rebel forces. He had made up another name, as we all had. He didn't talk about it that afternoon because he worried that others in the factory could hear us. We trusted no one outside our small family group. "We start to work tomorrow," he said, looking to see if the guard or anyone around was listening. He raised his voice a little louder. "I know you will all do good work for Angkar."

As he addressed us, he called us by our new names, and his message was clear—the intense look in his eyes emphasized it—*we must remember our new names.*

THE NEXT DAY BEGAN in the shadows before dawn with men in all black carrying rifles and shouting at us. "Wake up! Wake up! Time to work!" these angry silhouettes yelled. "You must work for Angkar! Hurry up! Outside, everyone!"

I sat up and could see that Dino, who slept at my side, was very excited. I worried about leaving him for the day. I petted him and scratched under his jaw. "*Angkouy,*" I said. He sat and looked up at me. "*Chhke da la-or.* You must stay here, Dino." He was a good dog, but I knew he was not patient enough to stay in one spot all day if left him alone. I hoped he would be all right and that if he ran around the village, he would not get into trouble. I did not want to leave him, but I had no choice.

We trudged barefoot out of the warehouse in the morning darkness and stood in a group. There was no more playing of the Cambodian national anthem, the song I had heard precisely at seven o'clock every morning of my young life.

We stood near Kim Ban, who was near a younger man in a military-style cap who looked to be in his mid-twenties. The man was next to a teenager with an AK-47. Everyone was dressed in black, but only the Angkar leaders wore hats. I stood by my mom. Kim Ban gestured to my mom, my sister Dy, Sakum, and their daughter Lin Ban to follow a woman in all black who stood across the common area. "Go there, with the woman," Kim Ban said. The woman had on a peasant farmer hat and held a piece of paper. She was screaming names and yelling for everyone to hurry.

Kim Ban gestured to me and his son-in-law. "We are going to work on tractors."

My mother looked down at me and patted me on the head. "Kim Ban will look after you," she said, patting me on the back and nudging me in his direction. "Be careful, my son."

My eyes teared up at the idea of my mom and me going different places. She smiled sadly and walked to the group of women who were gathering. I remember thinking that the screaming woman in the black hat was like a witch, and I worried about what she might do to my mother. I felt such love for my mother that I thought I was going to burst.

Our group of about ten men and a few boys walked behind the man leading us, a much smaller group than the large group of women and children who marched off in another direction. It wasn't until I saw the groups splinter that I realized that there were many more women than men in the families who had sought shelter in the factory. *Where are all the men?* I wondered. I was lucky that I was not going to work in the rice paddies, but I was sorry that my mom, my sister Dy, Sakum, and her daughter had to. I had never worked in a rice paddy, but I knew it was excruciating work, requiring one to bend over most of the time.

I walked next to Kim Ban in the group who traveled a short distance through Chroy Sdao until we arrived at a barnlike garage on the edge of town where the rice paddies began. It was two stories high, built of wood, and had about ten tractors and a few trucks parked in and around it. These vehicles had all been confiscated from farm owners and merchants when the Khmer Rouge invaded.

The young Angkar leader had not said a word on the walk. At the garage, he approached Kim Ban, standing very close to him and speaking loudly, only inches from his face. "You mechanic? You must get all these running." He had a strong country accent and very broken grammar. "Get to work."

"Yes, comrade," Kim Ban said, bowing and putting his hands together in the traditional Cambodian gesture of respect. "Yes, we will. Are there tools we may use?"

The Angkar leader looked at Kim Ban, tightening his lips. "You mechanic but have no tools? Where are your tools?"

Kim Ban paused but did not say anything. I knew he must have been thinking about what to say, about what would be the safest response. He knew better than to argue.

The angry man yelled again. "Where are your tools? You are a mechanic, but you have no tools?"

"I'm sorry, comrade, I don't have my tools with me," Kim Ban said. "We moved from our home, and I didn't have time to carry them with me. I was not allowed to take my possessions. I can try to find some. We can do the job."

"You better have made progress by the end of day when I come back. I expect a full report."

The man turned before Kim Ban responded and began walking toward the way we had come. We watched him go without saying a word until his black outfit disappeared. The teenager with the AK–47, probably only fifteen or sixteen, stayed with us. He found a spot in the shade of the garage wall and watched us stoically, his gun resting across his lap.

Kim Ban turned and looked at us. "Let's see if we can find any tools in this garage. There must be something here. And then we will try to start these tractors."

We found some rusty wrenches in the garage that despite being very old, would get the job done. There were cans of gasoline and oil too. The garage and surrounding farm had been abandoned by its owners only a week or two before, when the Khmer Rouge had invaded and seized everything.

Kim Ban instructed the men on starting up the tractors, and after a morning of evaluating them, we found that more than half of the tractors worked. He showed me and the other men, most of whom didn't seem to have any skills as mechanics, how to clean the carburetors and spark plugs and check the tires. He let me ride in his lap on the tractors when he took them for short test drives in the field near the garage. I put my hands on the wheel to steer, but he kept his hands on there too. It was a thrill for me to feel like I was driving.

Later in the day, after they fed us a bowl of watery rice soup, I heard Kim Ban and some of the men talking about the need for parts, especially spark plugs, and where they might get them. Kim Ban said he didn't want to ask the Angkar, but thought that maybe we could find parts on other tractors. We scoured the old garage in hopes of finding spark plugs, but we had no luck. I looked through old boxes and piles of trash but found nothing.

Late that afternoon, the teenage guard with the rifle who had been sitting in the same spot all day rose and began walking around us, shifting his AK-47, the muzzle pointing in our direction.

We wondered why he was in motion and looked to see the Angkar leader returning. Kim Ban smiled at the man when he approached.

"Comrade," Kim Ban said, "seven of these tractors are in good shape. They are ready to start plowing." He pointed to the running tractors that he had lined up on the side of the road across from the garage. "These three do not run, but we can work more tomorrow, and we can fix them. Thank you for this opportunity to work for you."

I was in a happy mood because I thought we had done a good job, getting seven of the tractors to run, but the Angkar leader did not see it that way. "You are mechanic, and you cannot fix?" He pointed at the broken-down tractors, some of which must have been thirty years old. "Why should we not kill you all now? To kill you all would be no loss." He looked at Kim Ban and then over at the expressionless teen with the rifle, who adjusted the strap on his shoulder and raised the muzzle as though he were waiting on the order to fire. "If we kill you, we won't have to feed you."

"Comrade," Kim Ban said, "we can work on these tomorrow." His voice was pleading. "These seven are good to go to work in the fields tomorrow."

The Angkar leader stared at Kim Ban for a long time, and then he put his angry gaze on me before passing it over all the men and boys in our group. "We give you another chance tomorrow. But you better fix these. Many more tractors coming here. Now we return."

He turned and walked back toward the factory where we would sleep. We followed him, none of us saying a word.

When we arrived back about dusk, I was so happy to see Dino outside the warehouse, waiting for me. He ran up to me and licked my hand and face when I picked him up. "Good boy," I said. "Good boy."

I held him and petted him and was so happy for his love. After a while, I carried him into the warehouse to see if my mother was there. She, my sister Dy, Sakum, and her daughter Lin Ban were lying on their mats. They looked dead tired, their faces red from a long day in the sun. My mom sat up and smiled and gestured to me, and I put Dino down and went to hug her. "My son," she said, holding me tight. "I am so glad to see you."

I STAYED WITH MY MOTHER that night and for many that would follow, sitting next to her and petting Dino while she lay there and rested from a long day working in the fields. She was not talkative on these nights but lay there with her eyes closed.

Because the rainy season had begun and the factory floor was starting to get wet, the Angkar allowed us to go out and gather enough bamboo to make small beds that raised us off the ground. Sleeping on the wooden surface was not comfortable, but it was better than wet concrete.

The watery bowls of rice the Angkar fed us during the day were not nourishing. Our hunger and the pains that went with it grew, bothering me the most when I tried to sleep. I had watched as three other boys about my age who had been staying in the factory went out each night. I knew one of the boys—his name was Nak—and we were friendly. I hoped he knew where there was something to eat and would let me share whatever they found.

One night I decided to follow them out. I told Dino to stay with my mom and be a good boy. The guard at the door paid no attention to me, and I went out into the night. It was dark, but there were low clouds, and soon I was able to see enough to get around. I saw the three boys turn and go behind the factory building, and I followed. I watched as they picked up bamboo sticks from the side of a wooden storage building.

I walked fast to catch up to them. "Hi," I said. "What are you doing?"

They looked panicked at first, as they had not seen me coming. When I got closer, they saw that I was just a boy like they were. They all looked at each other, uncertain if they could trust me, but then Nak, the tallest one, said to the others, "He's OK. It's Prou. I know him. He can help us."

He turned to me. "We are hunting the rice rats. They are all over here, coming out of the back of the factory and from the high grass near the paddies. Find a bamboo stick and a sharp wire or piece of metal. Stick the metal into the end. Like this." He held up his stick, and I could see a thick wire sticking out of the end.

He pointed to a corner beyond the factory. "There are some pieces of wire and scrap metal over there."

Because it had been the site of battles and eventually abandoned, the area around the factory had many piles of trash. I found a bamboo stick about four feet long and a piece of a broken radio antenna that I jammed into the end of the bamboo. It seemed to hold pretty tight and made a handy weapon.

"I'm ready," I said, rejoining the group. They were already starting to fan out around a thick mound of grass and garbage a few hundred yards from the factory.

"Go there," Nak said, gesturing to a spot on the opposite side of the grassy mound strewn with garbage. "Get ready. If a rat runs out, stab it."

I did, holding my stick ready. I was excited to be a part of this group and to have a mission. It reminded me of the fun I'd had catching fighting fish in rice paddy ponds.

Nak stepped toward the pile of high grass and jabbed his stick at something and stamped his feet. A rat darted out, its teeth bared and hissing. I could see its eyes gleaming and its long white tail straight up and jerking around. I tensed up and was ready, but the rat ran toward one of the other boys who stabbed at it with his stick, spearing it, to my amazement, on the first try. The rat let out an ungodly squeal as he pushed the stick with the wire in deeper. The other two boys ran to him and began swinging their sticks down on the rat. I joined in, swinging my stick down on the speared rat as hard as I could.

After it was certain the rat was subdued—the boy had poked the bamboo stick all the way through the rat and into the ground—Nak found part of an old brick. "Hold it there," he said to the boy who had speared the rat. He gestured to me and the other boy. "You two, move back." He stepped forward and brought the brick down hard on the rat's head. The squealing ended. I could see part of the rat's brain and blood glistening in the near-dark.

The boys all relaxed. Nak took the stick with the impaled rat from the other boy and held it up to show off the kill. He smiled and looked at me. "Time to eat. Do you know how to skin a rat?"

"No," I said. I had seen my mom clean fish, but I had never learned. And I'd never seen anyone clean a rat before. We often had been poor and hungry, but never hungry enough to eat city rats, which we believed were diseased.

"I will show you. Watch." He grabbed the rat by its neck and pulled out the bamboo stick and the wire, slick with blood. He walked over to a clear patch of ground and squatted, gripping the rat from the top of its back, just below its crushed head. He pulled a razor out of his pocket. It was a just a blade, no handle, but it looked sharp. He made a deep incision starting at the rat's throat and cut all the way down through its belly to its anus. Using both hands, he stripped its fur and skin off.

He stood up and looked at me, holding the bloody carcass up to show it to me. "Have you ever eaten rat?" He had a devilish smile. The other two boys were laughing.

"No," I said. I was not smiling. I thought about running back to my mom, but I didn't want to appear scared. I knew they were testing me.

"Then you will get the first bite," he said. "We can build a fire back there, beyond those trees."

We walked back behind a thick group of low trees that were away from the factory and the center part of the small town. Nak and the other boys stacked up some kindling wood, and one of them had pieces of cotton that he had soaked in kerosene. He started striking two rocks together to make a spark to start the fire. It took him many times to get it to catch, but eventually it did. Soon the wood started to crackle as the flames took hold.

Nak skewered the rat meat on a piece of bamboo he held over the fire. It started to sizzle, and it smelled delicious, as hungry as I was.

After a few minutes, he decided it was ready. He held the skewer over to me. "Eat it. It's good."

I stepped forward and took it from him and took a bite. It was warm and moist and delicious. I could have eaten all of it, but I knew that I should share it. I handed it back to Nak.

"What do you think of your first taste of rat?"

"It's delicious!" I said. "Let's go catch more." They all laughed. I had passed my initiation.

We caught and ate three more rats that night. I felt full for the first time in weeks.

I FELL INTO A ROUTINE. In the morning, we would all be awakened early and I would go with the men Kim Ban led to work on the tractors. My mother, my sister Dy, Sakum, and her daughter Lin Ban would go to work in the paddies, planting and harvesting rice in the muddy fields.

During the day, I stayed with Kim Ban, who was a knowledgeable mechanic. More tractors were brought to the garage every day. Most did not run and were towed by a truck or another tractor. Kim Ban would evaluate each tractor and teach the men what to do to fix it. Most he could fix, but some he could not, mainly due to a lack of parts, especially spark plugs. Some of the tractors were ancient, dating back to World War II and beyond. Those he would take parts from to use on the other tractors, sometimes taking off so many parts and tires that there was not much left of the skeletons of the broken-down tractors. We would drain out the old oil and use it in the tractors that still ran.

Kim Ban spent much time explaining to me how the tractors worked. I held wrenches and handed them to him when he asked. I was glad to have a job to do, and I asked him lots of questions. After about a month, he started to let me work on tractors on my own, just like the men. I was honored to have the responsibility, and I tried hard to do a good job.

When work on a tractor was complete, I often would ride on it with one of the men from our group to deliver it to the rice paddies. Many of the drivers were very kind and let me take the wheel and steer, unlike Kim Ban, who thought I was too young to drive without his hands on the wheel. Even though I could not see over the top of the tractor hood when I sat in the seat, I leaned to the side to see what was ahead. When I was on the main roads, I sat up as straight as I could and looked at the far top of the road in the distance and steered that direction. Other than an occasional motorcycle, the roads were mostly quiet. After many times behind the wheel, the drivers started to trust me. They would sit back and let me drive. I loved it and felt like I was accomplishing something.

I still held out hope that I would see my pa again. I thought about him all the time, and whenever I was on a tractor and saw workers in fields or passing along roads, I looked for his face on every person I saw. I wanted him to see the good work I was doing and the things I had learned.

I knew he would be proud of me.

EACH EVENING after the sun went down, I would go out hunting rice rats with the other boys. We formed a good team of rat hunters. We ventured farther and farther away from the center of the Chroy Sdao village where we could build small fires to cook the rat meat. I relished eating rats after a long day of nothing but a bowl of rice soup and, if I was lucky, a few pieces of a hay mushroom found during the day while working on tractors.

Every night, we chased rice rats in the fields, stabbing at them with our bamboo-stick weapons. We sloshed through the mud and got soaked by the rain when it came down, as it often did, especially in the summer months and early fall. We began using small lanterns with old bottles, a piece of cloth soaked in oil, to help us see. Sometimes we caught as many as five or ten rats, and we would cook them up and ate well. We talked about our concerns of being caught, but Nak said the rats were a nuisance and that the Angkar killed them whenever they saw them. "If someone catches us, we'll just tell them we are trying to save the rice crops and that we are doing it for Angkar," he said. "They hate the rats for eating their rice."

I had thought about taking some of the rat meat back to my mother and sister, but Nak warned me not to do that. "That might get us all in serious trouble," he said. "Let's keep it between us."

One night after we had been doing this for several months, we flushed an enormous rat out of a hole on the edge of a rice field. It was as big as a cat. I could barely believe my eyes at how large it was, probably three times the size of most of the rats we had caught. We surrounded it—there were five of us that night—and moved closer with our sharp bamboo weapons. It was a beast, flicking its long, straight white tail angrily. We moved more slowly, all of us watching Nak, who was not as quick to charge as he usually was.

My heart was pounding in my chest, and I was hoping that maybe Nak would back away and let this one go. But after staring it down—and getting our bearings on it in the dim moonlight—Nak charged. We all followed a split second behind him.

Maybe the rat decided on me, or maybe it was instinct because I was the smallest, but I became its target. It lunged right at me, hissing with its teeth bared. I felt its nose and the scrape of its teeth on my bare skin and yanked my leg away. I turned and ran, running as hard as I could, sprinting at least twenty yards, until I was sure it was no longer chasing me.

Gasping for breath, my pulse racing, I stopped under a gnarled hardwood tree with low-hanging branches and turned to look back. The rat was gone. I was glad of that. It had dashed off into the high grass. I slowly caught my breath and looked back toward my friends, who were all laughing their heads off, when I heard something moving in the tree branches above me.

I looked straight up and met the dark eyes of an enormous king cobra, curled around the branches. Its shiny eyes looked down into mine. It lifted up and fanned out its broad head, opened its mouth, and flicked its forked tongue at me. I set out running, this time back toward my friends, who laughed even harder when they saw me coming.

"Cobra!" I yelled and kept going, running all the way back to the abandoned rice factory where my mother and Dino and other family members were.

I was happy to lie down between my mom and my dog. I forgot all about my hunger that night.

The next night, I was right back out hunting rats. My friends joked with me, but I would do the same with them when rats turned on them and they ran. It was a great game we had, this hunting of rats.

AT THE END of each workday on the tractors, the Angkar leader would appear. He always threatened Kim Ban and the rest of us, saying that we didn't do a good-enough job, even though we had fixed many tractors. "I could kill you all, and it would be no loss," he said, repeating this phrase.

As time wore on, he started asking more questions of Kim Ban, about where he had worked before the Angkar took over Cambodia. Almost every day he would ask, "Did you serve in the army?" He would point to a large scar running down the side of Kim Ban's face and onto his neck. "Where did you get this scar? You look like you were hurt in battle."

"No, comrade," Kim Ban would say, smiling. "I was working in an abattoir and got cut. And these scars"—he would pull up his shirt, exposing his badly scarred torso—"came from a truck that exploded on me while I was working on it. I was never in the army."

The Angkar leader would ask him his name, almost every day, and Kim Ban would repeat his made-up name. After threatening to have us all killed and telling us that we must do better work the next day, the leader would walk us back to the factory.

ALTHOUGH THAT ANGKAR LEADER threatened us daily, working on the tractors had a special status and perks. The men often let me drive a tractor in the fields to plow under the old rice plants after harvest and to pull plows to flatten out the fields and cut small irrigation channels for when the fields were flooded. I proved myself to be a good driver, and even Kim Ban came to trust me behind the steering wheel.

Another upside is that some of the Angkar leaders I encountered while out working on tractors would give me extra food, such as pieces of dried fish and coconuts. I was treated pretty well compared to the women working all day in the fields. This was a great benefit, as food was becoming harder to come by, and the daily meals were skimpier and skimpier bowls of rice.

Working on the tractors, however, became more difficult as time passed. Most of the tractors were in terrible condition, and many were broken down beyond repair. The tractors often had been run too hard without enough oil and were burned up. Other times, tractors had sat in heavy monsoon rains or had been taken into deeper water in flooded rice paddies, submerging the engine blocks, which ruined the motors.

I often was taken to tractors in rice paddies that had died. Some had been there for months, rusting in the rain and the heavy Cambodian humidity. There was no fixing many of them, which infuriated the Angkar leaders. They berated us for not being able to work magic on these dilapidated machines. Our only solution was to remove parts from broken-down tractors and try to get one running tractor out of two dead ones. Sometimes that worked, but most often it did not.

ONE TIME, when I had a lychee fruit and a dried piece of fish in my pocket that I had been given, I was assigned to go to a distant rice paddy to check on a tractor. I was hungry—I was always hungry then—but not completely starving, so I decided to hold off on eating my food until later. I knew it would be all I had to eat that day.

I walked several miles and came upon a group of older adults in the edge of a rice paddy near a muddy road. Two old men were working slowly, standing up in the paddy. Sitting on the ground beside them with her head hanging low was an old woman who had wrapped her arms around her knees and leaned her head forward to rest on her elbows. Her arms were like toothpicks they were so skinny.

I touched her gently on her shoulder. "Hello," I said, bowing to show respect to an elder. "Are you OK?"

She slowly raised her head, and I could tell she was barely strong enough to do that. Her eyes were red and glassy. She opened her mouth to speak, but nothing came out.

I pulled the dried fish and the lychee fruit from in my pocket and offered it to her. "I can give you this food," I said.

Tears ran from her face as she smiled up at me. "Bless you, my son," she said, her voice barely audible. "Thank you. Thank you."

She took the dried fish and the lychee fruit and began chewing on the fruit. Her teeth were almost all gone and it was a struggle for her to eat, but she appeared to be happy as a little juice squirted onto her chin. She swallowed a bite before she spoke and pushed the juice into her mouth with bony fingers. "I have not eaten in days. They tied us all to trees for three days and nights and then let us go."

I looked at the two men who were standing there, picking at the top of rice plants that were not ready to be harvested, and noticed that they were in equally bad shape. I don't think any one of them weighed one hundred pounds.

"I'm sorry I do not have more," I said.

"Go, Son," one of the men said. "She will share with us. You must take care of yourself. There are too many of us about to die for you to help. You are a good boy. Be sure to be careful and live beyond this. There is no hope for us." His voice was very articulate, much like my Teacher Peo's had been, and I imagined that this man must have once been a teacher.

The woman, who was still chewing, found some strength to stand. Her skin was wrinkled and sagged on what was left of her pitiful body. "Come here," she said. She put her arms around me and hugged, and I could feel the coldness of death in her touch—a chill that came through even though the sun was hot and it was very humid. "I pray that you have all the blessings in your future that you deserve," she said, her speech also very proper. "Go on. Save yourself." I paused and started to ask another question, but she put her finger to her lips. "Go," she said. "You must go. You are a good boy, but please go."

I walked off and left them there. I encountered many more adults and children in desperate conditions as I traveled to different fields to tend to tractors. I always tried to help when I could, but there was little I could do.

As the summer of 1975 passed into fall, the Angkar began to move laborers more often. They never gave any prior notice. Kim Ban and Sakum's daughter, Lin Ban, was sent to a labor camp in a different area. Soon after, her husband, Jak, who had worked with us on tractors, was sent to Vietnam because he was part Vietnamese. The Angkar wanted to purge the fields of anyone who was not 100 percent Khmer.

At Chroy Sdao, the conditions of the tractors we serviced continued to worsen, and the Angkar leaders' anger was intensifying toward the mechanics. In one particularly bad week when two tractors broke down that we could not fix, one of the men in our group didn't show up one morning. "What happened to him?" I asked one of the other men who worked on tractors with me.

"They took him away," he said.

"Where?"

He gave me a sad look but did not answer. I didn't know where they had taken him, but I knew it could not be good. I was still naïve about what happened to people when they disappeared, but I was becoming less so.

The fleet of tractors the Angkar had in place was woefully inadequate in comparison to the acreage of rice paddies they were attempting to plant and harvest. This effort to plant more and more rice expanded and put thousands upon thousands of workers into the fields, but the number of tractors was limited. Many of the tractors would never run again.

In lieu of tractors, the Angkar also used oxen to pull plows, as Cambodian farmers had done for centuries, but many of the animals were weak and dying. The Angkar had no plan to care for the oxen, as they had no plan to care for the well-being of the people. Just as there were no doctors or nutritious meals for the humans, there were no veterinarians or proper food for the oxen. In one field I saw an ox that had dropped dead and been left to rot in place. Laborers planted seeds around the carcass as vultures flapped down and chewed on it and flies swarmed about.

In other fields, where there were no tractors or oxen, the Angkar put men in harnesses and made them pull the plows. One day I saw two men straining to pull a plow through a recently harvested field, with ropes from the plow tied around their shoulders. Every step looked agonizing. An Angkar guard with a rifle and a black hat walked behind them, shouting, "Faster. Do not stop. Keep plowing."

They strained and sweated and pulled with all their might, but the men were skinny and small. The plow barely moved along through the field. Their strength was nothing like a tractor or a healthy ox. It was hard to watch, and I felt bad for the men.

As I traveled to other fields to try to salvage the dying fleet of tractors, I began to see many more near death's door—children with distended bellies lying on the side of the road, men and women so skinny their legs and arms looked like toothpicks, their heads hanging down so low that their chins touched their chests. I saw many people laboring in the fields who could barely stand, leaning on their tools, only occasionally making an effort to do some work.

ONE AFTERNOON I was making my way toward a distant field where I was told there was a tractor I should try to fix. The field was far away from where we usually worked, and it was a road I had not been down before. The other men who worked on tractors were busy somewhere else, so I went alone that day. I was glad for the assignment, happy to get away from where the guards watched everyone like a hawk.

I enjoyed the solitude of this walk in the country. Several hours after starting my journey, I began to smell a horrible odor. It smelled like an ox was decomposing. I kept walking, believing an ox had died and been left to rot in the sun. I hoped I would pass it, and the smell would go away.

As I moved on, I noticed off to the left of the road ahead of me a low, grayish mound of strange shapes that spread out for several hundred feet. The lumps were gray and brown and dark green, with patches of white here and there.

I puzzled on this until I got closer and could clearly make out a skull. I realized then what this was: a pile of bodies. Thousands were stacked beside the road.

The stench was terrible, but I didn't turn away. I also realized—and it was like a lightning bolt striking me in the heart—that the many people who had been taken away had been killed. All I could think of was my pa. Was his body here? I studied the pile more closely, and it was clear many had on the old green uniforms that Cambodian soldiers like my father wore. The cloth was rotting and faded and dirty from exposure to the sun and the rain, but I could identify that uniform anywhere. Flies buzzed on the corpses, and vultures fed on the remains.

It had been about five or six months since they had taken my pa away. Was this what had become of him? I had always hoped that he was working somewhere else or that they had kept him in a prison and taken care of him, but I knew, looking at these bodies—arms and legs twisted in all sorts of awkward angles—that there was very little chance my pa was still alive. He could be in this mass grave that they didn't even bother to cover with dirt.

I thought of all the men my pa had introduced me to on the army base in Battambang City. How many of them were here? Had all of them been killed when the Khmer Rouge invaded? I studied the faces I could see, but the skin on most had rotted away and the corpses were black. The bones of some skeletons were starting to show through, accounting for the patches of white I had seen. I doubted that I would recognize my pa in this condition.

I had known all along what a cruel regime the Khmer Rouge and the Angkar government they had created had been, but seeing the aftermath of this carnage made me feel like I was no bigger than a tiny bug waiting to be squashed.

I don't know how long I stood there. It seemed like forever. After staring at the corpses, I looked down, near the edge of the road. Beside the pile of bodies, I saw a pile of small metal dog tags, the identification that soldiers wore, dumped on the ground. The dull silver of these tags glinted in the searing sun. I looked more closely. There were thousands of identification tags, most on broken, lightweight chains that soldiers wore around their necks. The Khmer Rouge had stripped them off each soldier before they dumped their bodies.

I squatted by the pile of stinking corpses and searched through the dog tags, reading the name of every single I.D. I started on one end of the pile. On each one I hoped to see the name Lt. Oun Seuth, my pa. If it did not have his name, I tossed it and the broken chain behind me.

Part of me didn't want to find my father's identification. If I didn't find it, that meant he might have survived. Even though I knew in my head there was virtually no chance of his being alive, in my heart I still had hope.

I did not find his dog tag, but after several hours of reading the names, I found a dog tag for my pa's friend, Sreang. He had directed me to my father when I saw him that last time at the school. I thought about Sreang and remembered how downcast he had looked on that day. He had known what fate had in store for him. My pa had known too. I, however, had not known the depths of what the Khmer Rouge would do and how little they cared for human life.

I closed my eyes and felt like all of the Earth was pressing down on me.

After a while, I opened my eyes. I put Sreang's dog tag in my pocket. I wanted to show it to my mother and tell her what I had seen. I began making my way back toward Chroy Sdao.

When I got back to the garage around sunset, I told the Angkar leader I had gotten lost and could not find the field with the tractor. He was angry about this, but not nearly as angry as he would have been if I told him the truth about what I had found.

THAT NIGHT IN THE FACTORY, after we all lay down to sleep, I whispered to my mother, "Mom, I found a big pile of bodies. Of soldiers."

Her eyes, which had been closed, opened wide. She sat up and leaned close to me. "Where?" she said.

"Far north of here, when they sent me to find a tractor."

"How do you know it was soldiers?"

"They had on uniforms, like Pa wore. And I found this." I pulled Sreang's dog tag out of my pocket and held it up. It was dim in there, with only one low lantern in the corner of that spacious factory, but it glimmered a little in the low light.

She read it and got very upset, squeezing my shoulder hard. "You must throw that away, far from here," she said, her whisper fierce. "Do it tomorrow. They will kill us immediately if they find you with that."

She lay back down on her bed made of bamboo and cried.

I listened as she tried to control her sobs. I knew she was thinking about my pa, his body in a mass grave.

This was confirmation of the horrible truth we had known all along but didn't want to admit.

Darkness

MY DAYS WORKING on tractors and nights of hunting and eating rats continued for months, stretching into the fall of 1975. One morning when I awoke, my mom put her hand over my mouth before I could speak. "They took Kim Ban and Sakum away overnight," she whispered. Her jaw trembled.

"Where did they take them?" I asked.

"I don't know," my mom said. "They were very rough with them. We must stick to our stories. They may interrogate us. You remember Kim Ban's and Sakum's new names, correct?"

"Yes."

"Do not say anything. Be quiet. Tend to your dog." She looked toward the door, observing that the guard was looking in another direction, and then back at me. "Do not ask anyone about them," she said, grabbing my arm. "Act like nothing has happened. You know their stories. Stick to them if you are questioned."

I petted Dino, who had been beside me all night, as he was every night. He was smart and could sense something was wrong. He let out a soft whimper, as though he were trying to speak to me.

I couldn't imagine what my life under the Angkar would be without Kim Ban. He had become like a father to me. My mom loved Sakum, her aunt, very much. Sakum had helped care for me when I was a sickly baby, and I still thought of her as my other mother. I didn't know what would become of me and my mom without them.

The Angkar leaders began shouting at us to come out and line up for work. I stayed close to my mother. Dino, whose routine was to run outside and roam around Chroy Sdao when we left in the morning, stayed by me. He sensed that I was upset and that bad things were happening.

The group of men lined up to go to the tractors, but I did not join them. Everyone looked more scared than usual, and no one was talking. I noticed that some of the other men were gone too. I had seen a mass grave. I worried that could be Kim Ban's and Sakum's fate as well. I stayed right next to my mother, leaning against her side so I could feel her presence.

The angry woman who led the group of women and children was doing her usual morning screaming. My mom and sister walked over to her group, and I went with them. I did not want to leave my mom's side. Dino walked with me, but I looked down at him. "No, Dino, you can't go. Go play." I leaned down and petted him. His eyes looked up into mine, questioning me. I pointed at the fields around the factory. "Go. I will see you tonight. *Go.*" He ran away, looking back at me with concerned eyes.

I turned and walked across the common area and stood by my mom. The woman in the black hat saw me "*Good!* A new recruit!" she screamed. "Angkar will put you to work in the rice paddies. Line up!"

It was October by this time, when the monsoon rains were heavy. We had been held captive for six months.

The woman in the black hat began walking, and the group followed. We trudged along a muddy road that cut through fields that had been flooded. Nobody in our group of about thirty women and children talked. Everything was wet and damp and hot, even though it was early in the morning. It had rained hard overnight, and my bare feet stuck in the mud with every step. The open fields seemed to stretch on forever around us, most holding standing water. A few fields were green, but this was the planting season, I was soon to learn, when the heavy rains aid the growth of new plants. Most of the fields were flooded and muddy.

After walking about a mile, we arrived at an intersection of water-filled fields where two men in black hats were waiting by a small paddy dam, one of them holding an AK-47. The woman who had been leading us turned and screamed, "Get to work! Today you plant. Go to this field and pick seedlings." She pointed behind us to a field that was green with new rice plants. "That is the nursery field. Go there, grab a bundle of seedlings. Plant them in this field here," she said, pointing to an open field on the other side of the road that looked like a lake. "When you finish planting your bundle, get another bundle. Keep doing it. You must fill out this field today. It must be fully planted by sundown. Hurry up!"

"Follow me," my mom said.

She trudged into the field where rice plants had begun to grow. The water was about six inches deep, and her feet and ankles disappeared into it. "Come and watch me," she said. "I will show you how. We move the baby plants to the other field."

I followed her down into the rice paddy, my bare feet sinking into the mud. Everyone was barefoot, the only way to work in such a muddy field. It was not easy to walk in the muck. Each step required effort to pull my foot from the mud and move forward.

My mom moved to the edge of the growth of the rice seedlings, which looked like thick grass about a foot high. She bent down, grabbed a handful of plants at the roots, pulled them up, and slapped the bunch on the surface of the water to remove the mud. She stacked the baby rice plants she picked and let them float on the water behind her. She turned to pick more seedlings, slapping each handful on the water to get the mud off before adding them to her pile. "You do the same," she said. "You need to pick your own bundle."

I moved to a spot next to her and reached down beneath the water and felt the bottom. I squeezed a few plants and tugged. The seedlings came loose. "Good," my mom said. "Now get the mud off."

I slapped the plants against the water. The mud sticking to the roots came off. "That's it," my mom said. "Keep doing it until you have a good-sized bunch. Then we'll carry these over and plant them."

It was hard work, bending over, the sun bright on us, and it wasn't even eight o'clock in the morning yet. I was soaking wet and sweating. I kept pulling the plants and putting them in a stack on the water. No one in our group, which had spread out along the field of seedlings, was talking. Everyone had their head down. Guards in black were watching us from the road. After about half an hour, my mom said, "That's enough. Let's bundle these up and go to the other field."

My mom scooped up plants that she had picked and made a bundle that she tied with one of the stalks. She helped me get my bundle together and tied it for me. "Now we plant," she said. We walked up onto the paddy dam—most of the fields full of water were lined by these low, man-made dams that kept them from draining—and across the road and down to the paddy field where we had been directed. The woman who had led our group here yelled, "There! Plant. Hurry up. You are too slow."

Others from our group had started planting their seedlings, bending over and pressing the plants into the mud. This field was full of water, almost a foot high. The skies had clouded over and it started to rain, soaking us head to toe, but everyone kept working. I stepped down into water that came up almost to my knees. My mom moved past three other women and found a spot. She dropped her bundle to float on the water. "You come here, on this side of me. We will make a row." She gestured to indicate the line she planned in the soaked field.

"What you have to do is take a seedling," she said, picking one plant loose from the bundle and bending over. "Push it down in the mud with your thumb. With your forefingers, make a small hole in the mud. Then, with your thumb, you poke the root down in the mud and pack it in tight." She held the plant above water and showed me the motion, and then she planted the seedling. It stayed put, its top only a few inches above the water. "You do it now."

I pulled a seedling from my stack and bent down, putting about half of my body into the muddy water. I tried to do as she said, but my seedling did not stay. It floated up. "No," she said, "you must make sure you make a deep-enough hole for the root and cover it. They watch this. If you don't plant right, the seedlings will float everywhere. If that happens, the guards will accuse you of sabotage and kill you. I've seen them do that to others."

I tried again, and the seedling stayed. "That's better," my mom said. "Make sure you get them in there good. We will try to fill in this row. Plant them two by two and set a pattern." She bent back down and started planting, and I did the same. "Look," she said. "See how I have them organized? Two by two. It is important to plant them orderly." I stood up straight and nodded. I bent over again and continued to plant. My back was already tired, and we had been working only about an hour.

These rice paddies, often called paddy fields, were like many I would work in over the next three years. A rice paddy is simply a field with several inches of standing water in it. The standing water prevents weeds from growing and protects the rice from getting too hot or cold. Cambodia, being tropical, is the perfect environment for rice production, particularly the northwest region, which is often called the "rice bowl" because it is so fertile. Rice, which is a grain, looks like high grass when the plants are fully grown. I would learn about harvest time later. We were in the planting stage, however, when a rice paddy looks like a muddy, shallow lake.

I had eaten much rice in my young life, but I had never farmed it. It is grueling work when done by hand, which is how millions of Cambodians from the cities were now being forced to do it in the Killing Fields. The rural people whose ancestors had farmed this way for thousands of years had enslaved city people like me and my mom and sister and millions of others to join them in this ancient practice.

I looked ahead. The muddy rice paddy looked not like a field but like a brown ocean that I could never cross. Working on the tractors seemed like child's play compared to this task. The rain had stopped, and the sun was hot and the temperature rising. The humidity must have been nearly 100 percent. None of the workers had hats, and we all were dressed in black. I felt the sun on my back, heating my shirt. The only drinking water we had was the muddy water around our feet.

I felt a sharp sting above my ankle. I looked down and saw a slimy, black leech about the size of my little finger attached to my skin. I reached down to move it. It stuck to my fingers. I yanked my hand away, but it stayed on my leg. "Mom," I called out, panicked. "A leech is on me."

She looked at me but did not straighten up. "They are everywhere," she said. "I will scrape it off later. They are watching us now. Don't touch it. It will not hurt you. It will be OK."

I summoned up everything I had and followed my mom's lead, trying not to think about the leech sucking blood from my leg while I was planting the seeds that would contribute to the largest harvests of rice in Cambodia's history. The repetition seemed endless: Plant a few seedlings. Move a few steps through the mud and water with the bundle. Plant a few seedlings. Move a few steps through the mud and water. Plant a few seedlings. Over and over and over again. I did not feel the same sense of accomplishment that I had when working on the tractors. I was sick of doing this, but at least the bundle was getting smaller. At the edge of the field one of the men was watching us, and not too far from him stood a soldier with an AK-47. Someone with an automatic rifle slung over their shoulder always seemed to be in sight.

I looked at my mom's face, which she kept down to avoid the bright sun, her eyes squinting, as she bent over and planted. Her face was expressionless, resigned to this job for the day, for the week, for the month, for however long it lasted.

I kept pressing the seedlings into the mud. Occasionally I looked over and she smiled softly at me, nodding her head in encouragement.

We planted seedlings for about four or five hours and were almost finished with our bundles when we heard a bell ringing. "Lunchtime," my mom said. We headed out of the paddy and back to where we had started, walking along the edge of the rice paddy we had planted with seedlings.

"Come here," my mom said. She took a piece of grass, bent down, held it with two hands, and scraped it along my skin, knocking off the leech, which was fat with blood. Some blood trickled out of the spot where it had been on my leg, and my skin was red. "Some people tie the bottom of their pants tight to keep them from getting up their legs," she said. "But don't do it too tight. It can cut off your blood flow. And I don't think it works too well. The leeches are boneless, and they can get up there if they want to. Just let me know when you get one, and I will get it off."

She directed me down the road. The woman who was our group leader stood behind a big pot and a stack of bowls. "*Line up!*" she screamed. "Over here."

We joined the line. The woman ladled rice soup from the pot into dented, dirty metal bowls and handed them out.

I followed my mom and sister in the line. "Hurry!" the woman yelled. My mom took one and then I got mine as I walked behind her. I glanced up at the woman who was like a witch to me. She gave me a nasty look, her eyes staring straight at me and her mouth bunching up in a crooked smile. I looked down at my feet to break eye contact with her.

There were no chairs or tables where we could sit. We had no options of shade or cover. The day had grown cloudy again, but it was still very hot. As soon as I got my bowl, we heard thunder and saw dark clouds. A heavy rain began to fall, getting water into my already watery bowl of rice soup. I put my hand over the top of the bowl and leaned over it to keep the downpour out, but it still got much water in it.

My mom and sister sat down on the edge of the rice paddy dam in the mud, and I followed them. We sat in the rain and drank from the small metal bowls. My bowl of lukewarm rice soup was only half full, and I slurped down its contents in only a few seconds. There was very little rice in the soup and nothing else, not even salt. I longed for hay mushrooms, something to fill my belly, but none were in sight.

We finished eating what little we had received and sat there, staring down at the mud, holding our empty bowls, saying nothing, the rain soaking our black clothes. After only a few minutes, the woman screamed again, "Return your bowls and get back to work."

We filed by and put our bowls in a stack.

We spent the afternoon, often in heavy rains, picking the seedlings in the nursery field and making bundles and then planting them in the larger field. It seemed endless. Plant a few seedlings. Move a few steps through the mud and water with the bundle.

Repeat.

Over and over and over again.

I spent most of the day bending over. I was exhausted and hungry and dehydrated. I could tell everyone felt the same way. Many of our group began to slow down. I saw one woman just standing in the field, not moving, her eyes closed, sleeping for a few seconds at a time.

I began looking around to see if the Angkar were watching me. I thought about burying all my seedlings in the mud in one spot, but then I saw the man in the distance and the ever-present guard with the AK-47. I didn't want to get into trouble because I knew it would mean trouble not just for me, but for my mom and my sister.

I trudged on, praying for the day to end. Although it seemed like it never would, eventually it did. After the Angkar rang the bell to end the workday, we walked about a mile back to Chroy Sdao, where Dino greeted me happily. Dino's love and affection brought the only happy moments I had in that time. He could make me smile in spite of it all.

We collapsed onto the bamboo pallets in the rice-processing factory where we spent our nights. I was very hungry and thought about going out hunting for rats, but I didn't see my friends, nor did I have the energy. I was so tired that I just lay down and stared at the ceiling until I fell asleep.

This was the first of countless days I would work in the rice paddies, days that almost killed me.

EACH TORTUROUS DAY of work lasted for twelve hours or more. It was all we did when we were not sleeping. I planted seedlings over vast fields, muddy expanses that seemed to spread on forever and ever, each day walking through the mud in my bare feet. With each step my foot plunged ankle deep—again and again and again. I learned to live with the leeches, hoping they didn't drink all my blood before I could get out of the paddy to remove them.

I did everything you can do in a rice paddy, as did my mother and sister. We planted seedlings in what seemed like a million acres. When the harvesting season began, we worked with a small J-shaped knife blade to cut off the tops of the rice plants where the grains grew and fill up a bag that we would deliver to the Angkar for threshing. This was very hard because the bags became heavier as they were filled. The bags were never full enough for the Angkar's liking, but nothing was ever good enough for them. After the harvest was reaped, we went in the fields with long tools that were like a scythe except made of bamboo. We did our best with these crude tools to clear away the old rice plants and make way for the new. If an ox or tractor had plowed the fields, we took tools to smooth out the surface in preparation for flooding and the planting of more seedlings. It was a never-ending cycle of growing rice—always with a guard carrying an AK-47 watching us to make sure we kept working.

There were never any rest breaks. If you had to pee, you were expected to sit down and pee where you were, right into the rice paddy. If you had to poop, you asked a guard, who told you to go and be back quickly. If you didn't come back right away, the guard would find and punish you, often by denying any lunch at all. If they thought you were trying to escape, it was very bad. I saw kids and adults who were tied to trees for hours at a time as punishment. Sometimes their heads were stuck in plastic bags, and they were left to the point of almost suffocating. My mom had seen workers killed right where they stood, so we always obeyed. Often workers would be picked out by the guards and led away, never to be seen again.

This is how the months passed. Each day we awoke with the sunrise and got home about sunset. All we had to eat was the same watery rice soup they served for lunch each day. Some nights, in spite of my exhaustion, I went hunting for rats in the group led by my friend Nak. We caught rats and that helped with my hunger, but we were all gradually being starved and on the verge of being worked to death.

My mom had heard nothing about Kim Ban and Sakum, and we worried about them every day. Deep down we knew they were dead, just like we knew the truth about my father. We just didn't want to say it.

I DIDN'T GO HUNTING for rats every night like I had when working on the tractors. It wasn't as much fun as it had been, and the Angkar village leaders were becoming more angry and suspicious of us. Nak and the other boys and I worried about being caught, and we started going farther and farther from the village at night. Some nights, I was just too tired to hunt for rats, even though I needed more to eat. I would lie on my bamboo pallet in a daze, like most of those living in the factory, and stare at the rusty beams of the factory ceiling. Our lives were a hellish series of repetitions: Wake, walk, work, walk, sleep. I know my telling of this story is repetitive, but repetition was all we knew. We did not get a day off. They worked us like the slaves we were, seven days a week.

Nak would come to me every evening and give me a look, nodding and raising one eyebrow. He said nothing, but I knew he meant, "Let's go hunt for rats." Sometimes I would go, but many nights I didn't feel like it. I hated to decline his offer because I enjoyed his company and friendship, but many times I was just too tired. He was still working with the tractor group and had more energy at the end of the day than I did.

One morning, after a night when I had declined his offer to hunt rats with him, I walked out of the factory when the Angkar woke us up. I looked around in the early morning light and saw something that caused me to lose my breath and my blood to run cold.

Nak's body was hanging from a pole outside the factory.

His stomach and chest had been cut open and stuffed with straw. He was only about ten or twelve years old, but they had slit him down the middle and stuffed him like a scarecrow.

I had been out hunting rats with him only two nights before.

My hands and body started shaking. I turned my head away and got as far from his displayed corpse as I could. I didn't want to be close to his body, and I thought I was going to throw up. My eyes filled with tears, but I fought back the urge to sob or fall to the ground.

That could have been me up there.

None of the workers said anything about the presence of his body hanging from a pole in our midst, but when it was time to leave, an Angkar leader addressed us. "This is what happens if you try to escape," he said. "This is the consequence if you don't listen. This is the punishment if you break Angkar laws. You must be loyal to Angkar. If you are not, you will die."

I had seen Nak's mutilated body for only a split second before I turned my head. No matter how hard I tried not to think about it, it was all I could see as I labored in the rice paddies in the weeks and months afterward. Even today, it is deep down inside me, this picture of Nak hanging on a pole and stuffed with straw. I wish I could remove it, but it is a memory etched in my mind that will stay with me forever.

I CONTINUED to hunt rats occasionally with the other boys after Nak was killed, but I did it sparingly and we were extremely careful. I had to have something other than the skimpy bowl of rice soup they fed us each day, and I always looked out for hay mushrooms or wild vegetables or fruits we might find. The way the fields were cleared for rice planting and nothing else, I had little chance of finding anything decent to eat.

It was about this time that I resorted to eating bugs that I found in the rice paddies. I would collect them during the day, often being stung. At night I would cut off their heads and clean out the innards I knew I shouldn't eat and then roast them over a small fire if I could make one. They had no taste, but I liked the crunch. Eating a bug wasn't so bad when there was nothing in my stomach. Like the mushrooms, they were a good source of protein and other vitamins. If I couldn't make a fire, I would sometimes eat the bugs raw. It was better than not eating anything.

In addition to the lack of food, we had no clean drinking water. The only water we got to drink was rainwater that fell into a bucket or water we could scoop out of the rice paddy, which was very muddy. Often when it rained, I would look skyward and open my mouth to catch the raindrops.

With each long workday, we all grew more tired and skinnier, and our complexions grew darker, like those of the peasants. We didn't get to go to the river to bathe, so the only cleanliness we had came from the heavy rains that fell on us while we were working. In the long dry season of winter, we never got a chance to get clean.

The one joy in life I still had was my sweet dog Dino. He knew the time when I would be coming home, and every day he waited for me. In the past, he had waited for me after each school day. This time, he awaited my coming back to the rice factory from the fields. I could always count on him. I would trudge up and he would be so excited to see me, barking happily and jumping up and down. My step would always quicken when I saw his black-and-white face and I would forget for a moment how tired I was. I would pick him up and pet him and tell him that he was a good boy, hugging him tight. He would lick my face and wriggle with joy in my arms.

When I went inside and lay down to sleep, he would lie down next to me. I scratched his back and his belly and the top of his head, his legs wriggling with delight. He slept by me every night, and I was always fearful the Angkar would take him away. If I awoke during the night, he was always there.

Dino was getting enough to eat by hunting mice and rats around the village. French bulldogs are good ratters, and I think that's why the Angkar left him alone. He had plenty of vermin to consume. He was not getting skinny like we were. The families staying in the rice factory all came to love him too. He was a sweet dog and never caused any trouble.

Even when he wasn't with me, he helped sustain my spirit. During the long days in the fields, I would think about Dino. I would be going through the repetitive motions with my hands, but in my mind, I would picture how happy he would be to see me at the end of the day. I would imagine that I was petting him and he was licking my face. I would forget for a few minutes that I was a slave by visiting my dog in my mind.

After another long day, sometime in early to mid-1976, maybe four or five months after Nak had been killed, I walked home, exhausted as usual. We lived exhausted, as though we were sleepwalking through each day, more tired one day than we had been the day before. Time had ceased to have meaning, and one day was no different from the next. I was ten years old by this time, but that meant nothing in the Angkar world.

I approached the factory and looked to the spot where Dino usually waited. My heart lifted for a moment because I expected to see his sweet face—but he wasn't there. I walked around the factory looking for him, and then I went inside to the place where we slept on the floor.

He wasn't there either.

I retraced my steps and then went everywhere I knew in the Chroy Sdao village. I looked for hours with no luck, calling out his name when no Angkar leaders were nearby. "Dino. Dino. Where are you?" I thought maybe he had gone to sleep someplace where I couldn't find him.

I reluctantly went to bed, but I worried about Dino all night and didn't sleep.

The next morning, as we were getting ready to go to work, a man who worked on the tractors came over to me. He held his head down and spoke quietly. "I think your dog was shot and killed. He is over near the old train tracks, down that way about a quarter of a mile."

I walked off immediately, not worrying about getting in trouble with the Angkar. All I could think about was Dino.

I walked fast to the long-abandoned train tracks, and then I saw him—his body lay in a pool of blood. He had been shot many times.

It looked like they had used him for target practice.

I picked up his body and cried. *How could they do this to him?* He had done nothing to these people. He was killing rats that were eating their crops. I could not understand it.

I carried Dino's body to a spot behind the rice-processing factory where none of the Angkar or people gathering to go work could see me. His blood had soaked into my black shirt. I lay him gently on the ground, and I knelt and used my hands to dig in the dirt. The ground was soft from rain overnight, and I scooped out a hole in which to bury him. I cried the whole time I clawed at the earth.

Once the hole was about two feet deep, I put him in and pushed dirt over his body. Tears continued to pour down my face. I tried to be quiet because if the Angkar had seen me, they might have killed me too.

Dino was my very best friend and a family member. They killed him for no reason other than because they could.

I stood by the spot where I had buried my beloved dog and cried. I didn't know how I could go on.

I'm Not Going to Die Today

[MAY 1976–DECEMBER 1977]

B Y THE TIME DINO WAS KILLED, we had been living under the Angkar regime for a year or more. I had no idea that on the other side of the globe, the United States was celebrating two hundred years of liberty. We had no news from the outside world. While huge parades and parties took place in Philadelphia, where I would live two decades later, I knew nothing of freedom. All I knew was seven long days a week in the rice fields, starvation, threats, and exhaustion.

Although each new day was much the same, each day also was a little bit worse. We were getting weaker, hungrier, and more tired. Time and hard labor and lack of food and clean water were taking their toll. The Angkar's suspicion of the workers was growing more intense. We worried constantly about our identities as the family of a Cambodian soldier being revealed. My mom and sister recognized a few people from Battambang City working in the fields and feared that we would be reported. We could trust no one because the enslaved laborers often turned on each other in hopes of winning favor and protection from the Angkar.

This went on for many months. One evening my sister was walking back from the fields to Chroy Sdao when she was approached by another laborer. "I recognize you from Battambang City," the woman said, pointing at her. "I remember your father. He was in the army. Lieutenant Oun was his name, I think."

"No," my sister said, but she did not have a good poker face. Her eyes were wide. "You have that wrong. I am from Battambang City, but my father was not in the army. I didn't know my father. His name was Sin Rith. He left me and my mother. He was a taxi driver."

"No, I remember him. And you too."

My sister hurried away as fast as she could. She whispered the story to me and my mother so no one else could hear. Our concern grew even more. "Do not admit the truth," my mom said. "Remember our stories. You must remember."

A few days later as we trudged home from the fields under the setting sun, an Angkar leader approached my mom before she could go into the factory. "Come talk to me," he said. "In office."

He gestured to the brick office building the Angkar used as a local headquarters.

My mom left with the man, and my sister Dy began to cry. Dy ran into the factory, and I followed her. She lay with her face on her arms and sobbed. I sat beside her and didn't say anything, ignoring the stares from the others around us. I wondered if my mom would not come back, just as Kim Ban and Sakum and my pa had not come back.

We had watched as others in the factory had been called to the office and had not returned. We did not know who they were, only that they were gone.

I'm not sure how long we waited—it seemed like many hours, but it might have been only one hour or even less—but my mom returned to us after dark. The factory was lit by a few lanterns, so it was very dim in there after the sun went down. My mom's face was tight and her eyes tired, but we were thrilled she was back with us. My sister and I hugged her, and as we did, she whispered, "Remember our story."

We lay down on our bamboo beds and tried to go to sleep.

Only a few minutes after my mom returned, the Angkar leader who had questioned her appeared in the doorway. He talked with the guard, pointing at my sister. The guard came across the factory floor and pointed the muzzle of his AK-47 at my sister. "Angkar wants to see you. Now."

She got up and followed him out, her face taut with fear. My mom sat and pulled me to her and hugged me tight. A few of the families started putting out their lanterns, and it grew even darker.

My mom and I sat there—it was impossible to sleep, worrying about my sister Dy—until Dy came back. Again, it's hard to say for how long, because it seemed like an eternity. My mother had not said anything to me because she feared the surrounding families reporting us. She smiled quickly and softly when she saw my sister reappear in the doorway and make her way over to us.

I knew that I would be next. I waited and recited to myself all our new names, and I rehearsed in my head the story about my father being a taxi driver. I had never used it, and it had been more than a year since we had first planned it, but my mom occasionally had reminded me of it.

My eyes were wide open, staring up at the dark ceiling.

"Try to go to sleep," my mom said. I stretched out, but I was too afraid. I knew they would be coming for me.

I stared at the dark factory ceiling and waited.

A few hours must have passed before the guard at the door called me. "You. Boy. Come here." I rose and walked out. I saw my mom's face, her jaw trembling a little as I was led away. "This way," he said, gesturing with the muzzle of the AK-47.

It was sometime after midnight. I followed him out of the factory, across the common area, and into the brick building. It was poorly lit, with only a weak oil lantern in the hallway, and smelled of mildew and kerosene. The guard pushed me into the first room on the right. The man who had questioned my mom was sitting in an old bamboo chair. A dim lantern sat on the floor beside him. An old filing cabinet had been knocked over on its side, and stacks of paper and folders spilled out onto the floor in one corner.

The Angkar leader sat there in his black uniform and stared at me. The guard came into the room and stood at my side with his rifle. I stared at my bare feet, not wanting to make eye contact. I knew better than to speak before I was spoken to.

After what seemed like a very long time, he smiled like he was my friend. "Your pa. He was in the army, wasn't he? Lieutenant Oun Seuth, correct? In Battambang City?" He nodded, prodding me to agree with him.

"No. I never knew my father." I looked him in the eye, and for some reason, I felt strong. My mom had prepared me for this moment. "I am told he was a taxi driver. But I didn't know him. He left my mom before I was born."

I thought I had sounded convincing, but the man turned angry, rose up out of his chair, and shouted, "Liar!" He slapped me hard across the face. I fell to the floor under his blow, and tears filled my eyes from the pain. The guard with the rifle stepped closer.

"Get up!" the man yelled. "Tell me the truth! You will be in serious trouble if you don't."

I stood slowly but didn't say anything.

"What was your pa's name? He was in the army. We know. Several people have told us."

"I'm sorry, comrade, but I didn't know him. I'm told his name was Sin Rith and that he was a taxi driver."

He raised his hand as if to slap me again, but then he stopped as he thought better of it. "What's your name?"

"Sin Prou."

"Where did you go to school?"

"I didn't go. We couldn't afford it. I helped my mom by picking up plastic and aluminum. I never went to school."

"Don't lie to me, city boy. You have been to school. I can tell by the way you talk."

"No," I said. "I didn't."

"Wait here. Don't you dare move."

He left the room and came back with a framed letter. He handed the frame to me. "Read that," he said.

I could read it. It was a typewritten letter from Prince Sihanouk, written in the 1960s on fancy stationery. It was addressed to all of Cambodia's rice farmers, praising them for the good work they do, and it talked about building new canals for fresh water. The glass covering the letter had several cracks in it.

But I knew better. I looked at it and scrunched up my face. "I can't read."

"You can't read any words?"

I slumped my head and looked at the letter. I pointed at Prince Sihanouk's name and asked, "Does that say Khmer?"

He paused, studying me longer. I knew he was trying to decide if I was lying. I saw a change in his posture, and I think he must have decided that he believed me. "Do you like working in the fields? Do you do a good job?"

"Yes, comrade," I said.

"You must work hard for Angkar. Angkar is building a great society. If you work hard, we all will reap the benefits. If you don't, you and your family will die."

I nodded. "Yes, comrade."

"I better not find out you have been lying to me. I will check up on you to see if you are working hard. Now go."

THE NEXT DAY, we walked to the fields as usual, led by the angry little woman. We spent the morning harvesting rice grains, cutting the tops of the plants and filling up bags and carrying them to the drop-off spot to get another bag to fill up. We did this again and again and again. There was no end to it. We never seemed to make any progress. It was as if all of Cambodia had been turned into one infinite rice paddy.

At lunchtime, when my mom and sister and I were sitting after finishing our bowl of rice soup, the angry woman approached my mother. "Don't go back to the fields. You are moving to Nikum. Go back to Chroy Sdao and get your stuff. Angkar there will give you instructions on where to go. If you try to escape, you know what will happen to you."

A young man in black with a red-and-white *krama* and a pair of sandals made from rubber tires stepped forward. My blood ran cold. I didn't know what Nikum was or what the future held in store for us, but I knew it could not be good.

My mother didn't say anything. Her dark eyes looked at the woman, and she nodded. We started walking back to the factory. The soldier did not follow us but stood and watched as we headed down the road.

At Chroy Sdao, one of the young men who was an Angkar leader—there were so many who barked orders and they changed so often, it was hard to tell them apart—was waiting for us. He told us that we needed to report to Nikum. "It takes a few hours to walk there," he said. "Go down this road and stay on it. You will find it. Report to the village leader. If you do not, we will find you."

We gathered our meager clothes and sheets and blankets and tied them in a bundle. We couldn't carry the bamboo pallets we'd made to sleep on, so we left those behind.

We started walking in the direction he'd pointed, the afternoon hot and muggy with storm clouds threatening. After about an hour, we didn't see anyone. It seemed like we were walking to the end of the world. We walked for another hour, the afternoon getting late, and still we did not see anything.

My mom stopped. "I hope we are not lost," she said, her eyes nervous. "I thought we would have been there by now."

It seemed like we would never get there, but eventually a village came into view along the lonesome, muddy road. It was a hodgepodge of structures with thatch roofs built into a circle. Chroy Sdao, which had a brick building and the factory and other sturdy buildings, seemed modern and sophisticated compared to this primitive outpost.

A guard who couldn't have been more than sixteen or seventeen approached us with an AK-47. "Is this Nikum?" my mom asked.

He nodded.

"We have orders from Chroy Sdao to come here," she said.

"Wait here," he said. "Don't move a step." He went into the first thatched structure.

I looked at my mom, who rubbed her hand on my head. I started to speak, but she put a finger to her lips and shook her head.

The guard came out with a man who appeared to be in his twenties. His black pajama-like uniform looked new, as did his red-and-white *krama*, and he wore a military-style cap. His rigid posture made it clear he was the boss. "Tomorrow, you join new groups and work for Angkar," he said. He pointed to a hut in the circle. "Tonight you can stay in that hut. The third one. A widow lives there."

He turned to the guard with the rifle. "Tell the widow to lodge them for the night. And watch them," he said, gesturing to us. "Make sure they don't try to run away." He went back inside his thatched hut.

The guard went into the widow's hut and spoke to her while we waited. He came out and gestured for us to go inside.

We climbed up the four steps into the hut, not knowing what to expect. Inside the dim hut we could see that the woman was heavily wrinkled and had silver hair. She was very short, about my height, and I was short for my age. "Welcome," she said, smiling at us. It was the first smile I had seen from a stranger in many days. "Have you had anything to eat?"

My mother said that we had not eaten since a meager bowl of rice soup at lunch.

"I don't have much, but I can offer you a potato," the widow said. "I will cook it for you. And I have some water too."

She built a small fire in the tiny clay oven on the side of her hut and roasted the potato for us. She cut it into three pieces, which were not big, and gave one each to me, my mom, and my sister. I was so hungry and tired that I could have eaten twenty potatoes, but I was happy to have the one piece. We gulped down the cups of water she gave us.

After thanking her, we lay down on the bamboo floor of her hut to sleep. With the small bite of food in my belly and this thatched roof over my head and this woman's warmth toward us, I thought Nikum might not be so bad. It seemed comfortable and more friendly than Chroy Sdao had been.

I could not have been more wrong.

THE NEXT MORNING we were awakened by shouting. "Wake up, you lazy shits! Wake up! Everyone wake up!"

The widow was standing, looking outside her door, her face sad. "You should hurry," she said.

We rose and walked out to meet the day. There was a group of six Angkar leaders, all men, all in hats, all shouting. Behind them were four very young men with AK-47s, their faces full of hate as they watched us descend the steps of the widow's hut and join others gathering in the common area that was ringed by the circle of huts. The village was surrounded on all sides by rice paddies as far as the eye could see. Several dozen laborers were assembled, including two other families with several children about my age.

"You!" one of the men yelled at my mom. "You go to the female group." He grabbed her by the arm and pulled her toward a line of women who were waiting. The group had a woman leader who had a haircut and a disposition just like the angry woman we had left behind in Chroy Sdao. "Hurry up," she screamed at my mom. "We have to get to work."

My sister and I started to follow our mom, but an Angkar leader yelled at us. "Stay here. Not with her. You—" he said, pointing at me, "will go to the children group. To the left. And you—" he pointed to my sister, "will be in the hard charge group. I will come back for you and show you. Wait here."

Of all the fears I'd felt up to this point, none had scared me as much as being separated from my mom. She had been my rock. Her calm presence in the face of all this chaos had helped me keep it together as I lost my dad, my aunt and uncle, and my dog.

As strong as I was, I was still a little boy, and I loved my mom dearly. With the exception of Dino's death, I had been able to keep from crying most of the time. I was determined that we could survive. I was determined to be strong. But I couldn't bear to lose my mom.

Watching her being taken away from me, knowing that they could kill her and I would never see her again, tears poured down my face.

WHAT THE ANGKAR had in mind for these four groups—children, females, men, and the young adults, known as the "hard charge" group—was a competition to see which group could grow the most rice. Our groups were to work and live apart.

The Angkar leaders of the children's group I joined were a few men and one woman in black hats. They gathered us in the village and led us on a long march along a dirt road. About one hundred children were in the group, ranging in age from as young as eight to about twelve. We were all skinny, some of us more so than others, and a few of the younger children looked very frail. Several of the younger children cried constantly on the walk. The woman scolded them, "Hush your crying! You are not a baby anymore. You are Angkar! You must work hard for Angkar!"

"I want my mommy," said one little crying girl, who looked to be about eight.

"Shut up!" the woman yelled. "Angkar is your mommy now. And your daddy too. Your mom and pa didn't love you. They were just having fun when they made you. You were an accident. They didn't want you. Angkar wants you. Angkar is your family now."

The girl cried even harder, sobbing as she walked slowly along. She was skinnier than the others, and at one point she fell to her knees. "Get up," the woman yelled, smacking her on the back of the head. "You must get up. If you don't come to work, you will be killed. That goes for all of you!"

The little girl got up and kept moving. I wanted to help her, but I was afraid.

All I could think about was missing my mom, but I did not cry. I did not want to give the Angkar the satisfaction of breaking me. I did not want to let them win. I heard my pa's voice in my head: *You can do it, my son. You are a strong young man, and you can do it. This is not a forever life. You must be there for your mom.*

I vowed that I would survive and go back to my mother. I would not let her down.

After what seemed like many miles, we arrived at fields of rice paddies that had been harvested and were in the stage of being cleared for planting. The old plants were yellowing and had to be plowed under so the field could be flooded and flattened out for reseeding.

We were all given makeshift clearing tools—bamboo sticks about four feet long with a branch left on the end like a primitive hoe. Few of the children in the group were as tall as the tools we were given. The little girl who had cried so much could barely lift her stick, but the woman yelled at her, "Chop the plants! We must prepare this field for planting!"

I took my stick, and I thought about turning on the woman and bashing in her head, but I knew that would lead to my being taken away and killed. *I'm not going to die today*, I told myself, a line I would often repeat over the next two years.

I followed the children who spread out in the rice paddy and began chopping at the old plants the best I could. I realized right away that this was pointless work. Even at the age of ten, I understood that the Angkar did not know how to manage these farms. Only a tractor or a plow could do this job effectively. I went into the rice plants and swung the crude tool aimlessly, just enough to look busy and avoid being the target of the woman's screaming.

They kept us out in the fields all day long. We would spend the days pretending to work hard and keeping an eye out for when they weren't watching us. When they left, we would stand there doing nothing, and sometimes just sit or nap. But this was dangerous because if they caught a child sitting or lying down, they would pull them out of the field, tie them to a tree, and not feed them anything or give them any water. I was determined not to let that happen to me.

I had no way to relieve my misery. I didn't know if my mom and sister were dead or alive. I knew Dino was gone, and I missed him greatly when I thought about his sweet black-and-white face and how he had looked up to me. I wasn't sure about my pa, but I was mostly sure that he was dead. I also missed my baby sister Poch and was thankful that she had gone to a safer place before the Khmer Rouge had conquered the country. But we had no way of knowing that she was OK.

I could be sure of nothing.

The food the Angkar fed the children's group was more of the same, a skimpy bowl of rice soup each day. We ate out in the open, sitting on the ground, from bowls that were never washed. If it rained, it rained in our food. If it was hot and sunny, which it usually was, we sat in the sun without shade. Although there were many children, none of us ever wanted to play in the little time we had on our lunch breaks.

We had lost the desire to be children.

While the days were hellish, the nights were no better. During the first few weeks in the children's group at Nikum, we had no shelter to sleep under. We slept out in the open, on the ground next to the rice paddies where we had been assigned. I pushed together leaves and dead grass for my bed roll and lay down. We had no sheets or blankets. When it rained, we gathered up banana plant leaves to cover ourselves, but we still got soaked. I wished that my mom could be there to tuck me in and tell me good night. Although living in the abandoned factory had been unpleasant, at least I'd had a roof over my head and my mom and sister by my side. In Nikum, I didn't have anything, not even a roof.

When the nights were clear, I sometimes enjoyed the beauty of the heavens above. It was as though the sky were my movie and the wind and nature sounds my music. I'd lie there and look up at all the stars and the moon and listen to the crickets and birds singing. Lightning occasionally flashed, and sometimes an Angkar leader passed by with a torch or a lantern, but mostly it was just moonlight and starlight.

I would take in this show and think of my future. I consoled myself with what my pa had told me: *This is not a forever life.* I prayed for my mother's safety, my sisters' safety, and the return of my pa and Kim Ban and Sakum. I talked to my dog Dino, and told him how much I loved him and that he had been a good boy. I could see his sweet face looking up at me. I tried not to think about Nak and his horrible fate.

I tried to be positive and cheer myself up, but it was very hard to be optimistic when so many children around me were sick and dying. When a child in our group would not get up in the morning, the woman who led the children's group would berate them and sometimes slap them. My stomach often hurt, and I thought about saying that I was too sick to work, but I feared her anger and always went into the fields.

AFTER A FEW WEEKS of sleeping outside, the children's group was moved to a large thatched roof shelter. It had no walls, only a roof. It was better than sleeping without any cover, but not by much. The roof leaked in the heavy rains, and when the wind blew hard, rain would blow in on the children sleeping side by side like animals in a barn. In the winter, we had no protection from the cold at night. Many of the kids got sick, victim to the combination of the elements and lack of nutrients.

In the fields, the Angkar leaders yelled at us constantly to work harder and faster. They threatened our lives many times, and these threats often were based on their claim that we were losing the competition. "The children's group is losing!" the leaders yelled. "You cannot lose to the other groups."

It was never explained how we were losing, and the logic of a group of children competing with adult groups made no sense, but nothing about the world I was living in made sense.

On most nights before we went to sleep, the leaders gathered all of us in a circle and preached to us about the honor and power of Angkar. They walked around like politicians making speeches. "Angkar is saving the Khmer people!" they often said. "Angkar has stopped the corruption of the government. Angkar will restore the greatness of the Khmer!"

The Angkar leaders, a series of men and the woman who led our group, went on and on, pacing around and slapping their hands together. They made all the children chant, repeating "Angkar! Angkar! Angkar!" They also led us in songs, but I do not remember the lyrics or what they sounded like. Many of the children were inspired by this show and fell victim to the brainwashing. I clapped my hands and joined in the chants and sang, playing along enough to not attract attention to myself, but I knew that this was all a pack of lies. The Khmer Rouge had taken away and murdered my pa, they had taken away Kim Ban and Aunt Sakum and murdered them, and they had murdered my beloved dog Dino. I knew they would kill me and my mother and my sister if they knew who we were.

I hated the Khmer Rouge and the Angkar they had created. I vowed that I would never let them brainwash me. I had pretended I was someone else for a long time. I could keep pretending.

One night after his pep talk to the children, one of the men pulled me aside. "Smart boy," he said. "Where did you go to school? I can tell you are smart."

"Nowhere. I worked in Battambang City, picking up trash."

"You liar. I hear you talk. And I heard you knew how to fix engines in Chroy Sdao. You are a smart boy. You have been to school."

I didn't say anything because he was not asking me a question. To tell him he was wrong would get me at best a beating and at worst possibly tortured or even killed. Some kids who had been misbehaving or not working hard enough had been tied to trees in the sun beside the rice paddies. They were left there for hours, sometimes all day, without any food or water.

"Come with me," he said. He grabbed me by the arm and pulled me toward one of the thatched huts where the Angkar leaders stayed. The twilight was almost over and the night coming on.

He took me into a hut to see the village boss, whom my mom, my sister Dy, and I had seen when we had first arrived in Nikum. The village boss was sitting on a straw mat. The room was lit by a gas lantern and empty except for a few mats scattered on the floor.

"What have we here?" the village boss asked.

"I think he is a rich little boy who has been to school," the man who brought me in said. "You hear how he talks. He is educated. We cannot trust him. He is a spy."

The village boss stood and looked me over. "What is your name?"

"Sin Prou," I said. Long names like Sokomasath, my childhood name, were more common in the cities and often could get one killed simply for having too many syllables.

"Where are you from? Who was your father?"

I recited my lie, once again denying my father. It pained me to dishonor him again, but I knew he'd understand. I tried to tell my story in a peasant dialect with no regard for the grammar I had learned. I thought back to Teacher Peo for a moment, the lessons he had taught me, and I wondered what had become of him under this new regime that hated intelligence.

"Where did you go to school?" the village boss asked.

I told him about scavenging trash and said that I'd never been to school.

"He is lying," the other man said. "He does not talk like that. He speaks like a smart boy. He would not speak so proper if he had not gone to school. You have heard him. And his skin was almost white when he got here."

The village boss held his hand up as a signal for silence. He was quiet for a bit, waiting a minute or two before he spoke to me. "I have a quiz for you. If we have twenty tractors, and six break down, how many working tractors are there?"

I knew right away that the answer was fourteen, but this was a trap. I pretended to be confused and counted on my fingers. "Eight?" I said, shrugging my shoulders.

He smiled. "Count to ten," he said.

"One," I said slowly. "Two. Three. Four . . ." and stopped.

The village boss laughed. "He is from city, but this boy is dumb."

"No," the man said, "he is lying!"

"I said he is dumb." The village boss stared hard at the man. It was as though he had slapped him.

"Watch him closely," the village boss said. "Make sure he works hard. Let me know if he does not."

He looked at the man, who nodded his agreement.

The village boss looked right at me. "I am sparing you because I think you are a good worker. You better not give me any reason to doubt this decision."

"Thank you, comrade," I said, bowing in the traditional Cambodian gesture and faking it as hard as I could. "I will work hard in the fields for Angkar."

On the inside, I screamed, but I knew I was saving myself. I knew I had to do anything I could if I wanted to live to see my mom again.

BACK IN THE FIELDS, the work was more grueling than ever. They woke us up before dawn, screaming at us to get up and get to work. "You're lazy! Wake up! Angkar needs you. You must plant. Angkar loves you. You must pay Angkar back."

I was becoming very skinny and was tired all the time. The longer the months of bending in the field to plant and chop and harvest went on, the more tired and the skinnier I became. The workdays grew longer, with all the children forced to work from dawn until sunset with only a short break for lunch. The leeches and the bugs were constant nuisances, especially in the monsoon season. Days and nights passed when I never dried out, and I never felt clean.

The children's group continued to gather for Angkar pep rallies at the end of each workday. I grew to hate these sessions more and more. I wanted to tell the children who believed the Angkar's lies what had happened to my family and how I felt, but I kept it all inside. These brainwashed children would report me to the Angkar. I knew that expressing how I felt would reveal who I really was, the educated child of a loyal Cambodian soldier whom the Khmer Rouge had killed. They would know that I resented them for killing my father and would one day seek revenge. They would want to kill me before I had a chance to kill them. They were my first enemy.

After working all day and eating very little, we sat as they carried on about how wonderful Angkar was, how they had saved us from the corrupt government of Cambodia. It was also said that the Angkar was saving us from the evil Vietnamese, who were jealous of our ancient and superior culture.

They repeated the same things over and over and over.

After each night's pep rally, they would individually talk with the older children in the group, especially the boys. One of the men called me over. "You should move up to the hard charge group," he said. "You are getting too old for the children's group. The hard charge group will get you ready for the army. Angkar needs strong fighters. They will train you. You can defend the honor of Angkar."

"Thank you, comrade, but I am not ready. I am too young. I will do it when I get older."

"You should not be scared! You will be a great fighter. I see how you work. You are strong!"

This man, who once had acted like he hated me, had changed his tactics. He was trying to encourage me through flattery, but I could see through him. "Maybe next year I will be ready," I said.

"You can do it sooner. I will not let you forget."

I saw other children my age and older who were moved up to the hard charge group. The man would come to me and have this same discussion every week or two, and every time, I said I was not ready. I played along, promising that maybe one day I would move up, but the last thing I would ever do was fight for Angkar. I decided that if they forced me into military service on behalf of the Khmer Rouge, I would try to run away, regardless of the consequences.

I WOKE UP ONE MORNING feeling very sick. I was feverish, and my stomach ached. I could barely stand, but I did so I could walk away from the other children and vomit onto the ground. I puked up everything in my stomach and continued to retch even though my stomach had nothing left to come out.

I lay down near where I had been sleeping in a small spot of shade cast by a tall palm tree. My head ached, and my body was so hot that I felt like I was going to die.

I could hear the leaders yelling at the children's group to get moving, and they were lining up to walk to the paddy. But I didn't move. I couldn't have moved if I had wanted to.

My eyes were closed, but I sensed one of the men standing over me. "Get up! There is nothing wrong with you."

"I'm very sick," I said. "I can't get up."

"You are weak! You must get up."

"I will when I feel better. Please let me recover."

He said nothing, and I could hear the man stomp away. I tried to get up, but I couldn't. I knew there were no doctors because I had seen other sick children neglected. I had seen no doctors anywhere since the Khmer Rouge had taken power more than two years before.

I lay there and ached and moaned. Fortunately, the leaders let me be.

I drifted off to sleep and got the first daytime rest I had had in years. I don't know how long I slept, but it must have been several hours.

I awoke to someone gently touching my arm and shoulder. I opened my eyes to see my mother. "Mom!" I said, so happy to see her. I thought for a minute that I was dreaming. I hadn't seen her for months, but it seemed like it had been one hundred years.

"My son," she said, and she leaned over and kissed me. "I cannot stay long, but I wanted to see you. I'm so happy to have found you."

"How did you know I was sick?" I sat up, and I felt better than I had earlier, but still very ill.

"A mama knows when her boy is sick. I brought you something that will make you better."

She held a small cup. She had brought a homemade cure, an old Cambodian medicine she made by boiling pieces of tree bark. She had given it to me in the past, and I knew it tasted terrible. "The more bitter the taste, the faster it will cure you," she had always said.

I started to take the cup when one of the Angkar leaders came out of his thatched hut and walked toward us. "Who are you?" he yelled, approaching my mom.

"I am his mother. He is very sick. I brought him some medicine."

"No. You cannot give him that." He snatched the cup from her and threw it on the ground. "Because of mothers like you pampering your children so much, that's why the children are so weak and lazy!"

My mother stepped back from me. "Go!" he yelled. "Go before I change my mind and punish you."

I looked at my mom's eyes, and they filled with tears. "Go, Mom," I whispered. "Do not stay here and get into trouble. I will come find you when I can."

She did not move. "Go," I said. "I will be fine."

My mom, her shoulders slumped as though all of the world sat upon them, walked away down the road. I watched her go. She stopped under a palm tree and turned back. I could see the agony on her face as she cried.

I wanted her to stay more than anything, but I waved for her to leave. I worried they might kill her. She moved on. I watched her walk down the dirt road until she turned into a black dot in the distance that disappeared from my view.

As sad as I was, I was heartened by the fact that my mom had found me. She was still alive. I was still alive. Just that fact alone made me feel a little better.

The next day I was back at work in a rice paddy.

THE WORK IN THE FIELD became even more intense later in the summer monsoon season that ran into the fall of 1977. We were pushed to clear and plant more fields, being woken up before dawn by the Angkar to get into the fields as light was beginning to creep above the horizon. We worked hard for six or eight hours, and then they fed us a miserable lunch, and then we were back in the fields for another six or eight hours until the sky became dark. When in past months and years they would call off the workers not long before the sun set, they now made us work until it was nearly impossible to see. They worked us through the rain and the wind. There were weeks at a time when I never dried off.

The children's group worked so hard that at the end of the day when we returned to the spots where we slept, we would collapse on the ground. We would lie there like zombies until someone screamed at us to get up again the next day. Sometimes we were forced to sit for an Angkar pep rally, but it seemed that the enthusiasm for the cause had waned. All the Angkar leaders had was anger and hatred that they inflicted on us by making us work longer and longer.

When they did do a pep rally, they talked more and more about the Youns, what they called the hated Vietnamese, and how the Angkar would prevail. But their voices belied what they said. They sounded scared and desperate. More older children were moved, recruited to the hard charge group to be trained for battle. They continued to ask me, and sometimes even the village leader would pull me aside, but I continued to say I was not ready. "I am only eleven years old," I said. "Maybe when I am twelve."

Children came and went from our group all the time. New younger children would arrive, and older children would be sent away. I never became very close to any of them, even though we worked side by side in the fields all day. We would be yelled at for talking, and we never had any opportunity to play, not that we had the energy to do so.

More and more of the children were getting sick. I often felt nauseated, and I don't know if it was from leeches that bit me in the paddy fields or bacteria in the water we drank or dirty bowls from which we ate rice.

After she found me on the morning when I was sick, my mom started to come see me about once every month or two. I never knew when she was coming, but she would find me in the paddy fields or where we slept on the ground. She would visit for a few minutes and then walk back to the fields where she worked.

My mom saw Dy occasionally as well and would relay news about her. She said that Dy, whom I had not seen for many months, had given birth to a baby, a boy she named Houeth. He was healthy in spite of all the difficulties. The Angkar had forced Dy to marry, my mom said, and encouraged her to have a child who could grow to work in the fields and fight for the Khmer Rouge.

I had a nephew. I was an uncle and I hadn't even known it. Under different circumstances, this would have been exciting, but in the condition we were in, this was not news to celebrate. I could celebrate nothing.

My mom looked skinnier each time I saw her. Her skin, which was getting darker from sun exposure, hung loose on her body, and her once dark hair was grayer. Each short visit ended with her crying, saying, "I love you, my son. Be careful."

I cried each time she left. I dreamed about how life only a few years before had been so nice in Battambang City, with my mom and my pa and my sisters and my dog Dino. It had been more than two-and-a-half years since we had been forced from our home. The lack of nourishment had taken a great toll, causing me to look like a skeleton, as did most of us who were enslaved. I was getting weaker, and I often had stomach pains that nagged me night and day.

IN LATE 1977, a new phenomenon took hold. I became as blind as a bat when the sun went down. This night blindness was due to a lack of vitamins, and it is something many of us experienced. The sun would go down, and I could see nothing. The Cambodian name given for it was *kwak mon*, which means "blind chicken."

When they forced us to work until dark, the walks back to where we slept were treacherous. Many of us with night blindness would hold hands in a chain and walk together along the muddy road, unsure of where we were going, trusting in those who could see to lead the way. It was very scary, taking one blind step after another. I fell down often, especially when it had rained and was muddy. Climbing blind out of the fields on the low incline of a paddy dam seemed like climbing Mount Everest. I went slow, taking very small steps, listening to the voices of others. I could see nothing at all.

I would make my way back with the group to where we slept. "Is this it?" I would ask. "Here?"

"Yes, we are here," one of the children would answer.

I would lie down on the ground, hoping to find a dry spot, and try to sleep. It didn't matter if I had my eyes open or closed—all I saw was blackness.

I went to sleep in darkness and woke up in darkness. I worried that I was going blind, but as soon as the sun rose each day, I could see again. I was relieved every morning to see the bright Cambodian sun that returned my vision. The relief, however, was short. The misery of working the rice paddies grew worse every day. The bags we filled in the harvest seemed heavier each time, and the number of seedlings we had to plant seemed endless.

I often thought that I could not take another step.

One afternoon when we were planting seedlings, a very frail boy not much older than me who had been vomiting earlier in the morning collapsed in the paddy. He was working about one hundred feet from me. I saw him fall into the water, which was about two or three inches high that day. He fell face first and did not get up. His bundles of seedlings floated by his body, and he was not moving. I knew he would drown if I did not turn him over. I left my bundle of seedlings and went in his direction. I thought that no guards had been watching me, but from behind me I heard one shout, "Leave him alone. Go back to work." I turned and saw a young guard, probably not more than fifteen years old, coming at me with an AK-47.

I did as I was told because the guard's eyes were fierce and his voice angry. I knew that he would be glad to have any excuse to shoot me. I went back to where I was and pretended to be busy planting seedlings, but I watched him approach the boy who had fallen. He used his foot to roll the boy over onto his back. He looked down closely and shook his head. He looked up at me, and I immediately turned my eyes away. I knew that the boy was dead. It probably would not have mattered if I had been able to flip him over.

I began to feel sick, as I often did on these long days with no fresh water and very little to eat. I stopped planting seedlings, taking a moment to gather myself, and I felt like I might fall. The sun felt hotter than ever. I tried to breathe deep, to keep from collapsing.

The guard had lost interest in the dead boy, whom he left to rot in the mud, and walked my way. "Get to work," he yelled, as he approached. "You are a lazy city boy, like him." He pointed at the boy's corpse. "That is why he died. He was lazy. You must work. Work harder. You do not work hard, I will kill you. It would be no loss. You and him will be fertilizer. That is all you are good for."

He lowered his gun at me. I looked at him, and for a moment, I thought, *Go ahead and shoot. What do I care? If you do it and I die, so be it.*

But that thought lasted only a split second. I wanted to live. I wanted to see my mom again. I wanted to see my older sister Dy and I wanted to reunite with my baby sister Poch. I wanted to find out what had happened to my pa.

I did not want to die. I feared death more than anything. That fear motivated me to start working. I mustered all the energy I had, which wasn't much, but it was enough. I continued to plant seedlings. The soldier turned and walked away from me.

I'm not going to die today, I told myself. *I'm not going to die today.*

A Torturous Ending to the Killing Fields

[JANUARY 1978–APRIL 1979]

THE TERRIBLE YEAR that was 1977 rolled into 1978 with no relief in sight. Conditions worsened as we all grew weaker from malnourishment and lack of rest. We were forced into the rice paddies early every morning, working in the dry season to clear and prepare land for planting when the monsoon rains would begin after the searing heat of April. I was often assigned to help dig ditches with a short-handled shovel. Sometimes I got so tired and felt so sick that I would fall to the ground. I would lie there for a few moments, thinking that this might be my last day, but I would always get up, repeating my mantra: *I'm not going to die today.* Every night I would stumble home in the dark and sleep on the ground, unable to see anything. My night blindness worsened. I was a blind chicken each night until the sun rose again. I would see the sun and repeat: *I'm not going to die today.*

The other children and I cleared fields by hand and dug ditches by hand because there were fewer and fewer tractors. The Angkar's poor treatment of the tractors over the years and their failure to invest in new parts and equipment meant that failing tractors were chopped up to use for parts for working ones. As tractors broke down, more were disassembled for parts to sustain the ones that still ran. One by one, tractors were taken out of service until almost all disappeared. Many of the men who worked on the tractors also disappeared, often accused of sabotage when tractors wouldn't run. One day they would be there and the next day they would be gone.

A boy about my age in the children's group knew that I had worked on tractors before they sent me into the fields. We were at lunch and had been digging a ditch that morning, when he asked, "Would you want to go back and work on tractors?"

"No," I said, shaking my head.

"I would if I knew how," he said. "I would do anything to get out of this job."

"You shouldn't do it. They would kill you for not being able to fix what can't be fixed."

Like the tractors, most of the oxen that pulled the plows had died. Very few oxen remained working in the fields, and the ones that survived were thin and diseased. More and more often I saw men strapped to the plows to pull them through the fields. It was a pitiful sight—skinny men straining to try to do a job that only an ox or a tractor could do.

As the year went on, the pressure on members of the children's group to move to the hard charge group and join the Khmer Rouge soldiers fighting the Vietnamese grew stronger. I was asked once a week to move up to the hard charge group, but I continued to say I wasn't ready. I said that I was sick and that my night blindness would keep me from being a good soldier. That was not a lie. I would have been an easy target if I'd had to do any fighting after dark. But I had no intention of fighting for the Angkar.

I hated them with all my being.

The threat of the Vietnamese invading became more pronounced. The leaders who oversaw the children's group talked more and more about how the Youns were evil and would be defeated by the powerful Angkar. Although they claimed that the Angkar was winning, the tension in their voices and the extreme way they repeated themselves showed how scared they were. This fear caused them to be harder on us, pushing us even more in the fields, screaming at us morning, noon, and night. More children were tied to trees and left in the sun as punishment. I saw many children slapped and beaten and kicked. I was good at pretending to work hard and obeyed when I was spoken to, so I avoided being singled out for extra punishment. However, every single moment I was awake felt like punishment.

MY MOTHER CONTINUED to come to see me whenever she could get away safely, which meant there would be a month or two between each visit. Our visits were very short because the Angkar leaders of the children's group watched her closely and questioned her. She knew if she stayed long, she would get into trouble.

Late in the summer of 1978, in the monsoon season, she found me planting rice. She waded into the water of the rice paddy and stood there talking to me, the water coming up above our ankles and hiding our bare feet, the rain splashing down on our heads.

"Hello, my son," she said.

"Mom," I said, surprised and happy to see her. I wanted to hug her, but an Angkar guard with an AK-47 stood nearby. He was next to a palm tree on the edge of the field. I couldn't tell if he was watching us, but we didn't want to draw his attention. No affection was allowed. "I can't stay long," she said, "but I wanted to see you." She asked me how I was doing, and I told her about my night blindness. Her face was sad, but then her eyes brightened. "I hear that the Angkar may not win the war with Vietnam. If things change, and I cannot find you, you should go back to Battambang City and meet at our home. I don't know what we will find, but that is where we should meet. Your sister will meet us there too."

"How is Dy?" I asked. I had not seen my sister since we were moved to Nikum, and I still had not seen my nephew.

"She is not doing well. She is pregnant again. They have carried her husband away to a camp, where she thinks they are torturing him and maybe have killed him. She has the blind chicken condition too. It's very bad. I am worried about her. But if the Vietnamese come, hopefully things will change for the better for all of us."

Although I was happy to hear the Angkar might be defeated, I feared what the Vietnamese, who for centuries had been mortal enemies of Cambodia, would bring.

My mom turned and looked at the guard, who appeared to be watching us from a distance. "I love you, Son," she said.

"I love you too, Mom. I hope we can return to our lives soon. I so much miss how it used to be."

"Me too, my son. Me too. I hope we can get back there and resume our lives. Be careful."

She turned and splashed off through the shallow water of the rice paddy. Every fifty feet or so she turned and looked back at me, her face long and sad in the rain. My eyes filled with tears, as did hers.

THE MONSOON SEASON ended in the early fall. As November passed into December, we began to hear bombs and gunfire in the distance at night. I couldn't see after dark, so I would lie on the ground and listen to the distant echoing percussion of warfare. I could only hope that the Angkar would lose and that the aftermath of these battles would mean freedom for us. What the aftermath would entail, I didn't know, but I was ready to try anything after all I had lived through. I was scared of the Vietnamese, but I hated the Angkar.

We continued to work during daylight hours, but fewer and fewer guards with AK-47s watched us, until one day there was none. Several of the men who oversaw the children's group had also vanished, and we were able to get away with working very little because of the lack of oversight. Only the woman was left to watch us, and despite how she screamed at us, something about her had changed. Where she once had been confident, she seemed desperate, and her verbal abuse rang hollow. There were too many of us for her to watch closely. We would lounge and sometimes even sit down until she approached.

The sounds of the fighting at night intensified. One January day we were working in a field harvesting rice, when we saw a platoon of Khmer Rouge soldiers marching rapidly down the road, some of them running. There were about eighty of them, most with AK-47s, and a few with bazookas. They were led by a man jogging ahead of them, shouting orders and telling them to hurry. They didn't stop but cut through our area, heading down a road that went in the direction of the mountainous jungles on the border near Thailand. It looked like the soldiers were running from something, their black sandals slapping on the dry dirt road. The confident posture they'd had when they had rolled into Battambang City almost four years before was gone. They were hunched, beaten, and scared.

That night we heard more heavy gunfire, closer than we'd heard in the previous nights and weeks. A few explosions were so loud that they shook the ground on which I slept. I imagined as I lay there that if I had my old vision and not the blind chicken disease, I would be able see fire in the sky as I had when the Khmer Rouge was fighting the Cambodian military. I thought back to that time and my father and his service. I felt as though I were a very old man, that these three years and eight months had aged me one hundred years. I was almost thirteen years old, but due to malnourishment, I was the height and weight of a younger child.

The next morning, after a night of fitful sleep, I woke when the sun rose. I sat up and let my eyes adjust to the light. Each morning I was thankful to see again. I looked around. The woman who led our group was gone. The children's group was left alone to fend for ourselves. I knew from his dialect that the boy who had asked me about working on the tractors was from Battambang City. His name was Prak. In another time and place, we might have become close friends.

With no adults to order us around, the children's group waited for a bit, afraid to leave. After about thirty minutes, when no one appeared to order us to work, Prak asked, "Do you think we will have to work today?"

"I hope not," I said. "I hope I can find my mom. I hope we can go home."

"Let's walk back now," he said. "I think we can make it in a day or two. I know Battambang City is south of here."

"What if they catch us?" I said. "They will kill us. I am not going to risk it today." He was eager to leave, but I was not going to die on my first day of freedom. I had seen what they would do to anyone they thought was trying to escape.

We waited a day under the cover where we slept, watching the road, which had many people walking back toward Chroy Sdao. I was worried we would see soldiers coming down the road with their machine guns, but we didn't.

The next morning, Prak again started trying to persuade me to leave. "We can tell them our group was abandoned and that we want to find another village to work in. But I think they are all scared and on the run. They do not care about us. They left us here."

I didn't say anything, thinking it over. "Let's wait one more day," I said. "One more day and I will go with you."

"OK," he said. "I will wait one more day. I want to go today, but I don't want to go alone. Do you promise you will go tomorrow?"

"Yes," I said. "Tomorrow, if the Angkar don't come back, I will go. It has only been one day. I am scared to risk it."

We spent another day lying around the shelter, and it was nice not to work. We saw more laborers than the day before straggling down the road, heading away from the farmland and toward Battambang City.

The next morning, as soon as the sun rose and my vision returned, I said, "Let's go. I want to see if my mom and sister are home. We can walk there."

"Great," he said. "I want to leave this terrible place behind."

"Do you have family you want to find?"

He didn't say anything, but stared at the ground.

Prak and I were among the oldest of the fifteen or twenty other children who were still at the shelter, waiting where we normally gathered to be taken into the fields each day. We set off down the dirt road toward Chroy Sdao in the dawn light. I turned to look back at the remaining children either sitting or lying on the ground. Two girls, both about eight, sat there and cried, holding each other's hands. They must have been sisters or cousins. I felt guilty, leaving them there, but I didn't know what to do or where to take them. I didn't know if I could take care of myself, so how could I help someone else? All I wanted was to find my mother. She was all I could think about. I needed my mom to protect me, and there was no way I could take care of another. Prak and I headed down the road and didn't look back.

As we walked through untended rice paddies, it was obvious things had changed. No one was working, where once every field had been busy. There were no signs of Angkar leaders. We began to see more and more of the laborers walking down the road, all going our direction, toward Battambang City. Many of the men and women we saw looked like zombies, their faces confused and their bodies frail, walking down the road in the sun. It was late January, and the heat was not too bad.

Prak and I moved faster than many of these dazed adults, passing by groups and not talking, keeping our heads down. We couldn't trust anyone.

After walking for a few hours, we came to the edge of Chroy Sdao, where my mom and sister and I had lived in the factory. Prak and I approached a number of huts and outbuildings, including one to raise chickens. Farther on we saw a big house where Khmer Rouge soldiers had lived. Some people milled around in the road, looking lost and confused.

"I need to poop," I said.

"Me too," Prak said. "Let's go behind that chicken house, where no one can see us."

We walked across the road and beyond the ramshackle hut made of wood and wire. There were no chickens, but it still smelled bad. No one from the road could see us, and I was glad to have a private place.

After we were done, we resumed our journey, passing by a few other huts and one building along the road.

I told Prak we were getting close to the factory where we had lived. "It is only a mile or so this way," I said. "The road from there goes on to Battambang City." I felt a lift in my step at the prospect of reuniting with my mom.

Prak started to speak, but we heard shouting from behind us. "*Stop! Stop!*"

We turned around to see three Khmer Rouge soldiers pointing AK-47s at us. They were men, much taller than Prak and I. "Why were you behind the chicken house?" the tallest soldier asked. "Are you *chhlop*"—the Khmer word for "spy"—"for the Youns?"

"No, comrade," I said. "We just needed to use the bathroom. We wanted privacy."

"You liar. Come with us."

They jabbed the muzzles of their AK-47s at us and pushed us farther down the road. They took us to what they called the station house, which before the Khmer Rouge invaded had been a two-story home that dated back to French colonial times. They forced us inside. It appeared that it had once been the home of a wealthy person, with high ceilings and expensive furniture and Persian rugs, but it was now trashed and dirty. Mud had been tracked everywhere. Many AK-47s stood lined up against the wall in the foyer. It smelled like sweat. They pushed us through a doorway on the right that led to a big dining room.

Two soldiers were seated around a long table, and they were even bigger than the first three. A soldier who wore a black cap and seemed to be in charge stood up and scowled. "Who are they? Why are you bringing them here?"

"I think they are *chhlop*," the soldier who led us in said. "They were sneaking around behind the chicken house, hiding away, watching this house. They might have been trying to steal food too."

"Take the big one down in the basement," he said, gesturing to Prak. His voice was like ice, and it scared me to hear him. "Take this little one upstairs. We will find out who they are and what they are doing."

One of the soldiers shoved me hard. "In the hall," he said. "Up the stairs." I stumbled and he laughed, his throat raspy. Once I had righted myself and began to go toward the front hall, he turned his rifle around and hit me in the back with the butt, knocking me down. The blow to the back of my shoulder hurt. I lay facedown in the hallway, stunned.

"Get up," he yelled, kicking me in the ribs. I struggled to my feet and went toward the stairs.

I looked back to see Prak going toward the back of the house. I wanted to make eye contact, but he was turned away from me. The soldier behind me pushed at me with the rifle butt again, not as hard, but in my neck. "Turn around, you little shit. Go upstairs."

I climbed the stairs to the top. Muddy boot prints covered the steps. Paint was peeling from the walls and ceiling.

"Into this room," the soldier said, pushing me again with the rifle into the first doorway on the right side of the hallway.

The room had one chair and a broken bed that was pushed into the corner. Mats and bedrolls were in disarray on the floor. Parts of the plaster ceiling had collapsed, exposing beams overhead beneath the roof. The house had experienced serious leaks in the monsoon season. Even though this was January, the peak of the dry season, I could smell mold and mildew. The glass panes had been broken out of the window. On the dingy white walls I saw bloody handprints. I realized that the mud stains I had seen on the floor of the stairs were not all mud. What I had walked through was a mixture of mud and blood forming trails on the steps and hallway that led into and out of this room.

The soldier leaned his rifle against the wall and pushed me into the chair in the center of the room. He took a piece of rope and tied my hands tightly behind me, hurting my wrists. He then tied the end of that rope to a bottom support on the back of the chair that pulled my arms down and behind me. It hurt my shoulders. Finally, he took a piece of rope and tied my feet together and to the chair. I could barely move.

I heard footsteps and looked toward the stairs to see the man who was the boss coming up in his sandals and shiny black pajama uniform. He had a red-and-white checkered *krama* tied about his neck, and I noticed that he wore a belt with a pistol and a very long knife. He was carrying a rope with a loop in it. "Let's use the noose on this one," he said. "It shouldn't take long to find out who he is."

He handed the noose to one of the soldiers, who tossed it up and over one of the exposed beams. The noose slid down until it hung about six feet high in the middle of the room. "I will move him," the boss said. He slid my chair over to where the noose was hanging. The pressure of the rope pulling my wrists hurt my arms and shoulders tremendously.

The boss took the noose and pulled it down more and guided it over my head and around my neck. He cinched it—tight, but not tight enough to cut off my breathing. "Give me that end," he said to the soldier. With the noose around my throat, he tugged on the long end that ran over the beam, pulling the noose tighter and forcing me to sit up as tall and straight as I could with my arms tied behind me. "Now, you little shit," he said, holding the end of the rope and walking around in front of me, "tell me your name."

My heart was pounding and my skin was freezing with fear. I couldn't speak, and I gasped for breath. I couldn't believe that I had been so close to getting free only to be staring death in the face of these Khmer Rouge soldiers. I thought about my mom and how I might not ever see her again. I didn't want to cry, but I couldn't help it. Tears pooled in my eyes.

The boss slapped me. "What's your name?"

I gulped and tried to focus. "Sin Prou," I said. I had hoped that I would be able to go back to my given name, Sokomasath, once the Khmer Rouge fell. That wish seemed like only a dream.

He slapped me again. "Liar!" He pulled on the end of the rope. It tightened the noose on my neck, pulling me up and lifting the chair momentarily off the ground.

He stood in front of me and leaned down close to my face. He wasn't talking loudly, but his voice was intense. "You are a city boy. I can tell by the way you look. You are just the kind to spy for the Youns."

I coughed from the choking sensation, but then I caught my breath. "No, comrade," I said, trying to shake my head as much as I could with the noose around it. "I am loyal to the Angkar. I am just trying to find my mother, to make sure she is safe."

"I don't believe you. Why are you not fighting for the Angkar? You are old enough to be a soldier."

"I have been sick. I can't see at night. I have blind chicken disease. My stomach is very weak. I am not ready."

He yanked the rope very hard and pulled the noose tight, but then he let it go, the long end hanging slack. I was able to get my breath, but then he leaned over and smacked me hard with his open hand. "Liar! You are a spy. I can see what you are doing. You are lying to me. You will sit here until you tell the truth or I kill you. I would be glad to kill you, but I want to know what you know. I am not going to kill you now. If you tell me who you really are and what you are doing, I might let you live. I know how to get answers."

He turned to the soldier with the rifle. "Get me a bamboo stick. A heavy one."

The soldier ran down the stairs. The boss circled me, staring intensely. He did not speak for several minutes, but then he said, "You will not be the first coward I have beaten the truth out of."

The soldier returned with a piece of bamboo that was about four feet long. He held it out to the boss, who was still standing in front of me. The boss did not reach for it. "No," he said to the soldier. "You hit him with it. I'll ask the questions. Hit him hard."

I couldn't see the soldier behind me, but I heard him moving. I braced myself. A hard blow from the stick landed on the back of my shoulders. The bamboo felt heavy and must have been freshly cut. He hit me on the side and once on the head. My eyes began to water and my teeth hurt from clenching with each blow. I bit my tongue and tasted blood in my mouth.

After about ten blows, the boss held up his hand to the soldier. I was sweating and hurt all over. The spots where I had been struck throbbed. The boss stood in front of me again. "Do you want to tell me the truth now? Or do you want me to beat you more?"

If I could have thought of a lie to tell him to make him happy and motivate him to let me go, I would have done it. But I couldn't see or think straight. All I could do was cry and try to choke out the words,

"No, comrade, I am just trying to find my mother. We were just using the bathroom. Looking for privacy."

"Bullshit! You were spying out on us, watching our soldiers. You were going to tell the Youns where to find us!"

"No, comrade," I said, choking out the words, crying with my mouth full of blood. I spit some of the blood out of my mouth and it landed in my lap. "I am loyal to the Angkar."

"Liar!" He turned to the soldier. "Beat him some more. Whatever you want. Work on him. Hit him hard but don't kill him. Not yet. I want him to think about the truth. Maybe his friend downstairs will tell us the truth. If he does, we can just kill this one."

He walked out of the room, but the soldier stayed. The soldier walked in front of me, cursing, calling me a "little shit" and "lying spy" and other names I can't remember. Each time he called me a name, he reared back and hit me with the stick. He hit me all over—in the shoulders, the legs, the arms, the neck, and once or twice on the head. My vision went blurry, and I thought I would pass out. I felt cold, but my body was soaked in sweat.

I don't know how many times he hit me or for how long, but it seemed to last forever, like a lifetime of blows and curses. At least the noose around my neck felt looser, and I hung my head forward and was able to breathe. It seemed that time had stopped and I would never make it out of this moment, that I was about to die. But then, after a few deep breaths, I remembered what I had said to myself in the worst of the moments in the Killing Fields. I repeated my mantra: *I'm not going to die today.* I said that to myself a few times, and then I thought of my mom. *Mom*, I thought, *I am going to see you again. I am going to survive. I'm not going to die today.*

The soldier eventually grew tired of hitting me. "You little shit," he said, winded from his exertion. He was taller and more muscular than most Cambodians. His dialect told me he was from the country. He was probably from the eastern part of Cambodia, where the villages had been bombed the heaviest by U.S. warplanes. He was uneducated and angry at how the war and his life had gone, a victim of the brainwashing of the Khmer Rouge, which he saw as his only chance of glory. He threw down the bamboo stick and cussed me some more, punctuating his last round of curses by spitting on my face. "You ain't worthy of my spit," he said. "I will be back to see you. You can count on that. I'll bring the scorpions next time."

He lifted his leg and kicked hard at my side, almost toppling the chair. The blow from the bottom of his foot hurt my arm and ribs terribly, and I winced in pain. The chair wobbled but stayed upright. I sat there with my head down, still in the noose, which thankfully was looser.

He walked around behind me, where he had leaned his rifle against the wall, and I heard him pause. He approached me from behind. I tried to figure out what he was doing, but when I felt the warm stream on the back of my head, I knew. He was urinating on me. "You ain't worth piss either," he said.

He left the room. His urine ran down from my hair into the back of my sweaty shirt and also onto my arms and hands. I was disgusted, furious. I tried to pull my hands loose. It was no use. I was tied tight and couldn't break free, but I kept trying. I wanted to get loose and grab one of the guns and kill him, kill all of them.

After wriggling for a bit, I gave up. I was exhausted. I couldn't break free of the knots. I took deep breaths and felt pain all over. I tried to stay calm, but it was terrifying not knowing what they would do when they came back. I didn't have a lie to tell. I believed that if I falsely confessed to being a spy, they would simply kill me. I had no idea what was happening with Prak down in the basement. I listened carefully but could not hear him. I heard many men coming and going on the first floor and many intense discussions among the soldiers. The boss's voice was the loudest. I couldn't make out much of what was being said, but I heard them talk about the Youns and that they could be arriving soon.

I sat there for hours, maybe three or four, before they came back to see me. The boss and the soldier returned. The soldier carried a bag made of thick white cloth about the size of a pillowcase in one hand and the bamboo stick in the other.

The boss walked in front of me and grabbed the loose end of the rope and tugged it. It pulled taut over the beam, tightening around my neck. I sat up straight and tall to reduce the pressure, but that caused my shoulders pain because of how my arms were tied behind me. "Your friend told us he was a spy. He said that you are a spy too. We let him go because he told the truth. He ran off down the road. Will you tell the truth now?"

"Comrade, I have been telling the truth. I did not know he was a spy. I did not know him very well. We only started walking together today. I am loyal to the Angkar. I only want to find my mother. I have been sick. I am not a spy. I promise, comrade, I am not a spy."

He frowned and shook his head. "You will regret lying." He looked at the soldier. "Open the bag on him."

The soldier put down the bamboo stick. He held the bag over my head, holding the opening with one hand so it wouldn't open too wide. He lifted the bottom of the bag and shook it.

A black scorpion, about three inches long, came out of the opening of the bag and fell onto my shoulder. It clung to a spot between the noose around my neck and my faded black shirt, its pincers holding on to my collar.

I felt its legs scurrying, and then its stinger dug into my neck and stung me right above my collarbone. The pain was intense—a burning, fiery bite on the right front side of my neck. It hurt like hell, and I cried out. The scorpion removed its stinger and climbed up onto the noose. It stung me again, higher on my neck this time, right below my jaw.

I cried again, louder this time.

"Keep crying, city boy," the boss said. "It won't help you. These are deadly, venomous scorpions. They are good for killing *chhlop*. Traitors deserve what they get."

I cried again, the pain burning in my neck. "*Please*," I said through the tears. "*Please* don't kill me. I want to see my mother again. I am not a spy. I have always been loyal to the Angkar. I worked hard in the fields. I fixed tractors. I have been loyal. I want the Angkar to win. I will be a soldier for you too. I am sick, I cannot see at night, but I will do my best."

The boss, still holding the noose, gave it a hard yank, and I began to choke. The combination of the noose tightening and the scorpion stinging caused me to wet my pants. I felt faint, and when I saw the soldier dumping more scorpions out of the bag, I passed out.

I REGAINED CONSCIOUSNESS LATER. When I opened my eyes, I was alone in the room. I could see through the window that the sun was much lower in the sky, probably less than an hour before sunset. I had been here all afternoon, maybe five or six hours. The noose was still around my neck, but the scorpions had crawled off me. I could see the scorpions on the floor, gathered in a corner beneath the window. I hurt all over, sore from the stings and the beating and the rope around my neck. My hands and legs and face were swollen, my fingers so puffy that they were twice as big as normal. It hurt to shift even a little. I stank from where I had peed on myself and the soldier had peed on me.

I worried about what would happen to me when it got dark, when I could see nothing. I tried again to tug at the rope tied around my wrists, but the knots were too tight and my arms were too weak.

I sat and listened to what I could hear downstairs. There was much more agitation, and it sounded like more soldiers were in the house. I heard them yelling that the Youns were coming. I could hear many footsteps going in and out of the front door.

I considered yelling for help, but I thought better of it. That might earn me more of a beating, or maybe they would kill me off.

After a few minutes, I heard footsteps on the stairs. It was one of the soldiers who had not been in the room when they were torturing me. "We have to leave now," he said. "Youns in tanks are coming down the road. They are not far."

He pulled a long knife out of his belt. I closed my eyes and braced myself, expecting him to cut my throat and leave me there to bleed to death.

I was resigned to this being the day I would die.

Instead, he knelt behind the chair and cut the ropes that bound my hands and legs. I felt instant relief from the tight knots that had held me. "You are lucky," he said. "Go home and don't let me see you again."

He ran down the stairs. I listened as I heard footsteps running out the front door. Soon, the house was empty. I could hear people outside on the road that went past, but no one was inside.

I removed the noose from my neck and shook off the ropes that had been cut. I listened. I heard nothing in the house. I slowly and painfully walked down the hallway and to the stairs, cautious for any movement. My clothes were wet, and I hurt all over. I was swollen in many places, especially my face and my fingers, which seemed as big as donuts. The spots where the scorpions had stung me throbbed with sharp pain. It was a slow descent, but I made it down the steps to the first floor.

All the AK-47s that had been lined up against the wall were gone, and the front door was left open. Out on the road I could see laborers who had left the fields, but I did not see any soldiers. I walked out of the house into the dusk and joined this beleaguered procession, hoping to get as far as possible from this house before nightfall when I would be able to see nothing due to my night blindness.

I did not know what had happened to Prak. I never saw him again.

I WALKED ALONE toward the center of Chroy Sdao. It was in the direction everyone was going. After almost four years of hell in the fields, everyone who was freed from the labor camps wanted to go back to the cities. Most were from Phnom Penh and had a long journey, but all the roads heading south went through Battambang City.

It was as if we were a parade of zombies, with many of the freed laborers consisting of little more than skin and bones. Old people shuffled slowly, while young people and kids with distended bellies walked with their heads down, their eyes red and glassy. I fit right in, glad to be among the laborers and not Khmer Rouge soldiers, who had gone into hiding, or Vietnamese soldiers, who were rumored to be coming.

It was getting dark, and my vision was starting to fail. A few of the people walking along had lanterns, but I noticed many other groups stopping by the side of the road to set up overnight campsites.

I ached from head to toe, but I kept going, watching for someone who might help me. I was very thirsty, my mouth dry, my lips crusty, and hungry too. I had not eaten for two days, not even a bug or a hay mushroom.

When I didn't think I could go another step, I saw a woman and two children who had stopped and put down plastic sheets on the side of the road. The woman reminded me of my mother, and I cheered at the likeness. I tried to smile at the children, a boy and a girl a year or two younger than me, but I knew I looked scary with my bruises and swelling. They cowered and avoided looking at me, moving closer to their mother. She looked up and made eye contact. Her mouth opened in shock. "Young man," she said, "are you OK?"

"Soldiers beat me and were going to kill me," I said. "But I escaped. I am very thirsty and hungry. I cannot see when it gets dark. I have blind chicken disease."

"Come," she said. "I can give you a little water and some rice. You can sleep next to us. We plan to keep moving in the morning, but tonight, you will be OK with us."

I squinted to see her as she handed me an old jug. I took some sips of water, and then she gave me a handful of uncooked rice. I let it soften in my mouth before swallowing it. It wasn't much, but it relieved my agony a bit. "Thank you," I said. "Bless you. I will sleep here."

I lay down on the ground a few feet from the mother, as tired and sore as I'd ever been. Even though many people passed on the road, often talking and crying, they did not disturb my deep, dark sleep.

I AWOKE with the woman shaking my shoulder. The sun was bright. I had slept through the night and past the dawn. "We are leaving," she said. "We are trying to get back to Phnom Penh. I wish you blessings and luck."

"Thank you," I said, sitting up. I was very sore, but I was thankful to be alive. "Thanks and blessings to you." I watched the woman and her two children walk down the road. It wasn't as busy with people as it had been the night before, but groups were still going in the same direction, heading toward the center of Chroy Sdao and then on to Battambang City.

I still felt much pain all over my body, but I was better than I had been the night before. I knew if I found my mom, she could take care of me. I rose and started walking.

I walked a short distance until the Chroy Sdao rice-processing factory came into view, along with the other familiar buildings. It had been about two years since we had moved from the abandoned factory to Nikum. My heart beat faster with the memories of living there with my mother and sister Dy and Kim Ban and Sakum. It also brought back memories of my dog Dino. I thought about how sweet a dog he had been, and I considered visiting the spot where I had buried him, but I knew that I must go back toward my home, where I hoped to find my mom. It was a full day's walk, and I hoped I could make it before dark. I got my emotions under control and began to move faster. I didn't have time to waste, and I worried that venturing away from the main road could be dangerous. I was safer out on the road in the mass of people.

I joined the procession of those who had survived years of starvation and enslavement. Although many of those in transit were sick and walking wounded, others were in high spirits, happy to be free from the labor camps and to be returning home.

Despite my stiffness from the beating I had endured, I made pretty good time. I put my head down and walked, passing many others who moved more slowly. The soles of my feet, toughened up after all these years of working and walking barefoot, were the only part of my body not sore from the torture I had endured.

I benefitted from more kindness of strangers on the road. A very old man gave me sips of water and an ear of corn. He reminded me of my grandfather, and I wondered how he was and if he had survived. I wished that I could find a bicycle and ride to him, but the Angkar had confiscated and destroyed most bicycles to keep their slaves from getting away.

I walked most of the day. My pulse quickened and my step sped up as I neared the outskirts of Battambang City. This was *home*! I had thought I would never live to see it again. It was getting dark. I had only about an hour before my vision would disappear.

I walked as fast as I could, coming down from the north through the city and toward our home on the east side, not far from the Sangke River. There were numerous burned-out and rusted cars and trucks and many shells of buildings that had been torched. I saw dead bodies, dead animals, and trash everywhere. I had to watch my step to avoid broken glass or sharp pieces of metal. Vietnamese soldiers were present, and I saw some of their tanks and trucks, but they were peaceful and did not bother me.

I passed by our market, which lay in ruins from fire and rain and sun and neglect. Many other buildings had been destroyed, and bullet holes punctured walls all along the street. Despite these conditions, it was good to be in the familiar territory of my hometown. I remembered these blocks in happier times. I was getting very close to our house. I feared what I would find, and I hoped that my mother and sister would be there.

I walked with great anxiety down the dirt road that led to the small community of simple homes where we had lived before the Khmer Rouge. All the houses there were in ruins, victims of ransacking and fire. Our house was nothing but charred remains, a black pile of burned beams. The only relic of my home that had survived was the tall coconut tree behind it.

My heart dropped. I stood where the steps had been and cried. I could envision my past in this shell of a house—my mom cooking on her side porch and my dad coming home from the war. I remembered the hammock that hung from the ceiling that my younger sister Poch had slept in. I had hoped to find my mom and sister here, but there was no one. I closed my eyes and wondered what I should do next. I had no idea where I was going to go.

With my lack of night vision, I would be helpless to go anywhere on my own once it got dark. I stood there in the dusk with my eyes closed, trying to bring back my past before the Khmer Rouge, not knowing what I should do.

I decided to go back into the busy part of town and sleep on the street by the market. I would be safer with people around. I got there as it was getting dark and my night blindness was taking hold. I found a spot on the street beside the market that seemed safe, and I sat down and leaned back against the building as it started to rain. The wall provided a little cover from the precipitation. I huddled against it and spent the night there, hearing many people passing by, but unable to see in the dark.

I spent much of the night thinking about what I should do. I decided that I should go back to Nikum to try to find my mom and my sister. I did not think my sister would travel with a baby, and I hoped my mom would be there too.

It was a long night, but no one bothered me. I was able to sleep in stretches while sitting with my back against the wall.

AS SOON AS DAYLIGHT BROKE and I could see again, I started walking. Getting back to Nikum would be a two-day trip, and this time I would be going against the flow of people leaving the fields and returning to the cities. I studied every face I saw, not wanting to miss my mom and my sister if I passed by them going the other way. I did not see them, but I saw many emaciated and troubled faces, thousands upon thousands of my fellow Cambodians who had endured torturous years in the fields just as I had.

I walked all day and slept on the side of the road, finding a spot close to a family of five who had set up camp. They shared hay mushrooms with me as well as a small drink of water. "Where are you going?" the father asked me.

"I am going to find my mom and my sister," I said. "I think they are in Nikum."

"Good luck, my son," he said. "I'm sorry I cannot help you, but we have to get back to Phnom Penh to find my parents and my sisters."

"Bless you," I said. "Thank you for the food and water."

The next day I started walking again. I felt horrible, exhausted from all the walking I had done and still sore from the beating I had received at the hands of the Khmer Rouge soldiers a few days before. As I walked, I kept a vigilant watch on the faces I passed, but none belonged to my mother or sister. I thought there might be a chance that I'd see my pa and Kim Ban and Sakum, but deep in my heart I knew better. Face after face after face passed by. I saw a sea of sad faces, many of them near death, their bodies barely able to move. I looked at every one and was disappointed each time.

I grew so tired and weak that several times I almost stopped. I felt like lying down and giving up, but I forced myself to keep going. *My mom will take care of me*, I said to myself. *My mom will know what to do.*

The image of my mom's smiling face, of my belief in the love she had for me, kept me going.

That afternoon I was relieved to see Nikum, the circle of thatched huts that my mom and sister and I had arrived at about two years before.

I approached the first hut and went up the short stairs to the open door. I looked in to see four women and about seven or eight kids crammed into the small one-room structure. They looked scared. I studied the faces, none of which was my mom's. "I am looking for my mother and sister," I said. "My sister has a baby."

I told them the names we had used, but no one seemed to recognize them. One of the young mothers, holding a baby, said, "There are other families here, in the other huts, but we do not know them."

I went from hut to hut in the village and asked each stranger I met if they had seen my mom and my sister. The huts were occupied by families with children who were too young to travel or by very old or sick people who couldn't move. No one in the first fifteen or so I entered knew anything about my mom or sister. I was worried I might not find them and would have to sleep outside. I also began to worry about the logic of my trip back to Nikum, that it had been a dumb idea and that I had wasted days and walked many miles unnecessarily.

I felt stupid and low and tired and lost. I was weary, so tired I could barely stand, but there were a few more huts. I wasn't going to rest until I had checked them all.

I climbed the steps to the next hut and repeated my query to the occupants, including the names my mom and sister had used in the Killing Fields. The inside of the hut was dim, and I could barely make out the figures of the families inside.

"Sokomasath," I heard a woman say. I could hardly believe it. It was my name—my original name! "Sokomasath," she said again. I thought I was dreaming.

A woman holding a baby wrapped in a white blanket to her chest stepped to meet me in the door. She looked very familiar to me, and I puzzled on her face for a second before I realized it was my sister.

"Dy!" I said.

I hugged her, wrapping my arms around my sister's waist. She looked so different: skinnier, her skin darker, her hair cut in the short bob that the Khmer Rouge forced on all women. She also looked much older, not like the teenage girl I had known.

"This is your baby?" I asked.

"Yes," she said. "His name is Loth. You are his uncle."

I looked upon my nephew with amazement. He was so tiny and wrinkled. I had not seen a baby in years, not since my younger sister Poch had been born.

"He is my second child," Dy said. "He was born a month ago. My first, Houeth, is two years old now. He is with his father's parents."

The names Houeth and Loth were tributes to my father's first name, Seuth. This brought tears of joy and sadness to my eyes.

"You should stay with us," she said. "There is one other family here. We have a little rice and some water and some lychee fruit we can eat."

"Thank you. I cannot see after dark. I have the blind chicken."

"Me too. Have you eaten?"

I told her that I had not, and she fed me rice and fruit and gave me a small cup of water. She breastfed the baby under her blanket, and then we all stretched out on the ground. I could see nothing, but I was next to my sister and happy to be in the company of family.

The baby cried for a while, and she tended to him. After he fell asleep, she told me her story, speaking very softly to avoid waking my nephew or bothering the other woman and two young children who lay only a few feet from us. She said an Angkar village chief had forced her to marry another laborer, ordering them to have a child who could one day fight for the Angkar and work in the fields. They had a baby. Soon after the Angkar turned against her husband and sent him to a prison camp where he was chained up and forced to break rocks with a sledgehammer. She thought her husband was still alive, and she hoped that he would be set free by the Vietnamese and that she could find him. He still had not seen his new son, their second child.

"What about Mom?" I asked. "Do you know where she is?"

She sighed and started to speak, but then paused. "What?" I asked. "Where is Mom?"

I tried to see her face, to read her mind, but I could only make out her shadow in the darkness. "I think that Mom is gone," she said.

"What do you mean *gone*?" I asked.

"When the Vietnamese were approaching, it was chaos at the village where the women lived. We could hear nearby shooting between the Khmer Rouge and Vietnamese troops. Everyone set off running in different directions. Some of the Khmer Rouge soldiers said they were going to the jungles, and they wanted women to cook and clean and grow vegetables for them.

"Mom and I stayed with my baby in this hut. We did not want to run with the baby. Two soldiers came to the door. They were going to take Loth from me and make me go, but mom said, 'No, take me. Please take me. Let my daughter stay with her baby and take care of him. He is not even a year old. I am a hard worker and a good cook.'

"She begged them to take her. The soldiers agreed. They let me stay with my baby, but they forced Mom to line up with some of the other women to go with the troops."

Dy paused for a long time before continuing. "I saw one woman who refused to go. They hit her with a hammer, killing her, right in front of the others. I couldn't believe they let me stay and that they let me keep little Loth."

She paused again and cried for a little while before resuming. "They have killed many babies. I have seen them do it.

"They marched the women, about ten of them, toward the border with Thailand, where there are mountains and jungles. They took Mom and the other women away three or four days ago. I have not moved. It's very dangerous to go anywhere with all the fighting. The Khmer Rouge has been defeated, but there are still many rebel soldiers left. They intend to fight and rebuild while hiding in the jungle. They will never quit."

I seethed with anger at the idea of my mom's enslavement by the Khmer Rouge. I asked, "Do you think that Mom will be able to get away? Do you—" and here I paused, unable to say what I was thinking, "do you—think they will kill her?"

"I do not know," she said. "I do not know."

"Is there anything we can do to help her? Maybe we can go get her? Help her escape?"

"I don't know how we could do that and live. We don't where she is. They would kill us right away. We should wait, and maybe she'll come back. I'm afraid to travel with the baby."

"Mom is strong," I said. "I bet she will survive."

But I was not optimistic. I was afraid to put into words my certainty that she was dead. I lay flat and opened my eyes, even though I couldn't see a thing in the dark. Of all the lows I had lived through, this was the lowest, knowing that I may never see my mother again. I didn't sleep a wink that night, enraged and heartbroken over my mom's fate, contemplating what my life would be like if I lost her.

I didn't think I could go on without her. I thought over and over again about the last time I had seen her in the rice paddy, speaking to me through the heavy rain. *I love you, Sokomasath*, she'd said. *I love you.*

MY SISTER DY and her baby and I made the shared hut our temporary home. The weather was getting warmer, and we often went to a nearby stream to bathe and find food to eat. My sister and the other family had some rice, and I caught fish in the stream that I cleaned and cooked on a fire near the shelter. I found lots of fruit and mushrooms too.

My wounds from my beating slowly healed, and with rest and food and baths in the river, I felt better physically than I had in years, even though I still could not see anything after dark. Emotionally, though, I was a wreck. I often cried when thinking of my mother, which I did all the time. I also thought of that boneyard of skeletons I had seen and how I was sure the Khmer Rouge had killed my pa. I grew more and more sure that my mom was dead, too.

I thought about the gods I had learned about from my mom and the monks in my Buddhist upbringing. I talked to these gods and asked them why this could happen to my mother and my father. I thought about trying to find my grandfather, but I knew he was too old to help. My grandmother in the other direction was caring for my little sister Poch. Poch had been one year old when I had last seen her, and by this time she would be almost five. But that would be a long trip, and I was worried about going into the country. The Vietnamese were in control of the cities, and we had begun seeing groups of their soldiers going up and down the road. They never caused any problems for us, but we heard that the Khmer Rouge was still battling in the country, relying on guerrilla warfare. I often talked about making these trips, but my sister said it was too dangerous.

Unable to do anything, I was overcome with inertia. Most of the day I spent lying on the ground near the hut. I remembered what had happened to my father when I was told they were going to take him to work on a farm. I began to believe that the same fate had befallen my mom. She would have been killed for no good reason other than the ignorant hatred of the peasants whom the Angkar had brainwashed.

A chill came over me. I was certain that my mom was dead. I knew by then that the people the Khmer Rouge took away did not return. They ended up in mass graves. I tried not to think about it, but I couldn't help it—I imagined my mom's body being dumped in a mass grave.

I could not comprehend my life without my mom. I didn't want to live without her. While I loved my father dearly and looked up to him like he was a god, there were many, many nights when he had not been at home. That had been no fault of his, of course, because he had been a loyal soldier and soldiers have to go into battle and leave families behind for long periods of time. He loved us dearly, but he couldn't always be there. But my mom was always there for me. *Always.* Every meal, every night tucking me in and singing me to sleep, every morning when I awoke to get dressed, she was there. No matter what I did or how bad I was as a child, she was always there for me with unconditional love.

Now she was gone.

I went through the motions every day of gathering firewood, looking for wild fruits and mushrooms to eat, and trying to catch fish in the river. I got a lot of rest just lying around, sleeping late, and doing very little. My vision at night, with the benefit of nutrition from a healthier diet and three meals a day, began to come back a little bit. I began to be able to see a little by lantern or firelight after dark, although my night eyesight was still very weak.

But I was unhappy as I had ever been. My mom dominated all of my thoughts. I was glad my sister was there, but she was preoccupied with taking care of her baby. I was happy that he was healthy, but I felt as alone as I had ever felt knowing that my mom was not in the world.

As the weather heated up in March and then into April, I spent more time at the stream. Other kids were around, but I did not want to play with them, nor did I spend any time trying to catch the colorful fighting fish. I had no desire to do much of anything.

I would swim alone, going in the stream to cool off, and sometimes I would just float in the slow-moving brown water and look up into the sky. For all the horror that millions of Cambodians had endured, I could not understand how the sky and the river and the trees and the landscape still could be so beautiful. Why would the gods let such a horrible thing happen to us, but then show us the natural wonderment of the world? Why would the gods let the Khmer Rouge kill my father and, near the end when we were almost free, my mother? I would close my eyes and go under the water, wishing sometimes that I would drown.

But I always floated back up, caught my breath, and went back to the hut. Life went on, even though I didn't know how it could without my mom.

As the months passed, Dy and I often talked about trying to go to my grandmother's, where our younger sister was, or to my grandfather's. She was afraid to try, and I didn't want to go alone. I had no bicycle, so the trip would have taken a full day or more on foot. I also felt responsible for helping her with the baby. My sister wanted to find her husband, but she had no idea of where to look. At night we could hear distant gunfire and bombs exploding. We were at a loss as to our next move, and we had no one to help or advise us.

Mom will know what to do, I often thought, but then I would remind myself, *She is dead*.

AFTER TWO OR THREE MONTHS had passed this way, one very hot afternoon I walked to the stream to take a dip and cool off. I sat there listlessly for a while until I decided to go back and check on my sister and the baby. I trudged along the dirt road with my head down. I had been thinking about trying to find a bicycle and going into the jungles where the Khmer Rouge were hiding and finding out what had happened to my mom, but they were hundreds of miles away. Earlier that morning, I had told my sister about this idea and she had said it was too dangerous. She had said she needed me to help her. I stayed, but I wasn't happy.

Back at the hut, my sister had built a small fire and was cooking some rice and a piece of fish. I watched the baby while she cooked. He was awake, wriggling around on a blanket on the floor and smiling at me. I tickled him on the stomach, and he smiled more.

I lost myself in playing with him and enjoyed his giggles. His baby laughter provided the only moments of happiness I experienced in that time.

My sister was occupied with cooking and I was playing with the baby, so we didn't hear the footsteps on the stairs and then someone standing in the doorway. We looked up, though, when we heard a voice. "Sokomasath! Dy!" a woman said.

I couldn't believe my eyes.

"Mom!" I shouted and jumped up from the floor. Dy also shouted for her, and we both ran and hugged her. I squeezed her tightly around the waist. "Mom! I thought I would never see you again. I am so happy to see you."

We hugged and hugged, all of us crying and talking at once, for many minutes. After a while, my mom said, "I want to hold my grandson. I thought I would never see him again."

She released us and picked up the baby and hugged him. She closed her eyes and snuggled him to her neck. He cooed at her, and she cried more tears of joy. "I love you, you sweet little baby," she said, her eyes still closed.

She hugged him some more, but then she opened her eyes and looked at me. "I love you too, Sokomasath," she said. "You too, Dy. You are my son and my daughter, and I will always be here for you. I was here for you when you were a baby like this one, and I am here for you now."

My heart filled with joy. This was the first thing that had gone right in my life in years. We were together again, and I was so happy to have my mom back. It was as if she had come back from the dead.

After we had settled down and Dy had tended to the food and fed us, she asked, "Mom, how did you get away? I worried they would never let you go."

Mom took a deep breath and began her story. "There were about four or five other women with me. They forced us far into the jungle. The Angkar have set up camps, but they move every few days. They made us cook and clean and scrounge food for them. When we moved, we had to carry heavy packs. It was very hard, and they yelled at us constantly, threatening to kill us the whole time.

"When we were getting ready to move camp again, a younger woman and I decided to leave. We said, 'We cannot keep walking.' I told her I have a son and daughter and a grandson to go see and care for. We snuck off in the middle of the night and walked back here. I decided if they caught me and killed me, then so be it. I could not wait any longer, and they might have killed us anyway. It took us twelve days, and we must have come more than one hundred miles. We ate whatever we could find along the way, mostly tiny dates and fruit from palm trees. We saw some step on land mines and die from explosions. We were lucky."

I was so happy that my mom and sister and I were together again and that we were free from the Khmer Rouge.

Of course, we still had serious problems. Our house was gone, and we owned nothing more than the meager clothes on our backs. We did not know where we would go or what we would do or how we would survive.

In spite of this uncertain future, we had each other. For the moment, that was enough.

PART III

REFUGEE SURVIVAL

Homelessness and Hellish Journeys

[APRIL 1979–FEBRUARY 1980]

A FEW DAYS after my mom's return, we left Nikum to return to Battambang City. The city was safer than the country, where skirmishes between the Vietnamese and the Khmer Rouge were ongoing, and my mother wanted to see the ruins of our old house. I told her that it had burned to the ground. "I want to see it for myself," she said. "Maybe we can restore it."

I bit my lip, reluctant to tell her it was beyond repair. Once again I embarked on the two-day walk from Nikum to Battambang City, this time in very hot weather, but at least I had the company of my mother and my sister Dy and her baby. We walked all day and then stopped under some trees beside the road at sunset and shared some rice and dried fruit. We slept next to each other on plastic sheets under old blankets. The baby cried much of the night, but I didn't mind. I was glad not to be alone.

When we reached Battambang City on the afternoon of the second day, we passed many Vietnamese soldiers and tanks, avoiding them as much as we could. They paid no attention to us as we walked down the streets we had frequented in the years before the Khmer Rouge had invaded. My mom's eyes were wide and her mouth tight as she viewed the widespread destruction.

Her step picked up as we neared our old community. I did not wish to see the destroyed house again, but I did what my mother said and followed her. I was glad that I had my mom to guide me and did not have to make any more decisions.

As the charred remains of our house came into view, my mom reached for my hand. She walked up to where the house had been and was silent for a few minutes. After a while, she spoke. "Your grandmother Proeung's tree has ripe coconuts." Her voice was weak, and her hand trembled. "You should climb up and get some for us. We can make a meal out of those. We cannot stay here."

The coconut palm, which my late grandmother had planted many years before, stood about thirty feet tall. I was tired, and a little scared to climb it, but I could not let my mom down. I did as I was told, scaling the tall trunk. I reached the top and twisted loose about five coconuts from beneath the fronds. The coconuts were hard to get free, but I turned them back and forth until they fell to the ground.

Before I scaled back down, I took a quick glance from high above at what had been our community. It was even sadder from this height, the circle of seven homes decimated by fire, followed by years of neglect. Wild shrubs and weeds were growing tall. It wouldn't be long until the community was lost to the brush and no traces of it existed.

Even if the home had survived, we had no proof that we had ever owned the house and the land. The Khmer Rouge had destroyed any semblance of government. We had no way to prove that this had been our property, the home that my parents had owned for more than thirty years. We were glad the Angkar had been overthrown, but we were scared of the Vietnamese and had no way to make a claim on our land. All over Cambodia arguments arose over who owned what. Fighting was the only way to settle these disputes.

After a long period of silence, my mom said, "We will go to the wat. I have a friend who lives near there. She has land and will let us stay. It will be good to go back to the wat."

We walked to Wat Dom Rey Sor, where I had worshipped with my mom while growing up. My mom did not find the friend she was looking for, but we found an open plot of land near the temple. Even though we had no formal claim, we decided to make it our temporary home until someone challenged us. We staked out a spot, cracked open one of the coconuts, drank milk from it, and ate some of its meat. We slept on plastic sheets under the open sky.

The neighborhood around the wat was chaotic, and we worried we would be forced off our spot. After a week, a friend of my mom's who lived in another section of town said we could stay near their house, across the street from them under a huge mango tree.

It was a safer, quieter place, and the tree had thick leaves and offered good shade and protection from rain. While my sister cared for her baby, my mom and I gathered bamboo stalks and grass and palm leaves, which we fashioned into a type of shelter to give us a roof beneath the mango tree. It had no walls, just a roof. The monsoon season was beginning, which meant heavy rains and flooding would make it hard to sleep on ground. We lashed bamboo stalks together to make a floor to raise us up a few inches, but that still wasn't enough to stay above the water when the rain poured down. We added to the shelter for several days, making it as sturdy as we could with whatever we could find. It leaked a little, but it was better than no cover.

We settled in this temporary place, but we didn't know what our next move would be. We had no income and no means of support. We walked back across town to attend crowded services at the wat, which had resumed after years of darkness, and we participated in the Cambodian New Year celebrations in April 1979. Many Cambodians were excited to return to the practice of Buddhism, which had been forbidden by the Angkar. Small amounts of food were offered to worshippers after the services, but it was a chaotic struggle because many were starving. The quantity of food was not nearly enough to feed everyone. There was much pushing and shoving, and we got very little. We were like so many who didn't know where our next meal would come from.

Finding food to sustain us was our number one objective. My grandfather, my mother's father with whom years before I'd watched battles from his porch, came to live with us and helped out. He was in his eighties and had survived the Killing Fields by growing vegetables in a garden. As a Buddhist lay leader who gave blessings at weddings and funerals and other religious ceremonies, he was paid with cans of rice at each ceremony.

He shared his surplus of rice with us, some of which we ate, but it also became currency for my mom. She would take the rice to the open markets that had sprung up and trade it for fruit, dried fish, and other items. She would turn around and trade this food for more cans of rice than she had received, turning a small profit. The prices in the city markets were excessive, and the supplies not good. Most days we ate rice soup. It wasn't much, but at least we had heartier and more regular helpings than the Angkar had fed us.

I began going outside the city during the day to the rice fields to hunt for something to sell to make a living. During that summer's rainy season, I searched and often found watercress greens that I picked to give to my mother. She would cook some and sell some. Even though I was thirteen—much older than I had been when I was salvaging plastic with my friends before the invasion—my mother worried about me leaving the city because we heard of kidnappings and murders committed by the remaining Khmer Rouge rebels who persisted in the jungles. "You must be careful, my son," she said. "The war is not over. Do not leave the city."

I would agree with her, but then I would turn right around and go beyond the city limits. I began running with other kids who strayed into the rural areas, and I continued to go out farther than she wished. I wanted to find food that would help my family. Sometimes I picked a lot of watercress, but other times I didn't find anything.

Later in the year, when the rice-harvesting season began, a city officer came around and asked me to come to work in the fields outside the city to pick the rice. "We'll pay you five cans of rice a day," he said.

I was not thrilled about working in a rice paddy again, but I didn't have any other options and I was glad to have a job. Each day for several weeks, I worked all day harvesting rice. My mom would take the rice they paid me and trade it for more and better things to eat. We would share some of this food—including cakes and other desserts she had traded for—when we went to the wat. As poor as we were, at least we were getting a small amount to eat in that period. It wasn't enough, but we shared with others in need when we could.

AFTER WE HAD BEEN BACK in Battambang City for a few weeks, my mom said, "Tomorrow you and I will travel to see your sister Poch." She had been with my father's mother in a farming village outside the city. I had not seen her since the days before the Khmer Rouge had invaded, when she was only one year old.

It was a full day's walk to get to my grandmother's small home in the farming village. The last time we'd made this journey, my mom had hired a motorcycle taxi driver who got us there in about an hour. This time, it took about eight hours of walking.

At the end of the long day, in the late afternoon, I could see my mom start to get tense as we approached the one-room house on the edge of a vegetable garden. We had had no way to let them know we were coming. I wondered if Poch would remember me or my mom.

We walked up the steps to the house and called out for my grandmother. Poch ran through the curtain that blocked the door—she was so much bigger than she had been when I had seen her last! She was five years old, and she looked surprised to see us. My grandmother came out, and her eyes teared up. "I didn't think you had lived! I am so glad to see you! Please come in!"

She and my mom hugged, and then I hugged my grandmother. She had my father's face, and it made me sad to think of him. "Poch," she said, "this is your mother and your brother, Sokomasath."

Poch looked confused and was shy. It would take her some time to get used to us. My mom just cried and cried.

We sat on my grandmother's floor, and she gave us water and some rice and fruits and vegetables. After a while, my grandmother looked at me. "Why don't you take Poch outside and play before it gets dark?"

Poch looked up to her, her face worried. "It's OK, Poch," my grandmother said. "He is your brother. He will look out for you."

Poch looked at me reluctantly, but followed me outside. I was not sure what to do, so we just sat on the steps of the house. I could hear my mom and grandmother talking.

"Did you get any news of what happened to my son Seuth?" my grandmother asked.

My mom paused a minute or two before speaking. "No. I know friends of his were killed. We think he was killed. All the soldiers were. We don't know where he was buried. We have no way of finding out."

I heard my grandmother weeping quietly, but no other words were exchanged. I tried to get Poch to play, but she was scared and stayed close to the house.

Later, after we went inside when it got dark, my mom and I stretched out on the floor near the door, while Poch and my grandmother slept on mats on the far side of the room. It was crowded in the little room with all of us there.

I was starting to drift off to sleep when my grandmother asked my mom, "What do you plan to do?"

"I need to find somewhere for us to live in Battambang City," my mom said. "I need to find work and a house."

"I know many are leaving for Thailand," my grandmother said.

"I know," my mom said. "But we want to stay. It is our home."

"I can continue to keep Poch for you until you get settled. She is a sweet girl."

"Thank you. I miss her, but I'm glad you took care of her and can continue to keep her. I will get her as soon as we have a home and a place to stay. Did the Angkar give you a hard time?"

"Not too bad. They took many of my vegetables from my garden, but they let me stay in my house. They did not know Seuth was my son, and I never said anything. I know I am lucky. So many others had it so bad."

"Yes," my mom said. "I didn't think we would make it. We saw so many die."

The next morning, after my grandmother fixed us breakfast and gave us a sack of vegetables, my mom and I hugged her and Poch, who was starting to warm up to us, and left to walk back to Battambang City. My mom cried during the first hour of the walk, and I held her hand, hoping that it would make her feel better.

I SPENT A LOT OF TIME with my grandfather in these days. I helped him dig a well for water, which was very difficult work as old and weak as he was. "Grandfather, please don't work so hard," I said. "Let me do most of the digging." I was thirteen and stronger since I had been eating better since the end of the Angkar regime, but I was still very skinny and short for my age. Our work turned out to be in vain. Water from the well, which was not too far from our mango tree shelter, was unfit to drink because of nearby sewage pits.

My grandfather and I also planted a garden of yams, squash, cucumbers, and long beans on another plot of land in the area near our shelter. The garden was productive, but it was a constant battle to keep rats from eating our vegetables. We built traps to catch the rats, and we caught one or two a night. We skinned them, cleaned out the innards, cut the head and claws off, and cooked the meat. Because of his strict Buddhist beliefs, my grandfather was reluctant to kill any living thing, but we did so out of hunger. My mom made many different dishes from the rat meat and my grandfather's vegetables and rice. Other types of meat were too expensive. Rice could only buy so much. The rats we caught and the vegetables we grew were free.

Not only did rice make up much of our diet, it was our primary currency. The Angkar had obliterated the financial system. There were no notes for money. In fact, there was no government at all. There was no president, prime minister, or king. There were no police. There were only Vietnamese soldiers, who were concerned only with winning the war against the Khmer Rouge, not running the city.

Although rice was effective, gold was the preferred form of currency. Small pieces could be used to buy items, and my mom traded rice for gold when she could. A tenth of an ounce of gold was known as one *gee*, and my mom acquired gold in these small amounts by trading rice and vegetables. Some traders had scales that would measure the gold, while others would look at the size and estimate the number of *gee*.

WE WERE DOING THE BEST WE COULD, but living in a lean-to under a mango tree was not good enough. We worried about being forced off the plot of land where we had settled. Many bandits and thieves and desperate people were also about. We didn't know what the Vietnamese, who had control of the cities and much of the country, would do.

My mom wanted better for us, and more stability. She learned about camps Cambodian refugees had set up in the jungles on the border with Thailand, about seventy-five miles to the west. Much trading in open markets had sprung up along the border. Thai merchants sold food and other goods at prices much cheaper than in the markets in Battambang City, where everything was scarce. Mom became convinced that we could make a lot of money by going there and trading for cheap goods to bring home and sell at higher prices. "Tomorrow I will travel to the border," my mom said. "I've made arrangements to go with a group from Mongkol Borey, north of here. You will stay here and look after your grandfather and your sister."

"No, Mom, I want to go with you," I said. "I will help you and look out for you. Dy and Grandfather will be fine here."

My mom did not want me to go, but I convinced her that with me along she could carry back more goods to sell. She finally agreed, and I was excited about the prospect of this journey.

Seventy-five miles in America would be an easy trip by car, something you could do in an hour if you had a good highway. But we didn't have a car. We didn't have bicycles. We didn't even have shoes. We would walk through war-torn land that was still in contention between the Vietnamese and the Khmer Rouge, land that was booby-trapped with land mines and bamboo-spike traps. We would walk through jungle wilderness where tigers, cobras, and elephants roamed. We would have to endure monsoons. It was dangerous, but we had no future if we stayed put. We knew of no other way to better our situation. The border was our best hope.

Many Cambodians who had survived the hardships of the Killing Fields had given up on trying to make a life in their homeland. The year after the Vietnamese forced the Khmer Rouge from the cities, an estimated three hundred thousand Cambodians starved to death. Hordes of refugees sought a new start in the growing camps on the border with Thailand.

The Vietnamese in control of the country did not want Cambodians to leave, and they tried to stop the exodus. Soldiers on the ground and in tanks often turned back refugees when they were traveling northwest toward the border.

The Vietnamese soldiers still had their hands full with the remnants of the Khmer Rouge who were waging guerilla warfare in the country, particularly in the northwestern jungles, where they had gone into hiding. They attacked Vietnamese soldiers any way they could, planting land mines and bamboo spikes along all the roads and trails. They also kidnapped innocent civilians to place into servitude in their jungle camps in the mountains, as they had done to my mom.

Of course, we did not want to go back to the Khmer Rouge's Killing Fields, but Vietnamese rule did not seem promising. They were an ancient enemy of whom Cambodian people had long been suspicious, and we did not view them as saviors. We were fearful of this new power ruling the country and had no faith that our nation could recover and prosper under yet another communist regime, one that had been hostile to Khmer people throughout the centuries. Cambodians felt stuck between a rock and a hard place. More and more elected to leave for Thailand and hope for a new future through the refugee camps.

But that was not my mom's plan. She did not want us to leave Cambodia permanently. It was her home, and she loved it and the many relatives and friends who remained there. She simply wanted to make money trading at the border to better our situation in Battambang City. She hoped that by trading at the Thai border markets, she could make enough money to stabilize our life back home. It was bleak in Battambang City, with many homeless, including parentless children who wandered aimlessly begging, and we often saw sick and dying adults and children right out in the street. In spite of this, my mom was optimistic that things would eventually turn around and that Battambang City would once again be a stable place for us to live.

ONE SUMMER NIGHT my mom and I began walking at sunset toward Mongkol Borey, a city about thirty miles north of Battambang City. Because of the fighting between the Vietnamese and the Khmer Rouge guerrillas, we traveled at night so as not to be seen. Others were on the road, and we looked for those we thought we could trust and stayed behind them. We carried hand-stitched backpacks that my mom had made. Hers held a small supply of gold *gee* that she had been accumulating over the previous weeks by trading in Battambang City, cans of rice for us to eat along the way, and a bottle of water. I carried a plastic sheet and blanket and a few cans of rice. We were both barefoot.

I had been eager and optimistic about this journey, but I realized only a few hours into the very first night how hard it would be to walk in the dark. My night vision had come back in the six months or so since we had been freed from the Killing Fields, but it still was not perfect, and my view was somewhat hazy.

We initially walked along on the side of a well-traveled dirt road leading out of Battambang City. It was muddy in many spots because the rainy season was coming on in the early summer. It was dark and scary and lonesome being out on the road in the middle of the night. The darkness seemed endless, and our trip so long it seemed as if we were the only people on Earth. "Stay close with me," my mom said when I lagged behind. "There are many bandits on the road, and there are Khmer Rouge hiding out. We have to look out for Youns too. Their soldiers are here too."

Most of that first night of walking we were passing through fields that had been rice paddies. A few times we heard Vietnamese soldiers coming down the road in a tank. We could hear the noisy rumble and feel the ground shake long before it got close to us. "Let's hide over here until they go by," she said. We walked off the road and sat or lay down if necessary to avoid being seen. Stopping slowed our progress, but it was nice to take off my pack and rest.

The sky was mostly cloudy and it rained on us some that night, which made me feel cold, but a few hours before dawn the clouds parted, the rain stopped, and I saw a full moon. I looked up at the moon and imagined that it smiled on us and was giving us a blessing of brighter light. I saw stars and imagined that they were like flowers in the sky. Crickets chirping in the fields, I imagined, were singing a song for us. These thoughts made the journey more bearable.

We traveled along like that for the rest of the night, walking, stepping off and hiding when a tank passed by, and then moving along when it was gone. We must have covered about twelve or fifteen miles in the darkness before the night sky began to lighten on the eastern horizon, which was behind us as we headed west. "We need to find a place to sleep and hide for the day," she said. She looked at the road ahead. "There are some trees up there. We can go there and eat and rest until it's dark again."

I was exhausted, my excitement at the beginning of this journey having long since faded. "How long until we get to Thailand?" I asked my mom.

"We have a long way to go," she said. "At least three more days of walking, maybe four. We have another day before we reach Mongkol Borey and meet our group." Her tone of voice with me was sharp, and without her saying so, I knew that she was telling me not to ask questions about the difficulties of this trip.

She looked me in the eyes and the stern expression on her face told me what I already knew: It was going to be hard, and it was going to be dangerous, and that was that. We were going to do it and we were going to survive and go back to Battambang City with goods we could sell. Complaining would not help.

We walked to a clump of trees and low-hanging brush near the side of the road as the sun began to rise. This would be a good place to stay out of view for the day and have shade from the hot sun. We shared a small meal of rice, a piece of fruit, and dried fish. We had walked the entire night without eating or drinking anything, mainly because my mom knew our journey would be long and she wanted to preserve the food and bottle of water she had packed.

Our journey that first night had been mostly through rice paddies and cleared fields around the flatlands of Battambang City that had been farmed extensively, but as we traveled the next night, the tree lines became thicker and closer to the road as we passed through dense jungles.

At Mongkol Borey, after two long nights of walking, we met up in the town center with a group of about ten to fifteen people, some of whom my mom knew. We would travel with this group to the border.

The paths we followed through the jungles were mostly flat. Many Cambodians went the northwesterly direction through the flatlands to avoid the mountains, which were even more treacherous, but it was not easy walking. The terrain was torn up from the tanks that had passed through and often was very muddy, sometimes with puddles as big as small ponds. Many roots poked our feet. We walked in a long single-file line because of land mines, with the first person in line holding a flashlight and looking carefully for other footprints that were safe. We all were told to watch for lumps in the ground where grass was not growing, because that was the sign of a land mine. The rest of the group followed the first person's steps as closely as possible. "Step exactly where I do," my mom told me many times as the miles piled up. It was slow walking in these groups who contemplated every step.

"WE ARE HERE," my mom said as dawn rose after our fifth night of walking. We had arrived at a crude camp in the trees on the border known as the Old Camp. The hills were dotted with many rough shelters that refugees had built out of leaves and tree branches on the hills. Others slept out in the open under the trees, and that's what we would do.

I stayed in the camp and slept while my mom went with others across the Thai border to a market. She came back that afternoon with a big bag of noodles, bread, and moon cakes. "You have been a good boy," my mom said, handing me a moon cake. "You can eat one of these—but only one. The rest we will sell."

Oh, how I loved moon cakes! They are mini cakes about the size of a donut, which some Americans would compare to a moon pie. It was the best thing I had eaten in years. They were light and easy to carry, and we could sell them back home for ten times what my mom had paid for them. I wanted more than one—I could have eaten ten—but I knew better than to ask.

One other purchase my mom made in the Thai markets was a cheap flashlight. It was a necessity for those making the journeys at night. It used two D batteries and emitted a dim light, but it was better than not having anything.

Our trading at the border complete, we slept and rested one night and day in the camp. The following night we joined the others and began the long, dangerous walk back to Battambang City. It took another five nights of slow walking, but we arrived home and sold our goods for gold and rice.

That journey marked the first of many. My mom was able to make a small profit each time, but we were lucky to survive the trips back and forth, which became more dangerous.

I think back to the ambition and the peril of these journeys, and I'm astounded by my mother's resilience. She was sixty-two years old when she led me on that first dangerous journey in 1979, but she was undeterred in her efforts.

Reaching our destination on either end of the trip—the markets at the border, where we found a place to stay in a camp, or our lean-to home in Battambang City—was always a tremendous relief. Many times on the way I thought we would not make it. I was always especially happy to get back to Battambang City and rejoin my sister Dy and her baby Loth and my grandfather beneath the mango tree.

We must have made that seventy-five-mile trip to the border and back to Battambang City ten or twelve times. We made the trips more often in the dry season, but we did a few in the monsoon season as well.

Each trip seemed harder than the last. The horrors and difficulties we encountered are etched in my mind.

WITH EVERY STEP we worried about land mines. I've read reliable estimates that as many as ten million land mines are buried in Cambodia, with half a million near the Thai border. Some of these land mines have been buried for years, dating back to the earliest days of the Khmer Rouge civil war against Lon Nol's forces. Others were buried by the Khmer Rouge to fend off the Vietnamese. The Vietnamese buried some to catch the Khmer Rouge. Land mines are everywhere.

One time in the middle of the night on a narrow trail through a thick jungle pass, we were in a group of about ten people who came up behind a family of two children and two adults. Both of the adults had flashlights, the cheap, dim kind that most refugees carried. Our group was moving faster than the family. We got up close, only about ten yards behind them. The family's clothes were ragged, and they were all barefoot. The two adults had huge packs on their backs, and the children, a boy and a girl who looked to be about seven or eight, carried sacks they could barely lift. The little girl was very skinny and crying loudly. Her voice carried through the jungle. "Hurry up—and hush," her father said. "We don't have time to cry."

Our group leader stopped, so we all stopped. My mom, who was fourth in the line we had formed, turned off her flashlight. "Let's slow down and take a break," the group leader said. "We do not want to pass them. They are making too much noise."

Our group waited as the family moved slowly ahead, watching their lights disappear, the girl still crying and the father telling her to be quiet. After they rounded a curve, an explosion rang out and a high red-and-orange blast of flame illuminated the jungle foliage. The land mine was so powerful that the ground shook below our feet. The noise seemed to rattle the leaves in the trees, prompting birds to shriek and flap away. Because explosions would often bring Khmer Rouge rebels or Vietnamese soldiers to investigate and capture or kill their victims, our group scattered in search of places to hide. My mom grabbed my arm and pulled me off the trail. We hid in a thicket, as did others who were walking in our group. We lay down behind some brush and listened. All we could hear was a child moaning and calling out "Mom, Mom" in a weak voice, and then "Pa, Pa." I couldn't tell if it was the boy or the girl. The other family members were quiet, and soon the child's faint cries stopped altogether. I wished we could go help them, but to do so could have been a death wish. We could not risk the attention. My mom had been taken prisoner by the Khmer Rouge once before, and she had no intention of letting that happen again.

We waited a few hours, lying down to keep a low profile, and heard nothing. "Let's go," the group leader said after a long wait. "We can get to the next rest spot before dawn. But we must hurry."

My mom turned her flashlight on and we joined the group line and marched ahead, looking for footprints through the jungle path where the family who we assumed was dead had stepped.

My breath grew short and my blood ran cold. I knew we'd have to go around the dead family. "Stay right behind me," my mom said, as we got near the spot where the land mine had exploded. She slowed down and studied the footprints more closely. "There could be other mines right next to that one. Step only where I do. Don't look to your right. Act like this didn't happen."

But I couldn't ignore the smell of gunpowder and burns on human flesh and the earthy smell that I knew was blood. I also couldn't stop myself from glancing to see their bodies as we passed—it was only a millisecond of a glance, but I saw this family of four blown backward and off to the side of a hole in the ground. They had terrible wounds to their lower bodies and midsections. The mother was sheared nearly in half. All were still, and their mouths and eyes were open.

I paused, and my mom noticed my delay. She paused too. "Come on," she said. "We must move on."

I quickly averted my eyes back to my mom's feet and continued stepping where she stepped, wishing I could cleanse that memory of this family out of my head forever but knowing that it would be with me always.

I remember this incident clearly, and it would repeat itself in similar ways many times. We saw many killed or maimed by land mines on our journeys back and forth to the border. Each time, we knew it could have been us who were blown up by a single misstep. I often asked myself if these horrors would ever end. I worried every night that I might not live to see the next day.

At the same time, though, I said to myself, *I will live through this.* The Killing Fields had not killed us, and I was determined to keep going and survive. I was not ready to die.

THE LAND MINES were not the only tools of horror in the paths of Cambodians traveling to the Thai border. On another journey through the jungle, we heard a man in the distance begin to scream. He was about two hundred yards away, but he was yelling in such agony that we could hear him clearly. My mom clicked off her flashlight. I was puzzled. There had been no explosion. "He fell in a trap," she whispered. "We must hide. The rebels might appear to capture or kill him."

She pulled me off the trail, and we found a spot behind some thick grass and sat down. The man continued to scream. My mom whispered, "The rebels dig shallow pits and sharpen bamboo spikes as sharp as razor blades and place them pointing up. They cover the pit with a cloth and leaves to make it look like part of the trail, but once someone steps on it they fall through and land on the spikes. These often poke through the feet, the legs, or even the body if someone falls forward. I watch very carefully for these. That's why I keep you behind me."

These traps were common along our routes, and we would see and hear others who fell into the pits. When someone fell into the traps, we could hear them scream for help from miles away. I learned how the sharpened bamboo sticks—which in Vietnam were called *punji* sticks, a common weapon used by the Viet Cong against American troops— would cut through flesh and bones. Because of the nature of bamboo, there was no way to pull the sticks out of the flesh because the wood splintered and would cause even more damage while being removed. The only way to remove a *punji* stick was to push it all the way through. Another tactic was to smear the sticks with urine and excrement to cause infections in those who fell on them.

A few times we passed by victims of the pits who had been dead for some time—weeks and even months. I remember seeing rotted corpses and even a skeleton on sticks poking up from a pit.

THE WEATHER WAS OFTEN THREATENING and made our travels more difficult. Many nights we walked through the heavy rains of the monsoon season. The winds would blow and the rain would fall and we would trudge ahead through it, knowing that it might rain all night and that the mud on our feet would not dry. We would often see trees blown over, and with the storms would come lightning. Sometimes bolts of lightning would strike trees and the ground would shake. In these heavy storms, carrying a pack on my back made every step a struggle, but we had no other choice. It often would rain for days, so we couldn't afford to sit and wait until the downpour ended.

During the daytime when it rained while we hid and rested, we tried to find shelter, but we often were soaked. Some days it rained so hard that water flowed over the jungle floor in such volume that we could not sit or lie down. We had to stand while it rushed around our ankles. Sometimes we took vines and tied ourselves to tree trunks so we could try to sleep standing up. We'd stay that way until night fell, when we'd resume our journey. It was impossible to sleep for more than a few minutes at a time. We were always exhausted when we started walking again.

Yet another hardship on the journeys was that we often lacked fresh water and food, especially after the first few days when we had consumed our supplies. When we ran out of food, we ate what we could find, usually leaves from the thick jungle foliage. My mom taught me that leaves which tasted bitter or sour were safe. "The sweeter the taste, the more poisonous they are," she said. "If it tastes good, spit it out and don't swallow it. Eat only the bitter or sour plants."

In the dry season, when our water supply ran out, we would take whatever we could get along the roads and the trails, sometimes cupping water in our hands from puddles that settled in the footprints of elephants or potholes made from a land mine explosion. This water was dangerous to drink, but we often did it anyway to quench unbearable thirst. Many others on the road often got sick, and some died from contaminated water. I often felt very sick and threw up many times on these journeys. Sometimes fear made me vomit, but other times I'm sure it was filthy water I had consumed.

I also feared the wild animals of the jungle through which we passed. The shrieks of monkeys in the trees above us during the night were haunting as we walked, although the monkeys did not come close because they feared being killed and eaten by humans, a common occurrence in the jungle. At ground level, we knew there were tigers and wild elephants. Sometimes we could hear a distant tiger, its loud roar reverberating through the jungle, and see trees shaking where it ran. Other times we could hear heavy steps of elephants and their trumpeting sound. We knew cobras lived in many of the trees, and around the rivers and lakes we were wary of crocodiles. While the various birds of the jungle were no threat, their constant soundtrack of songs and calls was always with us. Even though the animals kept their distance and never caused a problem for us, I was scared of the animals surrounding us pretty much every moment of these long trips.

In addition to big animals that I worried about, the jungle had a vast population of insects and spiders, which included tarantulas and scorpions. When we traveled in the dark, we couldn't see these smaller creatures, many of which were venomous, but we knew they were there. Mosquitoes were also fierce in the jungle, and they bit us many times. All we could do was scratch and hope we were not infected with malaria. Thick flies were a signal that dead bodies were nearby. Sometimes we passed through huge swarms of flies or mosquitoes and did our best to ignore them and keep moving.

As many challenges as we had, nothing was as bad as coming into contact with humans. The closest we came to dying on these journeys— and many times our lives were in danger—was during our numerous encounters with gun battles between the armies. The Khmer Rouge was ever present in the jungle, fighting with the Vietnamese soldiers who had invaded and secured the cities but were unable to stamp out the roving guerrillas. We feared the Khmer Rouge based on our hard experience. We knew well what they were willing to do. We feared the Vietnamese based on history. In addition, when we neared the border, we feared the Thai soldiers, who were opposed to the Khmer Rouge and the Vietnamese. The Thai soldiers often threatened Cambodian refugees with violence and frequently harassed and raped women. Finally, small, independent paramilitary groups had sprung up, including some made up primarily of former Cambodian soldiers from the pre–Khmer Rouge era. These independent groups protected the makeshift refugee camps that sprang up along the border. At any time, soldiers from the Khmer

Rouge, the Vietnamese and Thai armies, and paramilitary groups could be fighting with each other, ensnaring us in the cross fire. That's why we traveled only at night, hoping to stay hidden.

On one trip home in the darkness of night we could hear a large contingent of Vietnamese soldiers and a tank. They were on the move, coming our direction, shouting in the language we didn't understand. The heavy tank and the footsteps got louder as they came our way—it sounded like there could have been fifty soldiers or more. My mom turned off her flashlight. Standing in the pitch dark under the cover of jungle trees, she grabbed my hand and pulled me off our narrow path and down a small hill until we saw a pond. "We must go into the water and hide," my mom said. "They will not think someone is there."

I followed her into the pond. We had wrapped the food we carried in our packs tightly in plastic in case it rained, but I didn't know if it could withstand being submerged. I worried that our bread, dried fish, and moon cakes would get ruined, but I did what my mom told me. We waded into water about four or five feet high, just high enough for us to stand and keep our heads above the surface. The water felt cold. I needed to sneeze, but I stifled the urge.

We had just gotten into the water when the Vietnamese soldiers opened fire on a troop of Khmer Rouge soldiers they exposed. The Khmer Rouge returned fire with rifles and rocket launchers and grenades, which the Vietnamese also had. The noise of the exchange was deafening, vibrating the water in the pond where we hid. We heard the staccato roar of the machine guns, the concussive bursts of grenades, and we saw the occasional fire in the sky when a grenade or small rocket landed. My mom put her arm around me and held me close, trying to warm me up. We kept only our faces above the surface, ensuring that we could breathe.

We waited there for an hour or so, a time that seemed like it would never end, watching the fire in the sky and listening to the bombs and bullets fly. After a few hours, the fighting became more distant as the Vietnamese soldiers moved on, chasing the fleeing Khmer Rouge rebels through the jungle. We could hear the battle moving farther from us until it faded away into the night.

Once my mom was confident the soldiers had moved on, we climbed out of the pond. We were soaked to the bone and everything we carried was drenched, although the food in the plastic had fared better than I expected. What did get wet, we saved and dried out later and ate ourselves if it was not fit to sell. My mom's flashlight got ruined, so she tossed it away. We walked on in the dark in wet clothes, covering another six or eight miles before dawn, when we found a place to hide and wait again for the cover of darkness.

Oftentimes we would hear soldiers in the jungle and would hide in a lake or a pond or a river if one was nearby. Hiding in water was my mom's preferred method. We were well practiced at submerging ourselves in water for safety. If there was no water to offer protection, we would lie down in the thickest brush we could find and keep quiet. We worried about being captured and either taken prisoner or executed on the spot. Sometimes we lay there hour after hour before the soldiers departed. Other times we were caught in the middle of firefights that went on for long periods of time. A few times we laid down for an entire day and night, not even lifting our heads and peeing in our pants instead of standing up. After the gunfight was over and we knew for sure that no soldiers remained, we would get up and run to hide in a safer place. We would resume our journey when my mom deemed it clear.

The closest we ever came to getting caught was once while we were cooking rice. Two Khmer Rouge soldiers sneaked up behind us. They pointed their AK-47s at us and shouted, "Raise your hands! You must come with us."

"Run!" my mom said, grabbing my hand.

We left the food, water, and our other belongings behind and took off running through the thick jungle foliage. My fear caused me to throw up as I ran, but I kept going.

I was surprised and relieved that they didn't fire on us or chase us through the jungle. We ran until we were out of breath and didn't hear them anymore. We were out of food and water and had lost our belongings. We had another three days of walking ahead of us before we reached home.

THE CLOSE CALLS were so many. One time near the border, when we were staying temporarily at one of the camps while my mom traded, I was chased by Vietnamese soldiers in a tank.

I had been walking through a dry field with a group of other young teens from the camp who were about my age. The tank appeared on the horizon, and it started speeding toward us.

The trees in the field began to shake. I saw some small trees fall to the ground as though they were cut down with imaginary saws. I realized that the soldiers were shooting machine guns at us.

We all ran as fast as we could.

A few boys were felled by the gunfire and didn't make it.

I kept running and didn't look back. To try to save the wounded would have been suicide.

I ran down a hill and dove into a muddy pond, submerging myself until the tank passed.

I don't know how many died. All I know is that I survived.

OFTEN ON THESE JOURNEYS and at the border, we saw the aftermath of battles. We saw dead and decomposing bodies of soldiers who had been killed in gunfights. We saw bodies of men, women, and children who had died after stepping on land mines. We saw those who looked like they had starved to death or died of disease alongside the trails through the jungles. There were no medics and no doctors and no care for anyone in these desperate times. No one bothered to move the corpses. If someone died, they rotted where they lay on the jungle floor, attracting flies, vultures, and sometimes wild animals that fed on human flesh. There were so many bodies that it was not surprising to come upon the dead, but it was always upsetting.

Once, when a Vietnamese tank came by very close to us when we were passing three or four bodies on the side of the trail, we had nowhere to hide.

We lay facedown next to the bodies, which had only begun to decompose, and pretended to be dead as the tank rumbled past. The stench was terrible, and it was hard not to vomit, but we lay quietly with our eyes closed until the tank was gone.

We survived to live one more day.

Border Camps

I N EARLY 1980, after yet another perilous journey, my mother decided to stay at the border camp with some friends and make as much money as she could there. She was resourceful and could sell food she bought in Thailand to the hordes of refugees who were gathering in camps on the Cambodian side of the border. She said the repeated trips to and from Battambang City were too dangerous for us to continue. She also was physically exhausted. She hoped we could stay in the border camps until things settled down, and then we would return home.

The first refugee camps where we stayed on the Cambodian side of the border were known simply as the Old Camp and the New Camp. They were only a mile apart, and the new one sprang up when the old one became overcrowded. Both were unsanitary and poorly planned and were swelling with thousands of people who constructed their own lean-to shelters with leaves and sticks and grass, as we did. Others created huts out of whatever materials they could cobble together. It was as rough a shantytown as you can imagine. No relief organization was involved. This camp was simply desperate Cambodians banding together. The conditions we lived in were no better than barnyard animals. I fit right in. I had not had a haircut in about a year, and my black hair was long and wild.

Although filthy with dubious water supplies and open sewage areas that attracted enormous swarms of flies, these refugee camps offered some basic protection. A militia had formed to protect the camp residents from attacks by the Khmer Rouge, the Vietnamese, and Thai soldiers. Many of the leaders of this militia were from the Cambodian military under Lon Nol—the army, defeated in 1975, in which my father had served. These ex-military refugees formed the militia and recruited young men and boys to protect the camps because no one else would. They enlisted all the young males they could to patrol and protect the camps, including young teens and even children. Some of the youngest soldiers carried AK-47s that were longer than they were tall. They did not have enough training. When there weren't enough rifles to go around, these soldiers carried machetes. In spite of these limitations, this militia was not afraid to stand and fight anyone. They were brave and fearless.

When we decided to stay at the border, we stayed only about a week in the Old Camp before we moved to the New Camp, where there was more space. We put up a lean-to shelter of our own. My mother established a daily routine of sneaking across the border to the villages in Thailand to buy bread, noodles, rice, cookies, and other food items to bring back to the camp to sell or trade.

She would go very early in the morning and then come back and sell everything she had bought by the end of the day. She was making some money this way, but it was dangerous. Thai soldiers patrolled the border in an effort to keep Cambodian refugees from crossing. She had to sneak across each time.

I went with her to the Thailand markets a few times. Once, when we were leaving a market with our purchases, a convoy of Thai soldiers pulled up in three jeeps. They shouted at us, firing their rifles, and chased us down a sandy road. We could not run fast because of the soft sand. They drove behind us, their engines revving and their guns firing. My mother was carrying a big bag of food. "Go ahead," she said to me. "Don't let them catch you. Don't worry about me."

I ran ahead of her a little way, but then I paused, refusing to leave her. When one of the jeeps got close to us, we ran off the side of the road and down a dusty hill through some trees where they could not drive. We hoped that the soldiers would not chase us on foot. We'd heard many

stories in the camp about refugees who were caught and beaten and im-
prisoned—and of women whom the soldiers raped.

The Thai soldiers did not follow us off the road, and we made it back
across the border to the New Camp. The armed militia guards at the
camp recognized and welcomed us. The camp was becoming a home
with protection we valued. We had not had any sort of protection for
almost five years.

The very next morning, my mom went back across the border to buy
more goods to resell. It was the only way she knew to try to improve
our situation.

IN THE NEW CAMP, we had reconnected with Ath Yonn, my aunt
whom I considered to be one of my other mothers. My mom and Ath
Yonn and I decided that we should return to Battambang City and bring
my sister Dy and her baby Loth back to live with us. She and her baby
were still at the shelter with my grandfather.

The journey back was fraught with much peril and seemed even
harder than the previous trips. We ran into many gunfights, witnessed
land mine explosions, and faced the usual assortment of snakes, tigers,
elephants, and venomous insects and spiders. We ran out of rice and ate
leaves. When we ran out of fresh water, we drank muddy water.

I walked barefoot. It was the dry season and very hot. My feet blis-
tered, my back hurt, my stomach was empty, and my body was tired.
When we stopped to rest, dirt was my bed, leaves were my blankets, and
branches of trees were my roof.

In Battambang City, we found my sister and her baby in the shelter
under the mango tree and brought them with us. It was sad to leave my
grandfather behind, but he was much too old to try to make the journey.
The family who had let us stay on the land said they would look after
him, and we shared a tearful goodbye with him.

During our return to the border, the weather, even at night, was very
hot and dry. At one point, my sister Dy had to hold her baby Loth above
her head as we crossed a shallow lake.

One morning we came upon a pond near our trail when we were
planning to hide and rest for the day. Unlike so many of the ponds and
streams we passed, this one had crystal-clear water. We were very thirsty

from the heat and all the walking we had done overnight. We rushed into it until the water was over our knees and bent over and cupped our hands and drank our fill. It was cool and delicious. I considered us very lucky to find water this clear.

After my thirst was quenched, I saw something floating near the shore. At first, I thought it was logs. Then I saw one with bright cloth on it. I walked over to look closer and realized what it was—a man, a woman, and a child floating in the pond. I saw their bodies, which appeared to have been dead for several days, and the smell of rotting flesh hit me.

I felt like I was going to vomit, but the water I drank didn't come up. I said nothing to my mom or Ath Yonn or my sister about the bodies. What would that do but upset them? When darkness fell, we continued our journey back to the border camp.

DY AND HER SON LOTH squeezed into our shelter in the New Camp. As time went on, violence inside and outside the camps escalated. Inside the camps, residents often accused others of having been members of the Khmer Rouge. When the Vietnamese moved into Cambodia, many of the Khmer Rouge members had fled alongside those whom they had enslaved. Practically every family who had survived the labor camps had lost family members to executions, as my family had, and our hatred for the Khmer Rouge and desire for revenge were fierce. There was much suspicion among the refugees. It was common to hear fighting and sometimes gunshots and afterward see bodies of those killed during the infighting. As more refugees poured into the camps, the crowded mix of lean-tos and crude huts was becoming more and more dangerous. We would hear fights begin and huddle in our lean-to to stay out of the way.

The camp also was in peril from outside attacks by Khmer Rouge, Vietnamese, and Thai troops. All three wanted to weaken the militia protecting the camp. The Vietnamese and the Khmer Rouge viewed the militia as a competing rebel movement, and the Thai soldiers sought to keep Cambodian refugees from crossing the border.

A number of times the Thai soldiers fired long-range artillery on the camp and the nearby Vietnamese troops, causing the refugees to scatter into the surrounding wilderness. The Vietnamese fired back with shorter-range weapons. The camp militia was caught in the middle. One evening as the sun set, the Thai soldiers launched a heavy attack. The camp militia fought back mightily, as did the Vietnamese, and the shooting was intense. My mom and my aunt Ath Yonn and I ran out of the camp toward a small hill that was nearby. It was overgrown with very thick brush and tall trees with spikes that were as sharp as needles. The thicket offered privacy, so residents of the camp often relieved themselves there. The ground around it was coated with human waste. It stank and was covered in enormous swarms of flies. But with the fear of bombs and machine guns firing into the camp, we didn't worry about the smell—we feared for our lives. With darkness upon us, we ran as hard as we could to the top of that hill and dove into a hiding space surrounded by thick brush behind a large tree. We couldn't see clearly what we were doing, but we were happy to find a dark space that seemed protected.

We hid there all night, lying close together surrounded by the thorny trees and shrubs, listening to the fighting between the militia and the Thai soldiers. The fighting continued for hours. As the guns fell silent in the predawn darkness, we could hear the cries and the moans of the wounded echoing around the camp.

When the sun rose, we were surprised to see we were in a spot hemmed in by trees and thick brush with briars and thorns. We were behind a big tree with three other trees right next to it, sort of a hollow in an impenetrable thicket. What was so strange was that it had no opening for us to leave. We didn't know how we could get out. We were trapped. We couldn't figure out how we got into that space in our panic, but we were there. We were not scratched or cut up, yet we could see no way to get out of this spot without cutting and scratching ourselves terribly. We had not even stepped in the feces that surrounded the area. It seemed impossible—like some sort of miracle that we had gotten into this spot unscathed by thorns and untouched by human waste.

We waited there, hoping someone with a machete might come by who could cut back the brush and free us, but we also were afraid of attracting the attention of Thai soldiers who could still be lurking about. We waited all day and then another night. The next day, after a night with no fighting, we were anxious to get free and find water and something to eat. We could hear some people on the hill who were searching for dead and wounded. They were speaking Khmer, so my mom called out. "Help!" my mom shouted. "We're stuck!" Ath Yonn and I joined in a chorus of cries. "Help! Help! Help!"

After we yelled for a while, two members of the militia came to our aid. They were looking for wounded from the battle. A young man with a machete approached us and spoke to us through the brush. "Are you in there?" he said. "Are you hurt?"

We couldn't see him, but we could hear that he was close.

"No, we are not injured," my mom said. "But we can't get out."

He studied our predicament a little more, walking all the way around the thicket where we had hidden, and then he began to laugh. We could barely make him out through the brush. "How in the world did you get in there?" he asked.

"I don't know," my mom said. "We were running from the bombs."

"It might have saved your life," he said. He turned and yelled to another young man with him. "Come look at this! You won't believe it."

The other man came up, and he also began to laugh. "I don't see how that's possible!" the other man said. They both were laughing. They laughed so hard they had to sit down for a while. "I don't see how that happened!" the second man said. "I can't believe it!"

They laughed so much, that we began to laugh too. It *was* a ridiculous situation. We were fortunate that we didn't suffer any injuries. The smiles and the laughter of the men were so great that we forgot our hunger and desperate thirst for a few minutes.

After the men stopped laughing, one of them said, "OK. I guess we need to cut you out of there. Stand back."

With their machetes, they cut an opening through the vines and brush to give us a passageway out of the trees. It was thick and took them awhile. We were happy that this spot had magically opened up for us.

I still can't explain how we got in there, but I'm glad we did. As much as I've gone through, I feel that gods have looked after me to help me survive. This was one of those times when someone was watching over me.

SOON AFTER THAT BATTLE, workers from foreign relief agencies began to visit the New Camp as its population continued to swell with thousands upon thousands of Cambodian refugees who had come to the border. They brought supplies of rice that they gave out to families in the camps, measuring out portions with empty milk cans. We lined up and got our share. The relief efforts included visits by doctors and nurses who helped those in the greatest need, although they could help only a fraction of the refugees. The militia who guarded the camp—and it was heavily guarded in this period with all the fighting that had been oc-curring—had reached some sort of agreement with the Thai troops that allowed the relief workers to enter and help the refugees. It was the first time I saw the kindness of people from around the world.

The conditions in the camp started to get a little better, but the vio-lence had not abated. Fighting inside and outside the camp continued to escalate. One minute it would be quiet, and the next minute bullets would be flying. Often when shooting began, I was running around the camp and playing with other young teens about my age. I was thirteen going on fourteen, but I was skinny and short and looked younger. I would hide or lie low until the fighting stopped. I remember many times lying on the ground and hearing the whizzing sound of bullets passing over me. After the skirmish ended, I would return to find my mother in our lean-to shelter. "Why are you running all over the place?" she would ask, angrily. "You are going to get killed. You need to stay near me, stay safe."

I never blamed her for being tough on me. I was lucky not to have been killed. Many others in the camp were killed in the random fire-fights that popped up all the time. It was common to see the bodies of dead and seriously wounded lying about the camp after these battles.

IT ALL CAME TO A HEAD for us one night near the end of the dry sea-son. A tremendous gunfight engaged all four armies in and around the camp. The Vietnamese kept pushing in, and the Thai were fighting back. Khmer Rouge rebels were involved, and paramilitary fighters protect-ing the camp did their best to fend off all three groups. Shots were fired relentlessly in all directions.

My sister Dy, her baby, my mom, and I were right in the middle of all these warring parties, who fought nonstop for three or four days. Of all the intense battles we had witnessed, this was the worst. We found some trees and lay down behind them, huddling together and praying not to be hit. We stayed flat on the ground to avoid being struck by bullets or shrapnel. The ground rumbled beneath us with the vibration of explosions that were very close, and many bombs hit the camp. We were afraid to even lift our heads, and we peed in our pants where we lay. Loth, Dy's baby who was more than a year old, cried and cried and tried to wriggle away, but she held him tightly. It seemed like the battle might never end and that these could be our last moments on Earth.

We stayed that way for three or four full days—but it felt like forever. I thought that it might be the end of us, but late one night the fighting finally ended. It was calm for many hours, but we were still afraid to move.

When the morning came, the sun was bright and the clouds of smoke that had filled the camp cleared. We heard others talking and moving about outside. It sounded safe, so we stood and surveyed the camp.

Bodies lay all around, some dead, others wounded. It was a gruesome sight.

Then we saw something that surprised us. Near the back of the camp, a line of ten or fifteen trucks driven by a contingent of relief workers approached from the direction of the Thai border. The trucks were midsize, with big open beds surrounded by rails on the back.

The trucks pulled up into the camp and parked, including one very close to us, and relief workers got out. They were Europeans and Americans and Australians, men and women, all wearing matching jackets like the ones we had seen on relief workers who had visited before to bring food and improve the camp's sewage system. They had Cambodian translators with them who carried clipboards.

A tall European man and his Cambodian translator approached us. He smiled kindly and bowed his head. My sister Dy wanted to turn and run, but my mother grabbed her arm and told her to wait.

The translator spoke to us in Khmer while the tall man smiled. "You guys cannot stay here anymore," he said. "It is too dangerous. You have to go."

"Where are we going?" my mom asked.

"To a United Nations refugee camp in Thailand," he said. "We want to help you. You'll get shelter and food and more protection. It will be much safer than here. Come around here to the back of this truck."

We were too tired and shell-shocked to ask any more questions. We had nothing to lose, so we went along.

The tall man guided my mom and my sister, who was carrying her baby, to the back of the truck and lifted us into the bed one by one. We were all so skinny that it seemed to be no effort at all for him to pick us up and drop us in the back.

We stood and waited until the truck filled with about ten more refugees whom he lifted up to join us. When there was no more room, the truck's engine roared to life, and we began rumbling down the road. We left Cambodia, heading west, bound for the distant I Dang Mountain. We didn't know where we were going, but soon we would find a new home in Thailand.

Freedom inside Barbed Wire

[JUNE 1980–OCTOBER 1983]

I WAS FOURTEEN THAT DAY in June 1980 when the United Nations truck carried me, my mom, my sister Dy, and her baby Loth down a bumpy, dusty road under the hot Thai sun. We had to stand for the ride, jostling against others whenever the truck turned or stopped. My black hair was very long, hanging down my back, and my clothes, still the uniform I had worn during the last year of the Khmer Rouge reign, were ragged. The black was faded to a dingy gray and filthy.

We didn't know where we were going or what this trip held in store, but we were glad to be moving. I could see I Dang Mountain through the slats on the side of the truck. We had spent the previous four days lying still, hoping not to be shot or have bombs dropped on us. We knew our destination couldn't be worse than what we had endured for the previous five years—almost four years of Khmer Rouge rule and more than a year of homelessness in the chaotic aftermath.

It took only about twenty or thirty minutes for us to arrive at the camp known as Khao I Dang. Named for the mountain that hovers over the landscape, it was less than ten miles from the border. The sprawling camp was surrounded by thick barbed-wire fencing and consisted of thousands of thatched huts built in lines like military barracks.

Khao I Dang had been set up in 1979 by the United Nations Refugee Agency and was managed in partnership with the Thai government, whose soldiers provided protection, to deal with the exodus of Cambodian immigrants. Its population swelled to more than one hundred thousand refugees who were crowded into 2.3 square miles.

We climbed out of the truck with the help of the driver, who was very kind. He lifted us down with ease and told us to wait in line near the entrance where someone would take our names and show us where we could stay. The line grew huge with the arrival of more trucks and more refugees, as hundreds, if not thousands, gathered outside the entrance to the barbed wire–surrounded compound.

I leaned toward my mom and whispered, "What name do I tell them?" I had used the fake name Sin Prou in the Angkar years, but in the year after the Khmer Rouge was ousted, my mom had decided to call me Leuth. She was still reluctant to call me Sokomasath, my original name, for fear of reprisal. We had no official documentation of who we were and had not had any records of our lives for years.

We could have any name we wanted.

My mom thought about my question for a moment. "Tell them your name is Oun Leuth," she said. "That will honor your father. We should still be careful. We cannot say your father was a Cambodian soldier. We don't know who from the Khmer Rouge might be here."

"Oun Leuth," I said to myself. I had not thought about my full name in a year. "Oun Leuth."

I liked the name Leuth. It was inspired by Seuth, my pa's given name. My sister had named her first son Houeth, and her second son Loth, also honoring my pa's name. Even though my pa was gone, he would live on through us.

After many hours of waiting, we reached a table staffed by two relief workers, an American man and a Cambodian man who was his translator. "What's your name?" the translator asked. I was not familiar with his dialect, and I had a hard time understanding him.

"Oun Leuth," I said.

He seemed confused by my dialect.

"Oun Leuth," I said.

It was clear he couldn't understand me. I could barely understand him, but at least I knew he wanted my name. He turned to the American, and they spoke in English, although at the time I had no idea what language they were speaking.

He turned back to me and handed me a pencil and a piece of paper. "Write it down," he said.

I wrote it down in the Khmer script and handed it to him. He read it and looked puzzled. I could see they had a form, and they were translating the names into English. He shrugged and started writing.

I didn't know it at the time, but he would make a mistake that would set my name for the rest of my life.

In translating my new name, he dropped the *u* from Leuth, so it became Leth.

I've been Leth ever since.

AFTER THEY TOOK OUR NAMES DOWN, we were assigned to a hut. There were thousands of these small huts made of bamboo with thatched roofs built side by side. Each contained a single room of no more than two hundred square feet. All four of us would share one. It had a dirt floor, but after we had been there a few days, my mom and I cobbled together enough bamboo to make a floor. The best thing about it was that we knew we were protected from war. It was not luxurious, but it was the best lodging we had lived in since we had been forced out of our Battambang City home almost five years before on that fateful day in April 1975.

We felt safe for the first time in a long time.

We were given instructions on when and where to get our daily disbursements of food and water. This required standing in two separate lines, sometimes for hours, and it became my job for the family. Once you reached the food or the water, you had to give a relief worker your name and the names of your family members. They were very careful to check off the names, as they were trying to prevent unfair disbursement of water and food rations, which consisted of rice and dried mackerel. Many arguments broke out among the refugees in the lines, and often people tried to cut and got into fights. Thai soldiers, who provided security to the camp, would sometimes be called in if the fights got out of hand. I did my best to stay as far away from these conflicts as I could. Much of my day was taken up by standing in line and waiting, but I did not let it bother me. Compared to what I had seen, this task was easy. Although at night we could faintly hear the distant echo of bombs from battles at the border, we were too far inside Thailand to be attacked.

After I finished gathering our food and water—which I carried in two heavy buckets suspended on each end of a wooden pole I placed on my shoulders—I had the run of the camp. I walked around and met and played with many other teens my age.

Once I settled into this routine, I was happy and sad.

I was happy because for the first time in years we had freedom and security and enough to eat. This freedom was the greatest thing in my young life. I could talk, laugh, smile, and even sing—although I am not a good singer, I enjoyed it. I also found groups of kids, teens, and some young adults who would gather to play traditional Cambodian games, including *chaol chhoung*, an ancient game that involved tossing handker-chiefs that are folded into a ball with a tail. It was a game played during Cambodian New Year celebrations that brought young men and women together for the first time. The game has many different variations and also involves songs. I would stand near the game and watch as they all smiled and laughed and sang while tossing the balled-up handkerchief—perhaps the happiest they had ever been in their lives. I felt the same way about these joyous gatherings and was thrilled to express my happiness. I had missed many years of laughing and smiling.

In quiet moments, however, when I was lying down at night or waking in the morning, I was very sad. We had left my younger sister, Poch; my two surviving grandparents; and other friends and family members behind in Cambodia. I missed them and wanted to be re-united with them, as did my mom and older sister Dy. Dy also worried about her older child, Houeth, who was living with her husband, whom she learned had survived, and his family in Cambodia. She hoped they all could be together again. Family was the most important thing in the world to us—and ours was splintered. I found myself thinking about my father, recalling that last day when I saw him when he was a prisoner of the Khmer Rouge. I also thought about Kim Ban and Sakum and their disappearance in the middle of the night. I agonized over the loss of these family members who had died and the ones who remained alive but were separated by a vast distance. It was like a death, this separa-tion. It was hard knowing that they were alive and having no way to communicate with them. There were no phone lines or mail service. They did not have the protection we had, and we worried about their safety and health. This sadness weighed heavily upon us, as though the

I Dang Mountain that hovered over the top of the camp was sitting squarely on our shoulders.

I HAD TURNED FOURTEEN YEARS OLD a few months before, during the Cambodian New Year of April 1980. It had passed while we were living in the New Camp on the border, but we had no way to celebrate it then, as we were struggling to survive. We were thrilled to find that Khao I Dang hosted a wat constructed of bamboo that refugees packed to overflowing during regular Buddhist services, which my mom and I attended. It was such a joy to have this opportunity to worship again, and I could see a smile on my mom's face that I had not seen in years.

We prayed for those who had died as a result of the Khmer Rouge and wished for them to be reincarnated to a better life, to be a better person, to be free of sin. We also asked forgiveness from them and paid our respects. Respect is a powerful element of our tradition. My prayers focused on my respect for my parents. My father and my mother brought me into this world, a gift I could never repay. I also gave thanks and prayed about my respect for my two "other mothers" who helped raise me. They helped me overcome sickness as a child. They spent lots of money to heal me and to keep me healthy. They sent me to school and fed me and cared for me. One of my other mothers, Sakum, had perished, but Ath Yonn survived.

When I prayed, I was overcome with love for my mother, my father, and my other mothers. I still feel this way. They are my gods! I would not be here without them.

ONCE WE HAD FOOD, water, and a place to live, my mom and I began trying to find ways to make money. The camp grew more and more crowded with new arrivals every day. Refugees often traded with each other, and markets sprang up in the camp. My mom acquired scissors and sewing needles and cloth and began to make clothes by hand. She was great at it, and many people came to her for clothes. Sometimes she was paid in Thai money, and she used it to buy cakes made by fellow refugees.

In addition to the clothes she sold, she made new clothes for me and my sister and herself. She made blue sarongs for her and my sister and even one for me that I slept in at night.

I also wanted to contribute and earn money, and soon I found a way. I started waking up at sunrise and going up on I Dang Mountain to gather firewood. I used a hatchet to chop down trees and break them into small bundles. I sold most of the wood to the people in the camp, but some I saved for our family's cooking and warmth. After I made and sold the bundles, I stood in lines for water and food in the late afternoon. The camp was becoming more and more crowded, and sometimes the wait could be all afternoon and into the night. I had very little time to play, nor did I have time to go to the school that they had set up in the camp, but I was thrilled to be making money to help my family.

My mom and I made friends with many people in Khao I Dang. With everyone living so close and standing in lines together for much of the day, it was impossible not to know your neighbors. My mom became close to many of the refugees she made clothes for, and she also met many people at the wat. She was always very social and often talked with women and girls who lived in the camp. I befriended and hung around with many of the boys my age, and I met many adults in the camp when I sold them wood I had chopped.

Boys and girls in the camp followed the Cambodian tradition of staying separate and not intermingling—parents were strict about this—but I remember one girl fondly. She often came to talk to my mom. I thought she was cute, and I would smile at her from a distance. My mom never introduced us. I never learned her name, but I remembered her face.

Although I liked girls, I was not looking for a girlfriend. My mom would have scolded me if I had one. I didn't know it at the time, but this girl whose name I didn't know would play a big role much later in my life.

Khao I Dang began to get more and more crowded. Every day I saw hundreds of refugees coming through the entrance. More huts were built in the dirt of the sprawling community surrounded by barbed wire beneath the mountain. The lines for food and water grew longer and slower. The latrines grew more crowded and smelled terrible.

One fall afternoon, a relief worker came to our hut and told my mom and my sister that we were going to be moved to Sakaeo, another camp farther into Thailand. A few days later, they put the four of us and our few belongings in a truck. The move took us deeper into Thailand and farther from Cambodia. Although Sakaeo was only about twenty-five miles east of the Cambodian border, it seemed as though it were a thousand miles away.

It was a smaller camp than Khao I Dang, but our hut was very similar. Once again we were inside a barbed-wire fence that surrounded the camp. I realized when we settled in Sakaeo that I would never be able to go back to get our family members so we could all live together. This move marked the end of our hope of family togetherness. I felt great sadness and sorrow about this separation. It was a great burden on my heart, and I was overcome with homesickness for the land where I was born. Cambodia was the land that gave me language. The land where I learned respect for my parents. The land where my mom and my pa had started to teach me right from wrong. The land my father had given his life defending. I had hoped that we could go back to our lives before the Khmer Rouge, but that dream was lost.

I was losing the only land I had ever known.

IN SAKAEO WE FACED A NEW LIFE, but we did not know what that life would be. Our dream of the future was vague. We had no money, no friends in this new camp, and very little knowledge about the system for moving refugees to other countries. We knew relocation was a possibility and we heard many refugees talking about it, but we had no idea what would happen to us. As the only male in my family, I felt responsible for taking care of my mother, my sister, and her young son. I knew I had to be tough to handle whatever my family needed, and I believed I had failed in not being able to reunite all of us.

In spite of this pressure and these doubts, I never gave up hope that we could start new lives. In what country? We didn't know. And how long would we have to wait for that new life to start? We had no answers—only questions and waiting.

We realized right away that there was much more tension in Sakaeo than there had been in Khao I Dang. We heard rumors that many who resided in Sakaeo had defected from the Khmer Rouge, and I noticed that many of the refugees there still wore black. Years later I would learn that there were two Sakaeo camps. The first one had initially been set up by the Thai government and the United Nations for Khmer Rouge–affiliated refugees, but then refugees who had been victims of their brutal practices were also brought in. The first camp was closed in 1980, before we arrived, but Sakaeo II, as where we were is sometimes known, was opened nearby and many of the refugees from the first camp were moved there.

This combination of former Khmer Rouge members and those who had been their captives was scary. The anger and resentment of refugees who had been abused by the Khmer Rouge were palpable. Often fights would break out when one refugee suspected another of having been part of the Khmer Rouge, and sometimes there were accusations that one refugee had killed another refugee's relatives.

Because of this tension, Thai soldiers with AK-47s were prevalent throughout the camp, much more so than they had been at Khao I Dang. We had not been in Sakaeo long when one morning, as I was walking to get our daily disbursement of water, I saw three or four uniformed Thai solders shouting at a Cambodian man who was lying facedown before them on the ground. I steered as far away from them as I could, but I sneaked glances at what was happening. The man had bruises on his face and was bleeding from his nose and mouth. I could not tell if he was conscious or even still alive.

Who was he and what crime had he committed? I did not know, and I did not try to find out. After my hostage experience with the Khmer Rouge soldiers who had nearly killed me, I had no appetite for interactions with armed soldiers, nor did I want to get close to the fights between refugees in the camp. Most, like my family, just watched from a distance and hoped and prayed for the best. The Khmer Rouge had put dents on the Cambodian people's heads, including mine.

Although we feared the Khmer Rouge, we also feared the Thai soldiers who patrolled Sakaeo. They looked down on us as though we were animals. I was scared of being beaten and abused. I kept my distance from them and stayed quiet.

I wanted no more trouble with anyone. I did not want anything but to live.

IN CONTRAST TO THE THAI SOLDIERS, the relief workers at Sakaeo who provided food and water were very kind and generous. These people came from all over the world and represented many volunteer organizations. They had big hearts. They took care of us just like we were their family. They were a bright spot in our lives, and their presence helped give me hope.

After we had been in Sakaeo for several months, the situation in the camp began to improve. Best of all, the relief workers encouraged me to attend the camp school that offered classes from first grade all the way through junior college. It was such a joy for me to go to school again, and my mother encouraged me and was very happy about it too. Education had been important in my young life, and it was very important to my mom and my pa. I was thrilled every time I stepped into that classroom building constructed out of plywood.

Before the Khmer Rouge, many college students and graduates had lived in Cambodia, but afterward, few remained. Many teachers had been executed during the Killing Fields years, and many others who had avoided execution died of disease, exhaustion, and starvation. However, a few refugees at Sakaeo had enough education to teach, and I was thrilled to take classes from them. Although I had been prohibited from reading or learning for four years, I had retained much of the knowledge I had acquired in school in Battambang City. I fondly remembered my first teacher, Teacher Peo, and I was thrilled to recall the lessons in language, math, and science he had taught me. I studied hard, reading every page of the photocopied books they gave me, and it all came back very quickly.

I advanced rapidly in the Sakaeo school, moving through the high school to what they called junior college. I earned excellent grades and completed all the courses offered in the camp in less than a year.

After I had exhausted the classes I could take, I decided to apply to be a teacher to fill one of the many openings. The school had a hard time keeping teachers because many of the refugees who taught were often transferred to other camps.

I knew I was young to try to be a teacher, but I wanted to do my best and apply myself wherever I could. If I failed at becoming a teacher, that was OK. I wanted to try, and I was willing to fail. I took the teacher certification test—and passed! I was so thrilled and proud of my results.

The next step was a three-week teacher training program. I was fifteen by this time, but I was still much younger than all the others in the class. I also was only about five feet tall and looked younger than my age.

*My graduation certificate, which includes my photograph at the age of 15,
for a course I completed in automotive theory and practice at the Sakaeo refugee camp
in Thailand in 1981. This is the earliest surviving photo of me.*

I walked into the room on the first day of the teaching instruction and drew many stares from my classmates when I sat down among them.

"Who are you?" a man in his twenties asked me. "You should be in the high school, not the teacher school."

"I finished the junior college courses, and I passed the test to teach," I said. I sat up straight and held my head high. "I belong here."

He smirked and rolled his eyes, and I heard the others murmuring about me. Many of the older teachers in this class had seen me in the camp, running around with my shirt off and playing with other kids. A woman who was an assistant administrator in the schools said to me, "You don't belong here."

But I believed I did belong there, and I was determined to stay. I ignored the snide comments. I had lived through starvation and endless days in the rice paddies and a daylong torture session. I was not going to be deterred. I loved to learn, and I had completed the courses the Sakaeo school taught. Even though I was young, I wanted to teach.

I could see that the instructors had doubts about me, but I went to the class every day intent on learning everything I could. I was determined to do well and to become a teacher. I studied for hours each day, before and after the class, and regularly spent time in the camp's small library. I read every book I could get my hands on.

After a while, I earned the respect of some of the younger teaching students who were not much older than me, and I became friends with a few. We talked about where we were from, our lives in the pre–Khmer Rouge days, and our families and the cruelty that had taken so many lives. It was good to bond with them, although the older teachers and instructors remained skeptical of me.

I completed that course and was approved to teach. I was assigned to a high school class filled with about twenty teenagers. I'll never forget that first day when I walked to the front of the room with my lesson book and introduced myself: "Good morning, I am Teacher Oun."

Some of the students were older and taller than me. I could see the looks of surprise on their faces, which turned to smiles. "You are our teacher?" one boy asked, laughing. He must have been seventeen or eighteen and at least six inches taller than I was. His laughter spread through the classroom.

"Yes," I said, trying to stand tall and make my voice sound authoritative. "I am your teacher." I knew I had to impress upon them that I deserved to be here and that they could learn from me.

I took the one piece of chalk I had been given for this course and began to write numbers on the small slate blackboard that hung on the bamboo wall. "We are going to start with a math problem," I said. "Please let me know if any of you can solve this."

I thought back to the hardest algebra problem I had worked on in my junior college courses and jotted it down on the board. When I finished writing it, I turned around and their expressions had changed from smirks to surprise. They sat there tight-lipped and stared at the problem.

I held the chalk up as an offer. "Anyone want to come up and give it a try?"

None of them moved.

"Are you sure?" I looked around and made eye contact with each student. I paused for a long time.

I let the silence and their discomfort linger. After several minutes, I ended the stare down with them and turned to the board. "This is how you do it," I said, and I quickly solved the problem, working out the answer before their eyes.

I turned back around and could see several had their mouths open. A few were smiling kindly at me. After that, I had their respect and full attention, even though I knew some of the students did not like me, thinking I was a show-off. But that was all right. I had control of the room. It was a good class, and I shared with them many things I had learned.

I loved teaching and was very proud of the fact that I was by far the youngest teacher there—maybe the youngest of any teacher ever in the Cambodian refugee camps.

I spent a great deal of time preparing my daily lessons. I wanted to ensure that what was being said about me by a few of the other teachers—that I was too young to teach and could not possibly do a good job—was not true. Like all the teachers there, I taught every subject—math, science, literature, and other subjects. We followed a curriculum required by the school's administrators. Every week the principal checked my lesson book and would sign off or make suggestions. He was a man in his thirties, and he checked my work very closely. I could see he had his doubts about me because of my age, but he approved of my work and let me continue teaching.

Teachers earned about two baht, the Thai equivalent of a dollar, per week. I was thrilled to be making money. It was much more than I had been able to earn cutting firewood. By the standards of where I live and work today, a month's salary there would barely pay for a cup of coffee and a donut, but back then I felt like a rich man.

After school was over each day, I joined the student volleyball games. The relief workers had set up courts for the Sakaeo schoolyard, and I fell in love with the game. I had never played volleyball, but I learned quickly.

My students and I were all about the same age. Many times I stayed and played until late at night. I often went to play with the students from my class against other schools in the camp when games were arranged.

A few times other teachers at my school made fun of me for doing this. "Why are you playing with the students?" one older teacher said. "I thought you were a teacher. Maybe you should go back to being a student."

I ignored them. I kept doing what I was hired to do—teach. After class, I relished the volleyball games and supporting my school, which helped me develop camaraderie with my students.

NEW RESIDENTS WERE COMING IN and others were being moved along through the refugee camp system. We knew that one day our names would be called. A big bulletin board posted names of refugees who were being transferred. My mom checked it every day.

In early 1982, after we had been in the Sakaeo camp for about a year-and-a-half, the bulletin board showed that my mother, my nephew Loth (who was three years old by then), and I would be moving to Kamput, another refugee camp about seventy miles south of Sakaeo, close to the Cambodian border. My sister Dy had reunited with her husband when he arrived in Sakaeo. She had given birth to a third son a year before and was pregnant with her fourth child, so the camp officials did not want to transfer her. It was agreed that Loth would travel with us, and my mom would take care of him until Dy and her husband could join us with the new baby and their third child. Their oldest son Houeth was with Dy's mother-in-law, his maternal grandmother. Dy was hoping to bring them into the refugee camps as well so her family could all be together.

This move meant that we were moving closer to being resettled in another country in the refugee program. This was good news because we did not want to live in refugee camps forever, but each move also took us another step farther away from home. With each move we were reminded that we would never be able to go back to our homeland and that the hope of getting my younger sister, Poch, back with us became more unlikely. She was eight years old by this time, and we did not have the means or permission to travel to get her. If we left the camp system, we would not be relocated to another country. Fortunately, my mom believed that Poch was in good hands with my grandmother. We just hoped and prayed that God would find a way to reunite the whole family some day—wherever we landed.

Not knowing where in the world we might go was an odd feeling. The asylum countries we heard about were Australia, Canada, France, Japan, Switzerland, and the United States. My mom had been meeting with relief workers to establish our refugee status, and we knew we were in the pipeline, but we did not know where we might be sent or if it would even happen. It seemed like a dream, with America as the least likely destination. We thought Cambodia's weak relationship with the United States meant that we had no chance of going there.

We also worried what would happen to us if we were not granted asylum. What if we were forced to go back to Cambodia? Would we be treated cruelly under Vietnamese rule for leaving? What if the Khmer Rouge came back into power and learned my pa had been in the army?

Our future was uncertain, and many of the possibilities were frightening.

MY MOM, LOTH, AND I climbed into an old bus that drove us to Kamput with a few other refugee families. It took several hours. I had known that we would not stay in Sakaeo forever, but in some ways, I was sad to go. That camp had marked a turning point in my life, as I had returned to school there and even been allowed to teach. I had been so close to death only a couple of years before, and there I had taught school and played volleyball to my heart's content. I hoped that Kamput would be as good.

When we arrived at the Kamput Cambodia refugee camp, which had once been an old Thai military base, relief workers and translators who spoke English assisted us. The camp—like the others, surrounded by a high barbed-wire fence—made use of the old army barracks for housing, but it also had many hastily constructed shelters with thatched roofs.

A relief worker assigned my mom, my nephew Loth, and me to a space in the barracks, which was simply a large open room with hard wooden beds. Many other refugee families were there. The only way to have any privacy was to hang up sheets and blankets to create the illusion of walls. It was sort of like being back in the factory at Chroy Sdao, where we had first lived when the Khmer Rouge took over, although they had not allowed us to put up any sort of barrier between us and our neighbors.

The lodgings were not ideal, but at least we were not worried about communists coming to take us away and kill us. It was life inside barbed wire, but it was secure, and we knew we would not be there forever.

AFTER WE SETTLED IN KAMPUT, I started exploring the camp, looking for something to do. It didn't take long to figure out that Kamput was just like any other camp—dusty, hot, and dirty. We had limited amounts of water, but hygiene was the very least of my concerns. I wanted to find a job, and the job I enjoyed most was teaching.

The camp had schools for children, and I found the administrator's office and inquired about teaching. The principal looked at me skeptically. He said the list of teaching applicants was long, and the wait was indefinite.

I knew from his tone that I would not get to teach in Kamput.

I kept exploring and was happy to find a volleyball court, which was busy all the time with games. Many good players lived there, and sometimes they would bet on the outcomes. Some of the refugees in this camp had money that had been sent by relatives who had gone to the United States.

I would often wait for hours for a chance to get into a game on the court. I didn't have any money to bet, but I loved to play and chase the ball and hit it over the net again and again and again.

I sought out opportunities to make money, but refugees were not allowed to leave the barbed wire–encircled compound, so I couldn't go cut wood as I had done in Khao I Dang. With nothing to do, I spent many of my waking hours in Kamput watching or playing volleyball.

AFTER WE HAD BEEN in Kamput for a few months, I learned about English courses that were being taught in the camp. Unlike in Sakaeo, where the schooling had been free, the English classes in Kamput were set up independently by freelancers who required refugees to pay to attend. I made two friends who took the classes with support from family overseas. They would speak English to each other, and I was so impressed—Cambodians just like me speaking English! They seemed not like refugees to me but like wealthy people.

I had no money to pay for the classes, but I did not give up my dream of learning the language of the United States.

My friends told me when and where the classes were held. I would follow them and linger across the dirt path from the school and wait. After the students went inside, I would sneak up to the outside wall—it was a big hut with plywood sides and a thatched roof—and find a crack in the wall to peek in and try to hear. I didn't have the book the students were using, and I only had a broken nub of a pencil and cigarette papers on which to write notes, but I copied down what I could see on the blackboard in the room. I tried to say the words I heard the students repeating.

Learning English this way seemed impossibly hard, but I stayed with it.

A few other young refugees who also couldn't afford the classes started copying what I was doing. One day when I was eavesdropping on a lesson, I noticed the teacher, a Cambodian man who spoke English well, scowling at me through the crack in the wall.

The next time I showed up to listen to the class, he had covered the crack with paper. I couldn't see or hear anything. I scoured the building for another crack where I could follow the lessons, but they were all blocked.

That was the end of my English lessons in Kamput.

I GOT TO KNOW A MAN named Mr. Bo who put on traditional folk plays in the camp in the style known as *Lakhon Basak*. These performances drew on the ancient history of Cambodia and included elaborate costumes, music, and songs. Mr. Bo was one of the main actors and also directed the plays. He was a unique character and put on colorful productions in spite of limited resources. He also smoked marijuana regularly and often shared it with Thai soldiers who came to see him.

Mr. Bo's troop of actors put on nightly performances. It was the camp's only entertainment, and every performance was attended by large crowds. Each afternoon, hours before the plays started, I would take a mat or a plastic sheet to lay down in front of the stage to hold a seat. It got rowdy sometimes, with lots of kids jockeying for space by pushing and shoving, but the disagreements were not serious.

Mr. Bo also taught classes about Khmer literature in the camp's school. After I got to know him better, he would sometimes ask me to go teach his classes for him. Often this happened when he had had smoked too much marijuana and was unable to go. He paid me a little bit of money that I used to buy cakes and other foods for me and my mom and my nephew to add to the daily rations of rice and dried mackerel we received in the camp.

WE WERE ALWAYS in need of money. My mother continued her work of making and selling clothes, and she made a few baht here and there. I still hoped to save enough to pay for the English course, and that dream inspired me to work.

One stroke of luck was that we connected by letter with my father's uncle, Tim Yong, who had been relocated to Maryland in the United States. We had seen him two years before in Khao I Dang but had lost touch with him. In Kamput, we ran into his adopted son, who told us how to get in touch with him. Relief workers helped us send letters to him, and twice he sent us twenty American dollars.

My mom was meeting with immigration officials regularly, and they interviewed me about our story as well. We believed that we were moving closer to being relocated, and they said it was likely we would be going to America, but we still did not know for sure or where or when.

AFTER WE HAD BEEN in Kamput for about nine months, the passing of the calendar into 1983 marked two-and-a-half years that we had been living in the relief camps sanctioned by the United Nations and supported by many volunteer agencies from all over the world. They were safe, but it was a long time to live encircled by barbed wire. With the forthcoming Cambodian New Year, I would be turning seventeen years old. I was excited about the possibility of moving to the United States, but I was not convinced it would happen. So many bad things and hard times had befallen us that I would not believe it until I saw it.

As day after day passed, I became more skeptical. My number-one question was "When can we leave the camp?" My mother told me to be patient, but it had been a long time since relief workers had picked us up. We had been eating daily helpings of rice and dried mackerel for going on three years.

We also worried that our plans would not turn out as the workers said. In 1979, Thai troops had turned on forty thousand Cambodian refugees who tried to enter Thailand, shooting and killing many and driving them onto a dangerous mountain filled with land mines. That story was often told and retold in the camps, and it made us wary of the Thai soldiers who were supposedly there to protect us.

When we heard nothing for months, our concern grew. What could we do? We could only pray to our gods for help and ask them to keep their hearts and ways open for us.

A FEW MONTHS LATER, our prayers were answered. Our names appeared on the list of refugees scheduled to move through the Phanatnikom camp in Thailand's Chonburi province to a camp in the Philippines.

My mother was called for a long interview with a relief official who said we were being sent to a processing center for refugees bound for the United States. From Chonburi, he told her, my mom, my nephew, and I would go to a camp in the Philippines. From there, we would be resettled in America, in the state of California, where a church had been found to sponsor us.

America! It seemed true that we were really going to America!

TO GET TO THE PROCESSING CENTER in Chonburi, we had a long ride on a bus that traveled through Bangkok, the capital of Thailand. I had never seen a city so big or so much traffic. Lines of cars and trucks seemed to stretch for miles. It took quite some time due to the congestion, but we made it to the camp safely.

Phanatnikom was a small camp, designed only for short stays of two or three days. Once we piled off the bus, they fed us in a dining room that had great food. They served us unlimited portions of delicious pork and rice—more than we could eat! My nephew Loth ate so much pork that he made himself sick to his stomach.

The lodgings were not as nice as the meals. The place where we slept was unfinished, simply a shelter over a concrete floor with no walls. It rained and the wind blew so much that all the refugees staying there moved to the center to avoid getting soaked. Considering how they had fed us and our knowledge that this lodging was temporary, we did not complain. We had seen worse.

The second day, officials interviewed me and my mom, asking us to tell our stories yet again. By this point, my mom had told the story of my pa's abduction by the Khmer Rouge to various relief officials many times. It qualified us as political refugees who could be in danger if we were sent back to Cambodia.

On the third day, after more delicious and hearty meals, they called my mom and my nephew and me into the office and hung big plastic badges on lanyards around our necks. "Do not take these off," a relief official said. "You will be getting on the bus soon to go to the airport to fly to Manila."

I looked down at my badge. My name, LETH OUN, was in large print in both Khmer, which I could read, and English, which I puzzled over.

WE BOARDED A JET PLANE filled with other Cambodian refugees and flew to Manila. Many of the refugees got motion sickness and vomited on the flight. In Manila, waiting buses took us to the Philippine Refugee Processing Center near the village of Morong in the Bataan province, a ride that took several hours on winding, narrow roads that passed through high mountains. I looked out the window at very steep cliffs that dropped thousands of feet. The bus rode right along the edges of these cliffs—one wrong turn or a slip would plunge us all to our deaths.

More refugees got sick and vomited on the bus ride. So many threw up that the smell became nauseating and caused more to throw up, so much so that when the bus turned, puddles of vomit sloshed from side to side. My mom and nephew and I did not throw up, although we got close. It was a terrible ride, and I was so thankful when we finally arrived and were able to get off the bus.

This was our *seventh* camp in less than four years, and the fifth in the network of camps administered by the United Nations.

The camp in the Philippines was much like Kamput in that it was built like military barracks, with about eight houses in blocks, but no barbed wire surrounded this camp. The units had solid walls and afforded privacy, and my mother, nephew, and I were assigned one house all to ourselves that included a kitchen in the back with propane for cooking.

Celebrating the Cambodian New Year in April 1983 with my mother at the Philippine Refugee Processing Center near the village of Morong in the Bataan province. This is the oldest surviving image I have of me and my mom together.

Compared to how we had lived in the preceding eight years—going all the way back to April 1975—this was luxury!

Our Filipino hosts were very kind, unlike the Thai soldiers had been. The Filipinos did not carry rifles and look down on Cambodians but instead treated us with compassion and care and smiles. Food and water were plentiful, and the camp was not overcrowded as those in Thailand had been.

The camp had a wat for Buddhists to worship. On the Cambodian New Year, which came only a few weeks after we settled there, they helped us decorate a tent for a wonderful celebration and provided special foods and drinks for us to offer to the gods.

After we had been in the Philippines for about a month, my sister Dy and her husband and two youngest children joined us. My mom was thrilled to have her back with us, and she doted on her grandchildren, all boys. The oldest, Houeth, remained with his maternal grandmother, but they were now in refugee camps and making progress toward joining us.

This camp had many great things, but one of the best was its proximity to a clear stream and the beach on Subic Bay, just off the South China

*In the Philippine Refugee Processing Center in 1983,
from left, my sister Dy, her husband Han, and me. She is holding their
son Chhoeun. Their son Loth stands in front of me.*

Sea. We were allowed to swim and play. It was wonderful to have such
freedom. Occasionally, my mom would go with me and my nephew and
bring food for a picnic to enjoy on the beach. For people who had been
served watery rice soup by the side of a rice paddy where we had been
forced to work for more than twelve hours a day, a picnic on a beach
seemed like a beautiful dream.

The camp also offered free classes that were required of refugees in preparation for our move to the United States. I found learning English difficult, but I studied the alphabet and the sounds of new words diligently. I had a hard time with the grammatical structures, which were the reverse of what I knew. *English Essentials* was the book we used, and I still have my worn copy.

The camp also had classes that taught us how to live in America. They taught us many lessons, including not to throw any trash on the street, not to spit, and how kitchens and bathrooms with plumbing worked. "You can't go behind a tree to relieve yourself in the United States," a teacher said. It sounded so clean. I remember thinking, *Wow! I am going to heaven!*

The camp also offered doctors, dentists, and a pharmacy. They even had eye doctors who helped refugees who needed glasses. We had never been so well treated in our lives, and we took advantage of these services. Our health had been growing stronger in the camps where we had been fed, and my night blindness was gone by this point.

In addition to the beach to the west, the camp was bordered by scenic mountains to the east. As a way to make money, I often went into the forests in the morning to chop trees for firewood that I sold in the afternoons. I would come back to the camp with as big a load of logs as I could carry. It was hard work, and people often laughed at me because the wood I carried was much bigger and heavier than I was, but I didn't care. I was making money and enjoyed having this job to do.

With some money in my pocket, I could occasionally buy a can of soda. I loved the soft drink Mello Yello, which became a special treat for me. I also bought a pair of flip-flops, which seemed like a luxury after my years of going barefoot.

After an especially profitable few weeks of selling firewood, I splurged and bought a pair of sneakers. It was the first pair of sneakers I had ever worn. They cost the equivalent of fifteen American dollars. They were brown and were not a name brand, but they were the best shoes I had ever had. My feet felt so good when I was walking!

Life in the camp in the Philippines was so nice that many of the refugees often joked that if we stayed there the rest of our lives, it would be fine. But we all knew that we would be relocated eventually. My mom often had regular interviews with relief organizers who would help establish our destination in the United States based on groups that would sponsor us. Initially, we had been assigned to go to California, where a church was lined up, but shortly before we were scheduled to travel to America, my mom told them that my father's uncle lived in Montgomery County, Maryland, not far from Washington, D.C.

They said they could move us near him, but it would take a few more months to find a sponsor. She said that would be fine, especially because we were happy in the Philippines. She also knew having another family member to help us when we moved would be good for us. We waited, hoping that this dream would come true. Although we were optimistic and life here was good, we were wary of it all going wrong.

We went about our lives in the Philippine Refugee Processing Center, anxious about our future but enjoying the present while we could.

In early October 1983, my mom was called to an interview with a representative from the United States and a translator. He said we had all the necessary approvals to move to America and that a church in Maryland had agreed to be our sponsor. He did not know when we would travel, but it should be soon. We were so excited, yet we didn't know how long we would have to wait.

My mom had a daily routine of checking the community board for announcements. Two weeks after her interview, one hundred names of refugees who would depart for the United States the next day were posted. She scanned the long scroll, written in English and Khmer—and her name was on the list.

It was unreal! We would be traveling to America in only twenty-four hours!

The joy, the thrill, the excitement—everything that one could think of came out. We jumped up and down, hugged, smiled, and laughed. We were really going to America. It was a dream come true.

My sister Dy and her family were not scheduled to travel with us, but they were expected to follow in about a month. It was agreed that Loth, Dy's second oldest, who was four years old, would travel with me and my mom, and she would care for him until Dy and her family joined us in America.

That afternoon, my mom, Loth, and I walked around the camp to say goodbye to the friends we had made in the Philippines. These friends were like brothers and sisters. We had played together and laughed together. We had gone to school together and learned together. We had shared our anxiety about the future and the sorrow of the recent past. With this distant separation, it was unlikely we would ever see them again. Tears of joy and sadness ran down our faces.

ON THE MORNING before we boarded the bus to leave camp for the airport, all the refugees had to go through a physical examination with a doctor. We waited in a long, slow line and were called one at a time. I noticed that many of the girls came out of the examination room crying, and one or two fainted and had to be held up by family or friends who comforted them.

When I had my turn with the doctor and he asked me to take off my clothes and turn around so he could examine me, I understood. The purity of Cambodian women before marriage was sacred, so disrobing and submitting to a medical examination was traumatic for these girls. I was embarrassed to be examined in this way, but I knew for girls raised in Cambodia it was agonizing. Many cried long after leaving the examining room, casting a tense mood over the group of refugees waiting to depart.

After everyone had been examined, we gathered outside the camp's main office to wait for a bus. It took many hours—hours that seemed like days. We sat quietly on the ground and waited, something we had become accustomed to doing in refugee camps.

When the bus finally arrived, many of the refugees began to cry again, this time confronting the reality of leaving Asia permanently. Many, like us, were leaving family behind. My mom grew quiet, her face sad and her eyes tearing up. I knew she was thinking about my younger sister Poch.

I took my seat and looked out the window and prayed that we would all be together again. I also prayed that as the oldest man in my family, I could reunite us, but I said nothing about this to my mom.

The bus took us to Manila to stay for one night before flying out the next morning. The place where we stayed was filthy. We slept in an open shelter, like a gazebo, with sewage flowing nearby on the ground. The showers and bathroom were exposed and filthy, right in the middle of the mud and sewage. We didn't dare take showers there and used the bathroom only when we absolutely couldn't hold it anymore. Mosquitoes were everywhere.

My mother did not sleep at all that night, instead sitting by me and my nephew and encouraging us to sleep. We could not sleep well because of the mosquitoes, which feasted on us, and we slept only one or two hours at most. It was horrible, but because it was only one night, we had to bear it. We were not too far from the airport, and we could see and hear airplanes flying over us. We suffered through the long night, eagerly awaiting the sunrise.

Soon after dawn, relief workers brought us large, laminated name tags the size of a sheet of paper that they hung around our necks. These had our names and refugee numbers, as did the large canvas bags they gave each one of us for travel. I had so little to put inside my bag—just two changes of clothes and flip-flops—that it looked empty. "Do not lose your name tags," one of the translators said. "If you lose it, you will not go to the United States."

The bus ride to the Manila airport was short. A new group of representatives met us at the airport, and they were kind and professional. They seemed to understand where we came from and what we had been through. They walked us to the gate to wait for the plane and told us not to go anywhere. They also told the ticket agents at the gate to make sure that we didn't get lost.

When they called us to the plane, a giant transcontinental airliner, I looked at it in awe. I had never seen an airplane that big. We filed down the long rows inside the plane, walking to seats in the back. Some of the passengers who had already taken their seats in the front looked at us strangely, as though they were wondering who we were. The plane had rows that were ten seats wide. A big sign in front of our section said REFUGEE SEATING. We took our seats.

The flight attendants stood in the aisle and went through the routine of how to use life jackets and how to properly fasten seat belts. I had no clue what they were talking about.

Soon the plane began taxiing down the runway, and then it built up speed and lifted into the air. I looked through the window at the city of Manila and the coastline and the ocean below.

Overwhelming feelings of sadness overtook me. *Will I ever be able to return to my home? What will I do when I get to America? How can I make a living? Who will I talk to?*

At seventeen years old, I was almost a man. My past had been very hard—what did my future hold?

PART IV

AMERICA

My New Home

THE PLANE SOARED HIGHER AND HIGHER into the air until all I could see through the windows were clouds. It didn't seem real, as though we were in a dream. They had told us we were going to Seattle, where we would change planes for San Francisco, and then change planes to fly to Maryland, where we would live. None of those locations meant anything to us. We knew little about the place we would call home.

After several hours in the air, they served us a meal. The only thing I remember are mushy green peas. I had never eaten green peas. I took a bite and almost spit them out. I thought they were the worst thing I had ever tasted. I refused to eat anything else. For the remainder of the flight, all I consumed was Coca-Cola. "Coke," I said to myself after that first sip. I loved it. Whenever the flight attendant came around and smiled and asked a question I could not understand, I answered, "Coke."

I fell asleep some, but only for short bursts—twenty minutes or so. When I woke up, it seemed like the plane had not made any progress. We were still in a cloud, somewhere high over the Earth. I could hear the jet engines humming. If someone had told me we were flying to the moon, I would have believed them.

About fourteen hours after leaving Manila—fourteen hours that seemed like ten thousand—the plane touched down in Seattle. It was gray and rainy outside. We followed the other passengers and filed off the plane into the terminal. We still wore the big tags around our necks.

A small group of relief workers met us, including one who spoke Khmer. He was kind and instructed others with him to give us heavy winter coats. "It will be cold where you are going," he said. "You have never experienced cold weather like this. But you will do fine with these coats."

Someone handed me a brown parka. It was heavier than any piece of clothing I had ever seen. "Try it on," the man said to me in Khmer.

He helped me pull it on, and I slipped my arms into the sleeves. "Zip it up," he said, showing me how.

It was warm, swallowing my skinny body whole. I was scared by the sensation, but I didn't want to seem ungrateful. I was glad to take it off and put it in my big sack.

My mom and Loth got coats too. We smiled and bowed and put our hands together in the traditional Cambodian gesture, thanking him and the others, but we did not say anything. We were in shock from all these changes and too tired to speak.

The translator said he would take us to our next flight. I could sense people in the airport watching us, and I saw some boys and girls about my age pointing and laughing. My face didn't show it, but inside I hurt. Would this be how Americans my age would treat me?

Fortunately, we met others who were kind. They spoke to us in English, but I couldn't make out what they said. We nodded back and said, "Thank you" as best we could. At least we saw some smiles. We had gone for years in the Killing Fields without anyone smiling at us.

We waited a long time to board the plane to fly to San Francisco. A few other Cambodian families flew with us, and we sat together wearing our name tags. The flight attendants served us more food, but again, the plate had green mushy peas. I refused to eat, but I did ask for Coke. I drank one can as fast as I could and asked for another one, which they gave me.

When we landed in San Francisco, we met another translator. All of the people who helped us were generous and warm. I don't know what we would have done without their support. "This way," the translator said. "I'll take you to the flight to D.C."

My mom frowned. "No," she said. "We are not going to D.C. We are going to Maryland. We have family there."

He smiled. "It's OK. Washington is next to Maryland. You fly to that airport, and someone will pick you up. It's OK."

We trusted him because he sounded honest and spoke our language, but we were scared every minute. We knew from experience how badly life could turn out. Our fate was in the hands of a man we'd just met.

We were optimistic, but we were also terrified of what could go wrong.

WE WAITED HOURS in the San Francisco airport for our next flight. My mom, my nephew Loth, and I were all exhausted, having been awake for a few days with almost no sleep.

Finally the flight from San Francisco boarded, and the flight attendants ushered us to the back of the plane. The plane took off and seemed to stay in the air forever. The meal they served again had the green mushy peas, and I once again refused to eat. I worried that every meal in America would have these horrible peas. I did get another Coke.

The sky grew dark after several hours. My mom looked out the window the whole time.

Near the end of the long flight, the lights of Washington, D.C., and the surrounding metropolis came into view. It was beautiful—yellow and white with specks of red as far as the eye could see.

How could there be so many lights in one place?

We flew into Washington National Airport, fifteen years before it would become Reagan National Airport. Ronald Reagan was president in 1983 when we immigrated, but I knew nothing about American presidents. I would eventually learn much about presidents with the Secret Service, but on this night, I didn't even know there was a White House.

We got off the plane several hours after sunset. We walked into the terminal and stood. We didn't know where to go or what to do. Someone was supposed to be there to help us, but we were all alone.

I felt like a lost dog.

Crowds of people of all colors and ages passed us. They seemed to be cheerful and friendly, but we had no idea what they were saying. The English I heard people speaking was nothing like the English I had tried to learn in the refugee camps.

After a few minutes that seemed like forever, we heard someone calling to us in Khmer. "*Joohm-reap soo*," the voice said. "Hello."

We turned and saw a tall, slim Cambodian woman with gray hair. She was pretty and dignified in a blue dress suit. She seemed high class, as though she could be royalty. "My name is Sarah," she said, putting her hands together in the traditional Cambodian greeting. We did the same. It was such a great relief to have someone there to rescue us who knew our culture. "I will be helping you," she continued. "I have an apartment where you can stay. I will take you there. Tomorrow I will help you get established in this country. Come with me."

She walked us to her car, a four-door sedan, in the parking lot. My mom sat in the front seat, and Loth and I were in the back. She drove and asked my mom questions about our trip. I looked out the window in awe as she pulled out of the airport and onto the busy highway. I had never seen that many cars and trucks and motorcycles, all lit up and driving fast on wide, paved roads. Bright buildings and houses were everywhere too, more lights than I had ever seen.

So many lights in one night, I said to myself. It was unlike the darkness we had been accustomed to in Cambodia. This truly was another world. I was so enamored with this scene that I forgot all about being hungry.

Sarah took us to an apartment in Silver Spring, Maryland. Another Cambodian family was staying there, and we would be there temporarily until a space for us nearby opened up. They offered us noodles to eat, which we appreciated. I cleaned my plate quickly and would have asked for seconds, but I did not want to be greedy. I felt better with food in my stomach.

Sarah stayed with us while we ate and asked if we had any questions. We were so tired from the travel and in shock from the newness of it all, we didn't ask her anything even though all we had were questions.

Everything about life at that moment was a question.

My mom, Loth, and I would sleep in one small, unfurnished bedroom with a bathroom and shower. Sarah explained to us how the shower and toilet worked and apologized for not having mattresses for us, but there were pillows and blankets on the thick carpet. It seemed cozy and luxurious to us. I took a shower in hot water and it felt like a dream. I bedded down on the floor and slept like a baby.

WE AWOKE to our first full day in America. Sarah took us to the Social Security office and to sign up for food stamps. She translated for us as we dealt with the various government officials.

This new world seemed so strange and complicated. I knew that I would have to learn English to be able to navigate it.

That afternoon, my father's uncle, Tim Yong, and his wife, Peo, came to see us. They were older, in their seventies, and had been in America for two years. They took us to their nearby apartment for a meal. I called them Grandfather and Grandmother, terms of respect for older family members in Cambodian culture.

When I stepped into the apartment, I was surprised to see a young woman I recognized in their kitchen. It was the girl I had seen many times in the Khao I Dang refugee camp, and later I had seen her at Sakaeo. I had always thought she was very pretty. I smiled at her, and she smiled shyly back. We didn't speak to each other because that could have gotten us into trouble with my aunt and uncle and my mother. Young men and women were strictly prohibited from talking with each other unless married. But the smiles we exchanged that afternoon were enough. She looked beautiful, and the smell of the food she was cooking was fantastic.

I would learn that her name was Sophy. Her sister, Touch Yi, was married to Grandfather and Grandmother's son, Yom. My aunt and uncle had brought her with them when they immigrated to help cook and clean in return for giving her a place to live. Sophy's mother had been executed by the Khmer Rouge in 1975—about the same time my father had been killed. Her father, who had survived, stayed in Cambodia after the Killing Fields ended.

The noodles Sophy cooked that night made for the best meal I had ever eaten. I ate many servings. I cleaned my plate and she brought me more. It was such a pleasure to be in my grandparents' apartment and eat noodles and be together as a family. It was the first time my mom and I had had an opportunity like this since that fateful day when the Khmer Rouge had marched into Battambang City.

We had been slaves and refugees for more than eight years, but on this day we had family and homes to call our own. It was such a pleasure.

And though I may not have admitted it to myself—and my parents and grandparents would not have let me express it—I was falling in love with Sophy.

WE WERE FORTUNATE that in addition to my grandparents and Sophy, others helped us that first week. Sarah, our social worker, came to see us every day and helped us get established. She said our apartment would be ready soon and that pieces of furniture were being donated. She also said we could expect others from our church sponsor to stop by the apartment to help us.

Not long after she left one day, a Cuban American couple came to see us. "I'm Odina," the woman said. "This is Mario. We were refugees once too. Our church wants to help you out." They brought bags with food and clothes. Odina talked a lot and told us many things. I struggled to understand much of what she said, but she spoke slowly and repeated herself and made many gestures. We nodded and smiled and bowed and accepted their charity. They were so kind, and I'll always be grateful for the help they gave us.

In addition to Odina and Mario, an older couple from the church visited. Their names were Joseph and Maria Grant, and Joseph introduced himself as Elder Grant. They were Mormon missionaries from Utah. They piled me and my mom and Loth in their car, a Grand Marquis, and gave us a ride to the grocery store. I had never ridden in such a big vehicle! It seemed so luxurious and fit all of us with ease, as though we were in a limousine. They took us on a tour inside the grocery store and showed us how the store worked and how to use our food stamps.

Elder Grant and his wife also drove us to doctor's and dentist's appointments and anywhere else we needed to go. They were there for me in the doctor's office waiting room when I had my first physical in the United States, which recorded my weight as eighty-nine pounds.

Every time we called them, no matter if it was night or day, they came right away and never complained. Their love and concern for us had no bounds. They had such big hearts.

Odina and Mario also helped me make some money cutting grass. Mario showed me how to use his lawnmower, and I cut and cleaned up their yard. They gave me $20 for that and then helped me get work cutting grass for several of their neighbors. I made between $10 and $20 for each lawn I cut. I was thrilled to have work to do and to put some money in my pocket.

After we had been in America for about a week, Sarah picked us up and moved us to our own place: an apartment in the 1000 block of Quebec Terrace in Silver Spring. It was not far from where we had been staying. Our apartment was on the first floor of a four-story brick housing complex. The two-bedroom apartment was small and unfurnished, but it was ours.

My mom, Loth, and I had a place to call our own.

That afternoon Odina and Mario brought us a few old mattresses and beds and a small table and chairs. They said they would try to get us a couch soon, and maybe a television.

I was thrilled with the bed. It was the first time I'd had truly comfortable sleeping arrangements since the communists had taken over Cambodia. *Eight years and six months* had passed since then, when I was nine years old, until this fall night in 1983, when I was seventeen.

The mattress was so comfortable! I could feel my body relaxing, and I slept soundly through the night.

WHEN WE DIDN'T HAVE someone to guide us, I started to venture out of the apartment by myself. I walked around the block, but I did not go far. I stared at the street signs, but I could not read the names. I was afraid I might not find my way home, but each day I walked a little farther.

Cars and motorcycles and trucks were everywhere, and the paved roads were wider and smoother than any in Battambang City. *What a rich country this is*, I thought. I would stand on the street and study how the traffic lights changed from green to yellow to red.

Often I noticed people watching me. I felt self-conscious about my inability to speak English and understand what was happening.

I saw girls and boys holding hands—sometimes even kissing. My face got red with embarrassment when I saw this. It was something we could never have done in public in Cambodia.

Occasionally someone would speak to me. I would have no idea what they said. I would listen and smile and they would repeat themselves, but I could make out only a small percentage of anything spoken to me in English.

I felt like a baby starting life all over again.

My mother and I walked to the grocery store the Grants had shown us and did our best to figure things out. I was glad many of the cans and boxes had pictures. That was how we selected what we would cook and eat.

ON ONE OF OUR FIRST MONDAY NIGHTS in the apartment, not too long before midnight, we heard what we thought were guns and bombs, much like what we had heard when the Cambodian civil war was raging. We'd heard automatic rifles firing when the Khmer Rouge rolled into town. We'd heard grenades and machine guns in the camps on the Thailand-Cambodia border when battles were raging. We knew the sound of warfare, and we were convinced this was it. I was disheartened and terrified at what we were hearing here in Maryland.

"Turn out the lights and get under the beds!" my mom said to me and Loth. We all squeezed under, listening to the explosions outside our apartment.

I cried I was so upset. I had thought this life was behind us, that in America we would be safe, but here I was again, hiding from bullets.

The noise lasted about twenty minutes, and sometimes we'd hear people shouting. The voices were not angry, but joyous, like they were celebrating, which I found confusing. We worried about a knock on the door, but thankfully, it never came.

After it had been quiet for a while, my mom said, "I think it's OK for us to get out from under the beds. We can't go outside, but I don't think we need to hide anymore. We should keep the lights out."

I peeked through the blinds and saw the street was empty. Everything looked normal under the streetlights. Parked cars were undamaged in the small lot and on the street. No one was around.

I was surprised that there would have been such a gunfight, but I believed there had been some sort of small battle. Battles big and small had been part of my life from my youngest days, and it made sense that such fighting would be present everywhere. I had hoped we would be safe from warfare, but I decided that Maryland must be like the rest of the world.

I got into bed and tried to sleep, getting some rest, albeit fitfully.

The next morning it was still quiet, and my mom and I looked out the windows. We didn't have a telephone, or we would have called my uncle and aunt. I told my mom I wanted to find out what had happened. She told me I should wait, but I went outside anyway. I didn't want to stay inside forever, and it seemed quiet and safe.

I walked around the apartment complex and saw a group of people who looked happy, standing outside their building and smoking. A flag for the Washington NFL team was flying from a pole on a porch, and two men wore team jerseys. The team was very good when we arrived, having won the Super Bowl in early 1983, before we immigrated later that year. Of course, we didn't know the Super Bowl from a rice bowl.

I kept walking, not wanting to disturb this group. I saw a man I'd seen and spoken with before and approached him. "What going on last night?" I asked, struggling to use English. "Who fighting?"

"You didn't hear all those firecrackers?" he said.

I said, "What's firecrackers? You mean like a gun—pop pop pop?" I knew only the Khmer word for firecrackers—*phao*.

He looked at me for a minute and then said, "It wasn't a gunfight. It was a celebration. Happy." He smiled. "We won the game. It was *Monday Night Football*."

I realized the noises had not been gunshots but *phao*. I felt silly that we had hidden, but I was happy to know that we were not in a war zone.

I returned home and told my mother and Loth, who were relieved. Later that day, we went to my grandparents and told them and Sophy the story. They explained the popularity of the Washington NFL team to us, and we all had a good laugh about it.

That night also sparked my interest in American football. It took me a while to learn about the game, but I have been a Washington fan ever since.

AFTER WE HAD BEEN in Maryland for several weeks, my sister Dy, her husband, and her two youngest sons arrived, rejoining Loth, Dy's second son, who had been with me and my mom. (Her oldest, Houeth, and his paternal grandmother would join us six months later.) They stayed with us, which made our apartment very crowded. When Dy arrived, she was pregnant with her fifth child and due soon. Near the end of November, she gave birth to another son. Our two-bedroom apartment was noisy with all of these boys under the age of seven, but my mom was happy that we were all together.

As the year progressed, the weather got colder—the kind of cold we had never felt before. The coldest average temperatures in Cambodia were in the sixties Fahrenheit, and that seemed cold to us. When it had occasionally touched the fifties, we had felt like we were freezing. We had never seen sleet or snow. When the Maryland winter cold came, we stayed inside and cranked up the heat.

One day that winter it snowed heavily—about six or eight inches. We looked out the window in amazement at the white blanket that covered the streets. I had heard about snow but had never seen it. My mom asked me to pick up some food, so I set out to walk to the grocery store.

I was so naïve that I did not know how cold it could be. I wore my warm winter coat, but on my feet I had my favorite footwear—flip-flops—that I always wore around the house. When I first started to walk outside, it did not feel that bad, but after a few minutes, my feet began to get colder and colder.

I passed a few people who looked at me like I was crazy. A few of them said something to me, but I did not understand what they were saying and I kept walking. I picked up my pace as my feet began to hurt.

It was a relief to get inside. A few shoppers pointed at my feet and commented, but again, I couldn't understand. I stood there for a few minutes to get my feet warm and then picked out our groceries.

I walked back home as fast as I could walk through snow in flip-flops. My feet and my toes were so red, I almost suffered frostbite.

The next time it snowed, I put on two pairs of socks and wore my tennis shoes. I was cold, but not as cold as when I had worn flip-flops! I began to appreciate and even look forward to snow. I learned how to make snowballs and throw them with and at Loth and a few other kids who lived near us.

I was determined to make this country my home, even if sometimes it was freezing cold.

Working for the American Dream

[1984–1994]

AFTER WE HAD BEEN in America for a few weeks, a friend of my uncle's took me to register at Montgomery Blair High School in Silver Spring. They tested my English, and I did poorly. I had much to learn.

Even though I was seventeen, I ended up in a ninth-grade homeroom class. Although the American kids were three years younger, most were bigger than me. I was skinny and short, having been malnourished as long as I was. Fortunately, four other older Cambodians were in the class who were close to my age. They did not speak English any better than I did. The school assigned a language teacher to help us, and we sat in the back of the room.

I tried hard to learn English, speaking to everyone I saw even though I knew I was saying words incorrectly. Many of the teachers and fellow students at Montgomery Blair were very kind, and I am forever grateful for their support. Often teachers and fellow students would take time to correct me, figuring out what I was trying to say and then repeating it back to me.

Of course, some students laughed and made fun of me. That is how humans are—there are kind people and unkind people. I ignored those who ridiculed me—I had endured much worse. My goal was to learn what I could and do my best. I felt so fortunate to have this opportunity.

A GREAT JOY AT SCHOOL was making friends, especially fellow Cambodians. My friend Vanna and I became close. He had arrived in America about a year before I did, and he taught me many things about life in our new country.

He also helped me get a job working with him as a dishwasher at a Chinese restaurant. Every day after school, I would walk two miles to the Shanghai restaurant in the Silver Spring Metro station and wash dishes until it closed. About eleven or midnight, I walked home, another two-mile walk. I was scared walking alone, mainly because I worried about getting lost, but I always found my way. These were long days, and sometimes extremely tiring, but I enjoyed it immensely. Plus, they were paying me $3.15 an hour. That seemed like so much money!

At work, I got to spend time with Vanna, but I also made American friends there, including Reggie, a fellow dishwasher. He was a tall Black man in his twenties, and he was very funny. He often laughed at my attempts to speak English, but in a good-natured way. I would try to say something and he would laugh, but then he would tell me to say it again and correct me until I did better. He also told stories and jokes, many of which I didn't understand, but that didn't matter. I didn't need to know every word to enjoy his stories. I learned a lot of English from him that they don't teach you in school, including some words I won't include in this book.

I'll never forget my second paycheck—it totaled $78. I walked home proudly that night, planning to show it to my mother, but when I got home, my pocket was empty. I turned around and retraced my steps all the way back to the restaurant with no luck. It was dark, and the restaurant was closed when I got there, so I walked home with my head down, fighting back tears. About thirty hours of my work, like old dishwater, were down the drain.

My mother tried to calm me down, telling me that it would be all right. I was distraught, but the next day after school I was right back at work. I learned a lesson, though, and never lost another paycheck—and I would earn many paychecks from many, many jobs.

After about a month of work, I saved enough money to buy a used bicycle, which made my commute much easier. It was a simple ten-speed that cost $80. I got a padlock and a heavy iron chain, and I would ride to school and work and home with that chain draped around my neck. The commute that had taken about forty-five minutes now took only ten and wasn't as tiring.

I made another good Cambodian friend at Montgomery Blair named Horn. Horn helped me get a second job, this one at Tenley Mini Market, a convenience store and deli in Washington, near American University and the National Cathedral. I was thrilled because it paid $4.25 an hour! I stocked shelves, kept the coffee fresh, and cleaned. After I had been there a while, I worked at the cash register and learned how to make sandwiches. I interacted with many customers and enjoyed practicing my English with them.

The market was a much longer commute, about eight miles from our apartment. Because it paid so much more, I took all the hours I could get. The ride there was not easy. The route consisted of main roads packed with Washington traffic, especially Military Road, which was busy with big trucks. I often rode in fear, with cars and trucks within inches of me. The rides home in the dark were especially scary. I didn't have a light on the bike or a helmet.

One afternoon, after I had been working at the market for about a week, I was riding through an intersection on University Boulevard when a black Nissan sped through and hit me. The collision knocked me off my bike, flipping me onto the hood of the car and then off to the side of the street. The blow rendered me unconscious. When I came to, I was sitting up, leaning against a tree.

A small, older woman came up to me. "Are you OK?"

I was sore and bruised and my head hurt, but I was able to stand. "I'm OK," I said, getting to my feet.

I looked at my bike, laying on the edge of the road. The wheels were bent into figure eights.

The driver of the car, a big man who appeared to be in his thirties, approached me. His fists were clenched and his face angry, and he stood at least six inches taller and must have weighed one hundred pounds more than I did. "You need to watch where you are going!" he shouted, pointing his finger and poking me in the shoulder. "You damaged my car. You are going to pay for that."

I looked at the dent in his hood and at my ruined bike on the ground and got angry. I was not afraid of him. I was not in Cambodia anymore.

He did not have a gun. I positioned myself so that if I had to use my martial arts moves, I would be ready. "You should be paying me," I said.

"I'm going to get a lawyer and take your TV away," he said.

"Go for it," I said, repeating a phrase I had heard Reggie say at the restaurant. The man backed off, and I turned and picked up my bike and started carrying it home.

It cost $40 to get it fixed. I had to borrow money from my friends and grandparents to pay for the repair, but I paid them back the next week when I received my paychecks.

I started working at the market more than the restaurant during the school week, but on weekends and off days from school I would work part of the day washing dishes at Shanghai and then I would ride my bike to the Tenley Mini Market and work there at night. It was a long day, but if I worked eight hours at each place, which I often did, I could make more than $50 in one day and $100 in a weekend. I was proud to be earning money to help my family.

After we had been in America for six months, the public welfare programs required us to reapply. We had been getting $180 a month in public assistance and receiving food stamps, which had helped us get started. I will be forever grateful for this country's generosity to me. That money and the kindness of strangers helped me go on and build the life I have today.

We could have continued to take the assistance, but I was making money with my two jobs, so we decided not to reapply. "I have two jobs," I said in English during a meeting at the welfare office. "I will support us."

WE OFTEN SAW MY AUNT AND UNCLE—whom I considered grandparents—and Sophy when we went to their apartment for dinner. Sophy always cooked the best meals, and I would sneak glances and smile at her if my mother and grandparents were not looking. They sensed there was a spark between us, so they were adamant about keeping us apart. I know it sounds innocent and natural to Americans that two young adults might spend some time together, but in the traditional Cambodian way that was forbidden.

I did, however, figure out a way to talk to her. One morning when I was getting ready to leave at about seven o'clock, I saw her taking out the trash. They lived a few buildings away, in the same apartment complex. I watched her walk back into her apartment, but she did not see me.

The next morning I told my mother that I was leaving for school early. I walked my bike down the street and waited near the trash cans at the curb. I stood off to the side so if my aunt and uncle were looking out the window, they couldn't see me. It was a cold morning, but I had on my big coat and my tennis shoes, so I didn't feel too bad. I peeked around the trash cans, hoping she would come out. I waited for what seemed like a long time, and I worried she might not be coming, but after about thirty minutes I saw her step outside with a trash bag. When she got close to the trash cans, there I was.

"Sophy," I said.

She was startled at first, but then she recognized me. She was shy and smiled, but looked down.

"I wanted to see you," I said.

"We must be careful," she said. "Grandmother will be angry."

"I know. But I'm on the way to school. I'm not doing anything wrong."

"You are not supposed to be talking to me," she said.

"I know, but I've wanted to talk to you for a long time. I remember seeing you in Khao I Dang and at Sakaeo. I was so glad to see you here. You are a great cook. I love the noodles you cook."

She smiled and blushed, tilting her head down, but then she glanced up for a moment and our eyes met. We stayed that way for what felt like a long time.

"I . . . I have to get back inside," she said. "Grandmother will be suspicious."

"Can't you stay just a little longer?"

"I can't," she said, but she stayed.

"Do you take the trash out this time every day?"

"Yes," she said, nodding.

"I have to leave at 7:30 to go to school. I will come see you before I go."

She didn't say anything, but she just smiled and looked back toward her apartment. "OK," she said and turned and walked back fast.

I watched her return to the apartment, so happy to have found this way to speak with her. I went off to school in a great mood that day.

That began our daily ritual of meeting by the trash cans and talking about our lives. I told her about school and my jobs, and she talked about taking care of our grandparents.

I treasured these brief meetings every morning.

I CONTINUED MY BUSY ROUTINE of going to school and working at the restaurant and the market. I loved school. So many of the teachers were so helpful and kindhearted. I remember Mr. Malino and Ms. Katz, my English teachers; Mr. Klopp, my art teacher; and Mr. Hopkins, my auto mechanics teacher. My English was getting much better, and they were encouraging.

When the regular school year ended, my counselor, Ms. Ceide, said that I had done well with the ninth-grade curriculum. She said I could skip the tenth grade and move into the eleventh grade. "You have been doing great," she said.

I was thrilled at this news. I had told my mother that my plan was to earn a high school diploma and then go on to college. I thought about how proud my father, who had always regretted not being able to continue his education, would have been of me. In our early morning talks, I had started telling Sophy about my education dreams, and she seemed impressed. I knew to make it in America I needed to perfect my English and get a college degree. I told Ms. Ceide that I wanted to go to summer school and continue my education and not take a break. She was very supportive and helped me arrange the classes.

Life was good, much better than it had been a year before when I was living in a refugee camp without a penny to my name.

The only bad parts of my life at this time were the treacherous bike rides into Washington. The roads were so busy and crowded, and often there weren't sidewalks. I rode my bike in the rain and snow, and every return trip home was in the dark. I was nearly killed on several occasions by big trucks on Military Road. There were many close calls, and I always rode scared. I dreamed of having a car of my own, but I could not afford it.

After about a year, when I had saved up $250, I went shopping for an automobile. No one in our family had ever owned a car. There was a used-car dealer in Takoma Park, close to Silver Spring, that had bottom-dollar vehicles close to my price range. I rode my bike over there with $250 in cash in my pocket.

I strolled through the small lot, checking out the prices. There were a lot of junky cars, many of them from the seventies and a few from the sixties, but most of them cost at least $400. I found a dark-green, four-door 1975 Volkswagen Dasher that I liked. The price—$400—was marked in big white numbers on the windshield.

I had seen the car salesman watching me, but he hadn't spoken. I held up my shoulders, turned and looked at him, and thought hard about my English lessons. "I would like to buy this car," I said.

"It's $400," he said. "Can you pay cash?"

"Yes," I said, "but I only have $250. I will give you $250 for it."

"What?" he said, clearly not understanding me.

I pulled my cash out of my pocket, which was mostly tens and twenties. I held it up so he could see. "I will give you $250 for it," I said, saying *two hundred fifty dollars* as slowly as I could. "This is all I've got."

He didn't answer, but he stared at me, as though he were thinking it over. He looked at the car, and I thought of something I'd heard Reggie say: "Take it or leave it," I said.

He nodded, indicating he understood. "Hold on," he said. "Wait right here."

He went inside the small office. I could see him through a big window and watched as he made a phone call. He nodded and came back out.

"We can take $300," he said.

I spoke as slowly and clearly as I could. "I don't have $300. I only have $250."

He looked at me and back at the car. "OK," he said, "but there's no warranty and no returns. You can't bring it back."

"That is OK," I said. I was so excited on the inside, knowing that I would have my own car, but I tried to keep calm and not let this price get away.

We went into the office and I signed my name and showed him my driver's license, which I had received a few months before.

I opened the hatchback and squeezed my bicycle into the back. It was a great feeling driving off the lot, knowing I would soon be home and could show off my car and impress my mom, my aunt and uncle, and best of all, Sophy.

I LOVED THAT VOLKSWAGEN DASHER. It made getting to school and work so much easier, but, no surprise, a nine-year-old car with more than one hundred thousand miles on it had mechanical problems. The transmission emitted grinding sounds, but I knew what to do.

I had excelled in the automotive mechanics class at Montgomery Blair, and Mr. Hopkins, my teacher there, liked me. I drove the car into the class garage one day.

"Lath," Mr. Hopkins said (he always called me Lath, not Leth). "What are you doing with that car?"

"This is my new car," I said, proudly. "I'd like to work on it in the shop. Can I fix it here? It needs a new transmission."

I was in his Auto I class, the first of three classes in the automotive curriculum. "This would be an Auto III project," he said. "Do you know what you are doing?"

"Yes. I had an automotive class in a refugee camp in Thailand, and I worked on tractors in Cambodia during the communist time."

"OK, Lath," he said, laughing. "Don't let me stand in your way. Let's see what you can do, young man."

My friend Horn was in the class, and he helped me. The school automotive classes often received donations of used car parts, and we found an Audi transmission in the parts junk pile. We compared it to the Volkswagen transmission we removed and found that they were the same size.

We put it in the car and gave it a test drive, and it worked fine. I also did a tune-up and changed the oil, and the car ran much better.

Mr. Hopkins had watched us. "This is fine work, Lath," he said. "If you want to be a mechanic, I can help hook you up with a job."

"Thank you, Sir." I didn't tell him that I had bigger aspirations and that I wanted to go to college.

I TIMED MY DEPARTURE every morning to see Sophy when she took out the trash. I would park near the trash cans and sit in my car, waiting for her to appear.

We tried to be careful and not talk for more than five minutes, but we enjoyed each other's company so much that we often talked longer.

Five hours would not have been enough. Five minutes seemed like five seconds.

We packed a lot in, telling each other about our dreams of a better life in America. I cherished these short visits each day.

One morning, her grandmother caught us talking by my car. We were not kissing or holding hands, but we were standing close and smiling.

"Sophy!" Grandmother yelled. "Get inside. Now."

Sophy looked down at her shoes, and her eyes started to tear up as she turned and walked back. Grandmother gave me a steely-eyed look, but said nothing. I knew that my mom would hear about this and I would be in trouble. Even worse, I didn't know how I would talk to Sophy after this.

My heart sank. I was depressed all day at school and work. I worried about when and if I would see Sophy again.

I continued filling my days from early in the morning until late at night. I worked seven days a week, often not heading home until midnight. I was glad to have my car, which made the commutes pleasant.

Sophy stayed on my mind, but I had not had the chance to talk with her. My mom had scolded me severely after we had been found out. When she and I went to see my grandparents, they made Sophy stay in her room after she prepared the meal. I saw her fleetingly, but we were too afraid to even smile at each other.

After a few months passed, I got bad news from my mom. My grandparents, Sophy, Sophy's sister, and her brother-in-law were all moving to Philadelphia, where there was a growing Cambodian community. Jobs had been arranged for them.

I didn't know when or if I'd see or talk to her again—if at all. I was heartbroken.

I did the only thing I knew how to do. I kept going to school and working and tried to focus on my dream of getting a college education and a good job one day.

Sophy, however, was always on my mind.

WORKING AT THE TENLEY MINI MARKET was much more fun than the dishwashing job because I got to interact with customers who bought coffee and donuts and sandwiches. I enjoyed joking around with them and had a good time.

I noticed that some men who came into the market wore uniforms with white shirts and hats with gold stripes. They had pistols on their belts and badges and patches that displayed the White House, which I had learned about. Most of them were tall, and they had an air of confidence. I could read the name on their uniforms: U.S. Secret Service.

Many were very friendly, and I enjoyed interacting with them. One afternoon I asked a question of one of the officers who had always been kind to me. "What is the Secret Service?"

"We protect the president," he said.

"Oh, you guys are good, huh?" I said.

"That's right," he said with a laugh. "We are good."

I learned that the Secret Service had a substation office about a block away. Many of the officers who worked at that station stopped in every day to get coffee and something to eat. They would often chat with the market's owner, a retired police officer, and I got to know some of them well.

One of the Secret Service officers I first met thought I was Filipino. He was very outgoing and friendly, and as a joke he started calling me "Marcos." I liked the name and it stuck. I began introducing myself as Marcos, but soon I changed it to Mark. Americans had never understood the name Leth anyway. "Laugh?" they would sometimes say when I told them my name. Americans all knew the name Mark. It made me sound like I had been in Maryland all my life.

After I got to know some of the Secret Service officers better, I told a few of them an abbreviated version of my story about growing up in the Killing Fields. They were surprised to learn I was Cambodian, having thought I was Filipino all this time. Darrell Thompson, an officer who had a master's degree in English, offered to help me learn the language. We spoke almost every day, and he taught me a quick lesson every time he bought coffee.

Other Secret Service officers befriended me, and they always seemed glad to see me and showed interest in my life. Back then, I didn't know a police officer from a sheriff's deputy from a Secret Service officer, but I was glad to get to know these men. Although some would have found them intimidating with their uniforms and guns and badges, they were nice to me. They made me think of my father, who had worn a uniform and carried a gun all his adult life. It had been about ten years since he had been killed, and I missed him and thought of him often.

I wondered what he would have thought of this new life I had in America.

AFTER MANY MONTHS of living with Dy's family crammed into our two-bedroom apartment, we all moved into a larger three-bedroom apartment. It had more space, but it still felt cramped. I was happy to have school and friends and my jobs and my car to keep me busy and out of the apartment from early morning until midnight.

I was home one weekend morning before going to work when my mom said I had a phone call. She talked on the phone a lot and had been on for a while. I thought it must be my grandmother in Philadelphia who wanted to speak to me. I rarely got phone calls.

"Who is it?" I asked.

"It's Sophy," she said, smiling.

"Sophy?"

"Yes. Take the phone."

I could hardly believe my ears. Sophy had been gone for months, but I still thought about her every day. I was surprised my mom was encouraging me to talk to her. "Is it OK?"

"Yes," my mom said. "Talk to her."

I nervously took the phone. "Hello?"

"Hello, Leth," Sophy said. "How are you?"

"I'm—I'm fine," I said. I was so excited to hear her voice it was hard to get the words out. I could sense my mom eavesdropping on me from the kitchen.

"I wanted to tell you," Sophy said, "that several men here have asked Grandmother and Grandfather for my hand in marriage."

This pained me. I had feared she would get married in Philadelphia. I didn't say anything.

She continued, "I have not said yes to any of them, and there are none of them I want to marry. I don't like any of them the way I like you."

This cheered me up. "Thank you," I said, which was all I could think of to say.

"So," she continued, "if you want to ask for my hand in marriage, you need to talk to your mom and move quick. If you want to do so."

"Yes. OK. Yes." This had all taken me by surprise, so much so that I couldn't say anything else.

"I need to go," she said, and I could hear someone talking to her in the background. "These phone calls are expensive. But I hope to hear from you."

I put the phone down, and my mom looked at me and smiled. "Do you want to marry Sophy?"

"Yes!" I said. "Yes! Absolutely."

She hugged me. "I will work it out for you."

She called and asked Grandmother, who consulted with Grandfather, and they agreed. Our marriage was set.

A FEW WEEKS LATER, my mom, my sister's family, and I went to South Philadelphia, where there was a growing Cambodian community, for our wedding on August 28, 1985.

Sophy and I dressed in the traditional formal Cambodian wedding attire, elaborate clothes that my mom and some of her friends made. My outfit was a shiny gold shirt and suit, like what a Khmer king would wear, and Sophy wore an intricate red dress with a golden scarf like a queen. She looked so beautiful.

A Buddhist monk conducted the service at Sophy's sister's home, a row house into which twenty people crowded together on the first floor. After the service, we went out for our wedding dinner in a Chinatown restaurant. With my sister's family and Sophy's family and many Cambodian friends her family had made, we filled up about ten tables.

My mom beamed. She smiled the entire day. She loved Sophy and was so happy to bring her into our family.

I was happy too—incredibly happy. In less than two years, I had learned a lot of English, had two jobs and a car, and was on my way to earning a high school diploma.

But I also felt fear. I was nineteen years old and about to start my senior year in high school. I was learning how expensive America could be. Sophy's moving in with us would make ten people in our three-bedroom apartment. We had a new bill to pay every time I turned around.

Sophy and I married in Philadelphia in 1985.

I wanted to finish high school and go to college. How could I support a wife? I was so broke. My jobs paid minimum wage or slightly above.

I loved Sophy and was so happy to marry her, as I had thought it would never work out for us when she moved away. But the pressure of all this responsibility at such a young age weighed heavily on my mind.

WHEN SOPHY MOVED TO MARYLAND to live with us, she and I had a bedroom of our own, while my mom and my sister's family split the other two bedrooms and the living room. It seemed like someone was sleeping in every spot.

I kept working at the Tenley Mini Market and the Shanghai Restaurant, but I began looking for jobs with higher wages. I worked everywhere, including a McDonald's for a few days. When they hired me, they said I could be a cashier, but when I got there, they stuck me on clean-up duty. After a few days, I didn't go back.

I got a job in a 7-Eleven in Silver Spring, and although the pay was only pennies higher than minimum wage, I liked it. I liked working the register and talking to people who came through. It was good practice for my English. Some people were rude and didn't appreciate my efforts to make conversation, but others were friendly, and occasionally I'd meet a Cambodian.

Sophy also got a job, working in a chicken-packing plant. It was hard work and not pleasant, but she never complained. We were able to start saving some money and buy nicer food for the family.

It turned out we would need that saved money because in May 1986, Sophy told me she was pregnant.

This was, of course, happy news. My mother was thrilled when she told her. She hugged us both and kissed us and cried. My sister by this point had given birth to five boys, but they would not carry on my pa's name. But if my child were a boy, he would continue the line of Lieutenant Oun Seuth.

This was important to me and to her. It had seemed that years before in Cambodia that none of us would survive, and like my pa, we would all die and his family line would end. But here in Maryland, we were surviving and rising and living our own version of the American dream. We didn't think of it as an American dream, but simply as our dream of being safe and secure and having enough to eat—of being able to love one another and live freely without persecution and pain. That is what America allowed me, and I am forever grateful to this country for that opportunity.

Like my marriage, Sophy's pregnancy brought me great happiness, but also more anxiety. I had just turned twenty years old when we got the news, and I was one month shy from graduating high school. I knew that babies were expensive. I saw how my sister and her husband struggled to make ends meet.

I also did not want to give up on my dream of earning a college degree and of one day finding a job that would pay me more money to support my family. I was astounded at what some people in America earned in one year. Some players for the Washington NFL team in 1986 were making more than $400,000 a year! John Elway, the quarterback for the Denver team, would get paid $1 million! I couldn't imagine what someone would do with all that money—I was barely making $10,000 annually.

I knew that I could never play pro football, but I saw the kinds of cars many Americans drove and where some lived, and I knew there was a lot of money to be made. I also knew I needed a college degree to do so.

I GRADUATED FROM HIGH SCHOOL in the summer of 1986 with little fanfare. My counselors at Montgomery Blair helped me enroll and arrange for financial aid to go to Montgomery College, a community college. I started that summer, but took only one night class each semester. I needed to earn more because we had a baby on the way.

I worked all the hours I could at the Tenley Mini Market and the 7-Eleven. I started looking for other jobs, anything that would pay me more or give me additional hours to supplement my income. I took extra hours washing dishes at Shanghai when that was all I could get.

I worked days, nights, weekends. Anytime I could get hours, I was there. Sometimes I put in almost one hundred hours a week. Every paycheck I received, I put in the bank and saved as much as possible. I knew I'd need the money when our child was born.

My Volkswagen Dasher, which I'd had for two years, had close to two hundred thousand miles on it, but I kept driving it, rushing from one job to the other.

One weekend that summer, I loaned my car to my best friend Horn for a trip he wanted to make to New York. I would do anything for Horn, and he would do anything for me. On the return trip home, the car died on the side of Interstate 95, only about ten miles from home. Horn, like me, was a good mechanic, but he could not get it started. He left it there and got a ride back home. When we checked on it the next morning, we discovered the windows had been smashed and the radio was gone. The radio was worth only about $25, but it had been the best feature of the car. The Dasher had a serious engine problem, and we didn't have the means to repair it ourselves. I had it towed to a repair shop, but they said it would be a thousand dollars or more to fix it. I asked them how much they would give me for it, and they said $50. I took the money and left my beloved Dasher behind. I was not upset with Horn, because that car was old and had served me well. It could have died on me as easily as it died on him.

With the money I had been making, I had some credit and work history to show, so I bought a brand-new car. I found a black Plymouth Reliant made by Chrysler that I liked. The dealership gave me a loan with 18 percent interest. It added another bill for me to pay, but I had a reliable vehicle with heat and air-conditioning. I felt as though I were riding in style, and it would be a good family car. I had come to understand that to be successful in America, one had to have a good car.

SOPHY'S BELLY GREW through the summer and into the fall. Doctors at Washington Adventist Hospital in Takoma Park, which was not far from our home, said our child would be born before the end of the year.

We didn't know if we'd have a boy or a girl. My mother and Sophy and I all prayed for a boy. My sister Dy had all boys, so I hoped I could match her with at least one of my own.

I continued to work, as did Sophy. In December, it got to the point where the baby could come any day, but I couldn't afford to call out of work because I could lose my job or would not get as many hours. I was working at the Tenley Mini Market one night when my mom called me from a payphone. Sophy had gone into labor, and my brother-in-law and Dy had taken them to the hospital. Doctors said she would give birth any minute. "Can you come now?" my mom asked.

I was the only one on duty. "I will try," I said, "but I need to find someone to work for me." I tried calling my manager, but I could not get in touch with him. I tried calling the employee who would replace me at midnight, but he did not answer either. I tried calling other employees of the store, but I couldn't find anyone.

I knew that if I closed the store and left, that could be the end of my job there. I needed that job, and so I would have to wait until midnight and miss the birth of my first child. The minutes seemed like hours as I waited for the end of my shift.

My mom called me back when I had about two hours left to go. "It's a boy! It's a boy!" She was so happy, and I could hear her joyful crying. Tears pooled up in my eyes. Sophy and my mom and I had decided to name him Timmy, in honor of my grandfather, Tim Yong, who had helped us so much in America. Of course, he would be an Oun. Like me, and like my father.

When I finally arrived at the hospital, Sophy was in bed, holding him. He was sleeping, swaddled in a baby blanket, and seemed so peaceful. She handed him to me. I cradled him in my arms, and he seemed like a miracle.

Becoming a father was like no feeling I'd felt before, but it also set off new worries in my mind. All I had were low-paying menial jobs that would not feed a family. My English was not great.

I thought, *What am I going to do?*

I knew in that moment that I needed to work harder on my education and better myself to support my son, my wife, and my mother. I vowed to earn a college degree.

WITH THE NEW BABY, living in our apartment with my sister's family and my mother was challenging. My brother-in-law, who'd had a hard time in the Killing Fields, was drinking a lot and not working. He was bitter and had made no effort to learn English. Staying home all day was not helping his mood, and he began to turn on me.

One night after Sophy and the baby and I returned from a trip to Philadelphia, we found him very drunk in the apartment. She and I were talking, and he yelled, "What are you talking about?"

"I was not talking to you," I said.

"You know what?" he said. "I am sick of you. You get out of here. This is my house. My name is on the lease. Not yours. So you need to get out of my house."

It was true, the lease was in his name, although I had paid him to allow us to stay there. It had never occurred to me that family would kick me out. My sister Dy and my mom were scared of him, however, and did not argue with him. You could not argue with him when he was drunk.

The next day, I went out looking for somewhere for me, Sophy, Timmy, and my mom to stay. I could afford almost nothing, and certainly not a deposit. I spoke with my friend Horn. I was so choked up about having no place to go and not enough money to afford a new apartment for my family that I could barely speak.

"You can stay with us," Horn said. "You should come over now."

Horn and his mother greeted us at the door to their tiny one-bedroom apartment. "You can all sleep in the bedroom," Horn said. "We can sleep out here in the living room for a while."

Horn was that kind of friend, one who would give up his own bed. The kindness and generosity he and his mother showed us at that time meant so much. He would do anything for me, and I would do the same for him. More than thirty-five years later, he is still my best friend.

AFTER A FEW MONTHS WITH HORN, I had saved up money to get an apartment of our own on New Hampshire Avenue in Takoma Park. My mother, who had lived with us at Horn's apartment, stayed with us to help take care of Timmy while Sophy and I worked.

I also made the painful decision to take a break from community college. Because we had no other financial support, we had to work hard to pay all the bills: rent, insurance, car payment, food, telephone, taxes, and so forth. Life in America was more luxurious than it was in Cambodia, but it was much more complicated and expensive. Whenever I thought I was getting ahead, another bill would arrive and put me back down to barely breaking even. I knew that school would always be there, and it remained a goal, but I didn't have the time to take classes while working as many jobs as I could hold down.

Sophy also got good-paying work with her sister, picking fruits and vegetables for a market in Philadelphia, where she frequently traveled. She would sometimes be gone for a month, which was hard for her and me and my mom, who took care of Timmy while I worked. The money Sophy made was much better than minimum wage, so we did what we had to do, but I missed her terribly. The American dream, I was learning, doesn't come easy.

I bought the local newspapers and searched the want ads every day, looking for jobs that would pay me more money. I was hired at a Moto Photo in Rockville, Maryland, where I learned all about processing film and making prints. I liked working with the customers there, and often they enjoyed showing me their photos. It paid fifty cents an hour more than minimum wage and certainly was preferable to washing dishes.

In 1987, I landed a job that moved me up in the world when I became a bank teller at the Montgomery County Teachers Federal Credit Union. For the interview, I had bought dress clothes, including a dark blazer and a tie and slacks, that helped me fit in with the culture of the bank. I felt like I had it made, handling customer's deposits and withdrawals. I would straighten my tie in the mirror in the morning and smile at myself, thinking of how far I had come in only a few years. It was nice to have banker's hours, although I did continue to work nights at the Tenley Mini Market, 7-Eleven, and other places. Even with a job that required me to wear a tie, money was tight at home. We decided that Sophy should stop working in Philadelphia because we all missed each other, and she needed to be there for Timmy. I was thrilled for her to not go away, but we missed the extra money.

After a few years, my brother-in-law and I started talking again. He asked for my help in finding work and applying for jobs, and soon after that, he asked us to move back in with him and my sister and their five kids. He and Dy had their hands full and needed help. They had located a single-family house with four bedrooms in Takoma Park, not far from our apartment, which we could rent together. I did not want to do it—he had kicked us out and I will never forget that—but my mother wanted us to all be together. She missed seeing my sister's sons, and she could be more help to all of us if we were in one place. It would save us money, sharing the expenses. It also would be the first house we had lived in as our other homes had all been apartments. The proposed arrangement offered many benefits, but I still didn't want to sleep under the same roof as my brother-in-law.

My mom was insistent though. "Family is always family," she said. Nothing was more important to her than family, and so I agreed. She also knew that Sophy and I were having a hard time paying the bills.

In addition to our families, my "other mother" Ath Yonn, with whom we had always been close, moved in, and sometimes her family members would stay with us. On any given night, twelve to fifteen people were living in that house.

A great thing about living in a house with a yard was that it would allow me to have a dog. One day at the Tenley Mini Market, a Filipino man who had become a friend came in and said that he had some young puppies to give away. I had been more than ten years without a dog, but I still fondly remembered my dog Dino that I had loved so much. "I would love to take one," I said.

I knew that I would name him Dino in honor of my first dog.

That night I went to pick up the new Dino. He was a German shepherd, small at the time, but I knew he would grow big. I carried him home, and he cried all night. Everyone in the house wanted to kill me, but I was keeping that dog.

I trained Dino and he grew quickly, reaching about seventy-five pounds after a year. He became protective of our family and would sniff and bark at strangers who came into the house.

One day a year or two later, when most of us were away at work, he helped avert a robbery when a man broke into our home and tried to snatch a gold necklace from Ath Yonn's neck. Dino attacked the man and bit him on the arm. My mother ran into the room and pulled Dino away, worried that he might kill the robber. The robber ran off, his arm bleeding, and police caught him soon after.

Although they had all complained many times when he was little and barked, everyone in the house had grown to love and appreciate Dino—especially on that day.

THE LONGER I WORKED at the Tenley Mini Market, the more I got to know the Secret Service officers who stopped in to buy coffee and food.

Sometimes we just said hello and exchanged greetings, but other times they asked me about my life in Cambodia, about how I was doing in school, about my family. When Timmy was born, they were all excited about him and asked to see photos.

I also began to learn more about the Secret Service. When I had a chance to take classes at Montgomery College, I chose a few classes in criminal justice where I learned about law enforcement. I also talked with the owner of the market, and he told me stories about his time as a police officer in Maryland.

I decided that when I finished school, I wanted to work in law enforcement. I began to talk about this dream with the Secret Service officers I knew. "You should apply to come work with us, Marcos," Officer Jimmy Voelker said. "The service is growing. We need more officers."

"I'm a refugee," I said. "I can't work in the White House."

"If you are an American citizen, you can," he said.

That was around 1988, and I had not yet become a citizen. I had never even dreamed I could be a Secret Service officer.

I took the naturalization test in 1990 and became an official citizen of the United States. I studied hard in preparation, but the test was much easier than I expected. I passed easily and was thrilled to become an American citizen.

Not long after taking the oath of allegiance to the United States, I talked to the Secret Service officers about applying, and they gave me an application. However, I was worried because I had not yet finished college and all the officers I had met had bachelor's degrees. I wasn't even halfway through earning my associate degree, even though it had been almost four years since I had finished high school.

I talked with my mom about this application one night, and she said that I should try to finish college first. "That job will always be there," she said. "You have always said you wanted to earn your degree and improve your English. You should do that."

I told my Secret Service friends that I had decided to finish school before applying, and they all thought that was a good idea. Joining their ranks was a dream that I wasn't ready for—and I doubted that I ever would be.

Our daughter, Jenny, and son, Timmy.

TIMMY GREW FROM A TODDLER into a young boy and started school. Sophy became pregnant with our second child in 1992, and we were excited about growing our family.

On March 1, 1993, we had a girl. We named her Jenny—she was adorable. We were all so happy, and I felt fortunate that I had a boy to carry on my pa's name and a daughter who was precious.

A few years earlier I had taken a second bank teller job, this one at Potomac Valley Bank in Little Falls, Maryland, where I rose to head teller. The money was better, although not great, and because I worked so much, my progress in school was still slow.

As with Timmy's birth, I was thrilled at the miracle of a new child, but I worried about supporting a bigger family. I knew I needed to earn more money, and that to do so, I needed to finish college.

THE FOLLOWING YEAR, Sophy and my mom and I decided that my family should move to Philadelphia and my mom should come with us. Sophy's sister had a good job there and could help Sophy find work. My mom liked Philadelphia because there was a community of Cambodians in South Philadelphia and a wat that she liked to attend.

Sophy's brother-in-law arranged a job for me, and I also found a job working in a shoe warehouse. Most appealing, I was accepted into Community College of Philadelphia. It transferred all of my credits from Montgomery College and gave me a generous financial aid package.

So one afternoon, after living eleven years in Maryland, Sophy, my mom, and I packed all our belongings into a small U-Haul trailer, put our two kids in the car, and drove north on Interstate 95 to Philadelphia, the birthplace of American liberty.

Finding My Future in Philadelphia

[1994–2002]

W E MOVED INTO A ROW HOUSE in the 1500 block of South Sixth Street in Philadelphia. Thousands of Cambodian refugees had settled in this part of the city, which years later would become known as Cambodia Town. The closeness of all the families in the dense neighborhoods of row houses created a true Cambodian community. We could stroll past storefronts and restaurants with signs in Khmer script! It was a long way from Battambang City, and the climate was decidedly different, but in a way it was like going back home.

My mom loved it. She had felt lonely all our years in Maryland, with no one to talk to in Khmer except for her immediate family. She had not learned English and had been afraid to venture out on her own. In Philadelphia, however, she found many Cambodian neighbors with whom she could converse. Going shopping in the Asian market wasn't the mystery it had been in American grocery stores, and we lived within walking distance of a Cambodian Buddhist wat, where she often worshipped and participated in activities.

My mom babysat Jenny, who was only one year old at the time, and often took her out for walks around the neighborhood and to visit with friends. She also would babysit for neighbors. She acquired a used sewing machine and started making clothes.

With my mother at a wedding in the early 1990s.

Our home, which we took out a loan to buy for $34,000, had three floors and was always busy with guests. It seemed expensive to us at the time, but it was nice to own instead of rent. In addition to me, Sophy, Timmy, Jenny, and my mom, my sister Dy's sons often visited us and sometimes would live with us, as did other more distant friends and family who needed a place to stay. The sound of laughter was common in our house and in other homes down the street. Everyone was family. That was the way it had been in Battambang City, before the communists had ruined life as we knew it.

It was possible for me to not have to speak a word of English in this neighborhood. That was perfect for my mom, who was in her seventies and set in her ways. Other Cambodians also had found learning English too hard and given up, resigning themselves to staying in this tiny slice of the city where they could communicate comfortably.

I did not want to limit my options. I wanted to continue improving my English, and I was determined to earn a bachelor's degree and find a better job. I met with an adviser at Community College of Philadelphia and realized that if I worked hard, I could earn associate degrees in criminal justice and sociology in about a year.

I studied hard, but I also worked hard, putting in long hours. I worked early morning hours helping out my brother-in-law Yom Yong with a small grocery store he owned in South Philadelphia. I woke up about three o'clock every morning to go to the food warehouses and buy fruits and vegetables to help him stock the store before it opened at seven. Then I would go to school, where I was taking three or four classes each semester. I never missed a class, and I studied between classes when I was on campus. I found many helpful professors whom I visited during their office hours.

After school, I worked afternoons and nights and many weekends at a shoe warehouse in South Philadelphia, unloading eighteen-wheelers and organizing shoes in shelves fifteen feet high. The days were long. By nine or ten every night, after helping get Jenny and Timmy to bed, I collapsed for a good night's sleep. I was happy, knowing that I was making progress, that my dream of a college education was coming true. My grades were good, my English was getting stronger every day, and we owned our own home. I had never thought of the idea of the American dream until I started to write this book and thought the phrase made a good title, but when I look back, I realize that's what I was doing all along—striving for my own American dream.

Once I graduated from Community College of Philadelphia, I started applying to schools where I could earn a bachelor's degree. I applied to many different universities, including Columbia, Cornell, Temple, Villanova, Penn State, Penn, and Widener.

I knew of Widener University by a strange twist of fate. Once when we were living in Maryland and making one of our many trips to visit family and friends in Philadelphia, my Plymouth Reliant broke down in a heavy rainstorm on Interstate 95 in Chester, Pennsylvania, about fifteen miles south of Philadelphia. I guided the car under an overpass near an exit ramp. After the rain let up, I told Sophy, Timmy, and my mom to keep the doors locked while I went to find a payphone. I could see a sign that said Widener University, and far up on the hill, I saw a white dome atop an elegant four-story building that looked to be historic. *This must be a very nice college*, I said to myself.

Little did I know that about five years later, I would be a student there. Widener was the first college to accept me, and it was generous with financial aid.

In the fall of 1996, I began my studies.

CLASSES AT WIDENER were a vastly different experience from those at community college, which had included a mix of students of all ages and backgrounds. Most of the students at Widener were white kids in their late teens or early twenties. I turned thirty during my first semester, and I had two children. My classmates were going to parties and joining fraternities and sororities. A lot of them had sleek German cars their wealthy parents had bought them. I was working sixty hours a week in addition to taking classes.

I would listen to these kids talk about their lives and not say much. I was there to improve my English and earn my degree. Occasionally, a fellow student would ask me where I was from, and I would tell them.

"Is that part of China?" they would often ask. "Do you speak Chinese?"

I didn't try to explain to them the place I had come from and what I had been through and had seen.

I also introduced myself to everyone as Mark. I knew that they would have a hard time with Leth, and I wanted to fit into American culture as much as possible. Even though my legal name was Leth Oun, I put my name down as Mark Oun on all my papers.

The Widener classes were harder than those in community college. At times I had doubts that I could pass, but then I would say to myself, *You are just going to have to try harder.* If I was given a reading assignment, which would often be long, I would try to read whatever I was assigned twice. Because I read slowly and had to look up many words, this took me quite a long time. Some nights I would stay up past midnight studying and working on my assignments even though I had to wake up at three in the morning to go to work. The coursework was difficult, and I often would get frustrated, but I was not going to let myself fail.

Fortunately, I found caring professors in Widener's sociology department. My first semester, I took a class from Dr. William R. F. Phillips, a beloved longtime sociology professor at Widener who helped me in so many ways. He could see that I was struggling. "Any time you have a question, my door is always open for you," he said. "Please stop by and see me."

I took him up on that offer. I went to see him every day I was on campus, and he never once acted like he didn't have enough time for me. He always answered my questions and encouraged me. Dr. Phillips was understanding if I did poorly on an assignment or a test. He took a lot of time explaining concepts and offering encouragement. "You can do this," he would say.

He became like a father figure to me.

One afternoon I was walking to my car in a Widener parking lot when I saw Dr. Phillips waiting at a bus stop. "Dr. Phillips," I said. "What are you doing?"

"I'm waiting on the bus," he said.

"I can give you a ride," I said.

"No, that's OK. It's too far. I live in Philadelphia."

"I do too. Come with me. I will take you home."

He tried to dissuade me, but I wasn't giving up. Eventually he agreed and got in my Plymouth Reliant and I drove him to his apartment in Center City Philadelphia, only about ten or fifteen minutes from our South Philadelphia home.

I learned later that Dr. Phillips, who was in his mid-fifties, was suffering from ALS, also known as Lou Gehrig's disease, and that he couldn't drive. I was glad to help him out and gave him many rides home. It was not nearly enough to repay everything he did for me, and I enjoyed his company. He died in 2001, three years after I graduated, but his good work lives on in the life I've been able to lead.

He will always be remembered in my heart.

Vernon Smith and Dr. Barbara Ryan were also very supportive Widener professors. In Dr. Ryan's course, she assigned a paper about women's rights. I decided to write about my mother and all she went through in the Killing Fields after my father had been killed. Dr. Ryan was touched by my story, and she and I became close and have remained friends. When I wanted to write my book, she helped me get started with it, and she has been a valuable partner and editor on this project throughout the years it has taken to finish it. I can't say enough good things about Dr. Ryan.

Professor Smith, who was a great teacher, also played a big role in my life. Once he got to know me, he recommended I contact the Philadelphia probation office, which is known as Family Court, and let them know that I was Cambodian and spoke Khmer. He knew that the Family Court needed bilingual workers to help Cambodian juvenile offenders on probation in Philadelphia.

I ended up getting an internship that became a part-time job, and I helped many Cambodian teens who had gotten into trouble. I would go to see these teens and visit with their parents as well. The fact that I was one of them calmed them because they were afraid of American law enforcement, and the language barrier was challenging. I communicated with them in Khmer to help them understand not only what they needed to do to satisfy their legal obligations, but to be successful in this country. I told them they needed to learn English and study and work hard. I myself was a good example. It felt good to help Cambodians who had come to this country just as I had.

That job—my first in criminal justice—put me on the path to the job I have today.

I owe so much to Professor Smith. He helped this refugee more than I can ever repay. He and I stayed in contact after I graduated and became close friends, and I got to know his family well. We became so close that he even asked me to be godfather to his daughter Erika. She is a talented young woman, competing as a professional figure skater who performed with Cirque du Soleil. I am so proud of all she has achieved.

I often went back to Widener to speak in Professor Smith's criminal justice classes. He introduced me to my coauthor, Joe Samuel Starnes, who was the editor of Widener's alumni magazine when we met. Sam, as he is known, wrote a profile of me for the magazine in 2011, and we stayed in touch. He played a major part in helping me finish this book and finding a publisher for it.

In May 1998, I graduated from Widener. It was a thrill to wear the graduation cap and gown and sit out on the beautiful lawn behind Old Main, the historic building that I had seen years before when I was in search of a phone after my car broke down. What's more, I was recognized as the outstanding sociology graduate of my class. I don't want to brag, but that's not bad for a thirty-two-year-old refugee who didn't speak English fifteen years before!

My mom, Sophy, our kids, and many members of my extended family attended the commencement ceremony, and they threw a big party for me at our home. It was a celebration not just for me, but for all of us. We had all come so far from the Killing Fields and refugee camps.

Although I was a student at Widener for only two years, it was a transformative time, allowing me to become a criminal justice professional and fulfill my dreams. The kindness, encouragement, and support shown to me there resonates in my life every day.

AFTER GRADUATION, I landed a full-time job as a social worker with De La Salle Aftercare, a program providing services for delinquent youth that is part of the Catholic Foundation of Greater Philadelphia. I met many good people there, including Joseph Garr, who, like me, would go on to be an officer in the Uniformed Division of the Secret Service. Joseph, who ultimately became a special agent with the Secret Service, helped me get started at De La Salle. I filled a role there similar to the work I had done for Family Court.

My job with De La Salle took me into all parts of Philadelphia. One day I was in the federal building downtown and saw a posting for a job opening for a correctional officer with the Department of Justice.

I didn't know what my chances were, but I was always looking for ways to move up and better myself, and I knew working for the federal government would pay better than the social work I was doing. I had two young children, a wife, my mother, and other family members to support.

I applied, but after a few months went by, I assumed they had passed over me. I forgot all about it. But one day, I got a phone call from a woman with a heavy southern accent who said she was with the Department of Justice. My first thought was *Oh no, what did I do?*

I had a hard time understanding her drawl. "Why are you calling me?" I asked.

She said they liked my application and wanted to interview me.

"Application for what?" I asked.

"You applied to be a correctional officer," she said.

"What is a correctional officer?" I asked, because I didn't remember the details.

She was good-natured and patient with me. She explained the job, which was working as a guard in the federal detention center, and said they would like to interview me. "Be sure to wear a coat and tie," she said.

The interview process was grueling. There were stacks of paperwork to fill out and tests to take and a panel of high-ranking officers and even a psychologist who questioned me. I was so nervous during the group interview that my shirt and suit became soaked in sweat. Following the interview, they took my fingerprints. My hands were so wet I had to dry them with a towel before they could record my prints.

Despite my sweaty hands, I got the job.

I had taken the step from being a social worker to an officer of the law.

I WAS THRILLED with this new position, which I started in December 1999. It was a significant jump in pay, more than three times what I had been making at De La Salle Aftercare, and it came with full health insurance for my family and other generous benefits. I felt good about my future in the forthcoming millennium.

I went through a rigorous preparation program, including police academy training at Fort Dix in New Jersey. I learned how to handle and shoot pistols, shotguns, and SR-15 and M-4 rifles. I learned about many things, including riot formations, self-defense techniques, and prison-management procedures.

When I began my regular duties, I reported to the federal detention center at 700 Arch Street, then a new tower with more than one thousand inmates that is directly across from the William J. Green Federal Building and only a few blocks from Independence Hall and the Liberty Bell. My uniform consisted of a white shirt with my name on it, gray pants, and black steel-toe boots. It was an awesome feeling to be in uniform. I thought of my father, who had worn an army uniform for much of his life.

The detention center was a jail for federal detainees who were awaiting trial or transfers to serve sentences in penitentiaries. It held every kind of inmate—from white-collar criminals to murderers—and had male and female units. I was assigned to work as a correctional officer in the special housing unit, which everyone called "the SHU." (I quickly learned that the federal government has many, many acronyms that I needed to learn to do my job.) Inmates in this unit had violated the center's rules or gotten into fights with other inmates. We didn't know what these inmates were capable of doing. They could be a dangerous bunch, so we watched them closely and kept them isolated from one another. We made sure they were fed and stuck to the schedules and followed the rules. I learned how to use the center's computer system to document every action, and I began working in the control center that oversaw the entire operation for that floor. Many good fellow officers showed me the ropes.

At the time the detention center was a brand-new facility. I worked a lot of overtime, often taking on extra eight-hour shifts, which would put me on the job for sixteen hours at a time. During one period when they were shorthanded, I worked sixteen hours a day, seven days a week, for three months. I couldn't resist the offers for overtime—I was making what seemed like a great deal of money to start with, and overtime paid time-and-a-half. I couldn't believe how much money I was putting in the bank. I could earn in one day what had taken me several weeks of washing dishes and tending convenience stores to earn. The correction officer work was not physically tiring—nothing like what I had endured in my younger years. My only regret was all the extra hours took away from time I could spend with family and friends, but I knew I was helping all of them by making more money. I took every extra shift I could get. At this point, Timmy was going to West Catholic High School in Philadelphia, a private school that was expensive. I wanted to be able to give my children opportunities I'd never had, and working the extra hours enabled me to do so.

Other officers and my bosses were amazed at my stamina. "How can you work so long?" a coworker once asked me. "Don't you get tired?"

"My body is used to it," I said. "I have always worked hard." I didn't tell him about the interminable days I had worked in rice paddies with a Khmer Rouge gunman watching me, but I thought back to those days and how hard they had been. The work in the jail was easy.

After I had been there a year, I was promoted to officer in charge, or OIC, as it was known, of the special housing unit. The higher-ups put a lot of trust in me. I was determined to not let them down. Only the most diligent officers with excellent work records received that assignment, and I was proud to reach this level.

I continued to learn, participating in many specialized training programs the department provided, including weapons (I became an excellent marksman), self-defense, and riot response. I was assigned to the riot team, known as the PR-24 team, so named for the two-foot-long police baton we used. After I'd worked there about a year, I began receiving assignments to travel to transport prisoners from one institution to another. This included transporting NFL player Alonzo Spellman, who stood about a foot taller than me and outweighed me by more than one hundred pounds, when he was arrested for making terroristic threats on an airplane. He was friendly to me, however, and we got along just fine.

IN THE LATE SUMMER OF 2001, I was selected to take a self-defense class at a federal training site in Central Pennsylvania that would prepare me to teach self-defense to other officers. I enjoyed opportunities that gave me a chance to travel and meet new people and take a break from the jail routine. Because I knew martial arts methods from childhood, I excelled in self-defense.

We were in class on the morning of September 11, 2001, when the news of the terrorist attacks in New York and Washington broke. We stopped the class and watched the news. When I saw the World Trade Center towers collapse, I closed my eyes and prayed for the survivors and for the dead. I could not believe that anyone would attack *my country* this way. Although Cambodia will always be first in my heart, I had come to love the United States in equal measure. Uncle Sam and Lady Liberty had taken me in and cared for me and given me opportunities. I felt especially appreciative as an employee of its federal government. This country was taking good care of me and rewarding me for the work I was doing.

I decided on that day that I wanted to join the U.S. Army and fight for my adopted country. This country had given me a new life. I wanted to pay it back.

When I returned home, I called an army recruiting branch in Philadelphia and told the man who answered the phone that I wanted to join and defend my country. He sounded excited to hear this and said he had a few questions for me.

"Are you a U.S. citizen?"

"Yes! Since 1990."

"How old are you?"

"Thirty-four," I said.

There was a long pause.

"When do you turn thirty-five?"

"Next month. On October 10."

Again, there was a long pause. "I'm sorry, but enlisted men must be between eighteen and thirty-four," he said.

I thanked him for his time and hung up. Even though the army wouldn't take me due to my age, I knew there must be other ways I could help defend my country. I started calling people I had met along my journey, including Jimmy Voelker, the U.S. Secret Service officer I had met years before when I'd fixed his coffee at the Tenley Mini Market. I hadn't talked to him in a few years, but he called me back when I left him a message. "Where the hell have you been Marcos?" he asked, laughing as he used my nickname from the market.

I told him about my job with the Department of Justice and how I had wanted to join the army. "Why don't you come with us?" he said. "We protect the president and his administration. That's an important form of service to your country. You are already in the federal government. It shouldn't be that hard of a move, and we are hiring."

I took his advice and applied to the Secret Service Uniformed Division. I emphasized the training and experience I'd gained by working in the federal detention center. My bosses there were kind and willing to serve as references for me.

I was optimistic, but I also felt that I might be a longshot. Most of the Secret Service officers I had met were tall, white men who could have played cowboys in westerns. I was five-feet, six inches tall and Asian. But I didn't let that stop me from applying for that job and other federal government positions. The federal Drug Enforcement Administration, known as the DEA, had openings that valued bilingual job candidates. I also applied to the U.S. Marshal's Service.

After a few months, the Secret Service called me for a telephone interview. I did well enough that they brought me to Washington for in-person interviews. Those interviews also went well, but they made me take the National Police Officer Selection Test, known as POST, which tests reading, writing, and mathematics. I was very nervous, and I found it to be difficult. I knew that I did terribly on the test.

A month passed. I believed that I had done so badly that I was out of the running. But they called me back and said that they were interested in hiring me, even though I had failed the test. Before they could hire me, I needed to pass. "Would you be willing to take the test again?" they asked.

"Of course," I said. I would take that test as many times as they would let me. *I'm going to keep taking it until I pass*, I said to myself.

I retook the test in the summer of 2002. I believed that I had done much better, but I had to wait for my results.

Several months passed, and I began to believe I wouldn't get the job. One afternoon in late November, I got home from work and checked the mail. An envelope from the Secret Service was in our box. It had a gold star embossed on elegant paper. I stood on our stoop and opened it, expecting it to be a rejection, thinking that they would have called if they were going to hire me.

But I was wrong. I could barely believe the letter as I read it. They were offering me, Leth Oun, a Cambodian refugee turned American citizen, a job as a U.S. Secret Service officer. I read it twice to make sure I had read it correctly.

When I realized it was true, I started cheering and jumping up and down with my arms in the air. Sophy and my kids and mother and other friends all came running and congratulated me when I told them the news.

I would be protecting the president!

I TURNED IN MY NOTICE with the Department of Justice. My coworkers teased me, but my friends there were happy for my success.

Yet there was some sadness with this new job because it would mean my family, including my mother, would be moving back to the Washington, D.C., area when I began my training. We had been in Philadelphia for more than eight years and had made many dear friends. My mom would miss the Cambodian community, and Timmy, who was sixteen, and Jenny, who was nine, would have to change schools. But the career change was worth it. My sister Dy and her family were still

242 | A REFUGEE'S AMERICAN DREAM

in Maryland, and we had friends there, too, where we had spent more than a decade. I told my mom that we would visit Philadelphia often and keep our friendships there.

I would also miss the neighborhood. I had been a mentor there for many Cambodian refugees, helping some with paperwork and giving advice to many about various issues regarding living in America. I was happy to share what I had learned on my journey, and I was always willing to work with my people. I told my friends and acquaintances that they could reach out to me any time. "I will be only two-and-a-half hours away," I said.

THE WEEK after I accepted the job, Lieutenant Winward from the Secret Service called me to set up my orientation. He went over the entry process and told me a bit about the six months of training I would go through when I started. He set up a time for me to meet with him in Washington.

At the end of the conversation, I asked, "Sir, did you ever work at the substation?"

"How do you know about the substation?" he asked.

"Do you know the Tenley Mini Market?"

"Yes, I know that place."

"If you know Tenley Market, you must have known a guy named Marcos?"

"No way," he said.

"Yes, that's me."

He laughed for a good long while. "I can't believe it," he said, laughing some more.

"Yes, Sir," I said. "That is me. It is good to speak with you again."

"You've come a long way, Marcos," he said. "I'll see you when you get here."

From No House to the White House

[2002–2012]

EVEN THOUGH I HAD BEEN a Department of Justice correctional officer and worked in the federal system, I had to complete the full six months of Secret Service training required of new recruits. I was fine with that. I would do whatever they asked of me to be successful in this job.

The first three months I went through the training program at the Federal Law Enforcement Training Center in Artesia, New Mexico. Much of it was physically demanding, with a lot of running and other physical tests, such as getting through an obstacle course and doing certain numbers of push-ups and sit-ups. At thirty-six, I was the second oldest in my training class, and the oldest man. After a few weeks, the oldest recruit was injured and had to leave, so I became the senior member of the group. I was a decade older than many of my peers, most of whom were in their twenties, but the physical tests were no problem for me. I had started working out with weights and running regularly during my years as a correctional officer. I was very fit. Many of those in their twenties could not keep up with me. I had come a long way from the eighty-nine-pound refugee who had arrived in America almost twenty years before.

The training included self-defense classes, and I was able to show off my skills, particularly my knowledge of Muay Thai, which is very similar to the Cambodian martial art Bokator that I had learned as a child.

I know the techniques like I know the back of my hand. I had taught it to my son Timmy and he had participated in competitions and often won. To me, Muay Thai is the best martial art—and lethal if you need it to be. You have eight weapons—two fists, two elbows, two legs, and two knees. The most deadly are the elbows, which are sharp and can cut someone's face like butter. I had to use it a few times while working in the jail to subdue an inmate who attacked the guards. It was always effective, even against much larger men. The trainers and my fellow classmates were impressed when they saw me in action. None of them wanted to spar with me. I might have been the shortest and the oldest man there, but they didn't view me that way after they saw what I could do with Muay Thai.

I also did well on the shooting range. I had honed my weapons skills in the regular monthly training required of correctional officers as well as individual practice I had done on the federal shooting ranges. I could handle pistols, shotguns, and rifles with ease and shoot targets with high levels of accuracy.

I earned a lot of respect from my fellow trainees and became good friends with a number of them. It was also a relief that the class was a fairly diverse mix that included men and women of all races and not just tall, white men. I was the only Cambodian, but there were others of color, including a few fellow Asians.

While the physical and weaponry requirements were not a problem for me, the academic assignments were difficult. The most challenging thing for me is language, and taking tests has always been hard. I don't want to make excuses, but not beginning to learn English until I was seventeen has often put me at a disadvantage.

Many reading assignments led up to three tests I would have to pass. These covered the seemingly endless number of federal policies and the U.S. Constitution, as well as federal law enforcement procedures. I took copious notes in class and read my assignments twice and studied hard, but I worried about taking the tests when the time came. If I didn't pass, they said, I wouldn't make it. I went through many pens and pads of paper.

Also difficult was the three-month stay in New Mexico, which was hard on me and my family, who had stayed in Philadelphia. We had decided not to move until I was through training and Jenny and Timmy had finished the school year. I was getting paid, and the money was good, but I missed Sophy and my children and my mom terribly. It was such a long trip and the weeks so demanding that I did not come home on the weekends. I stayed in the dorm and studied as much as I could. I missed their smiles and kindness and the wonderful Cambodian food that Sophy and my mom cooked. There was nothing to do in southern New Mexico except to walk around a Kmart. Every night the entire town smelled like the nearby oil refinery. It was depressing. I talked to Sophy and my mom on the phone every day, but that didn't replace seeing them. I told them and myself to be patient, that this would be for the better and soon I would be home.

I also worried more and more about the tests. I didn't tell my family about my concern, but my mom sensed my worry. She had learned more about what the job entailed, and although she was impressed I would be assigned to protect the most powerful man in America, she worried that I wouldn't be able to handle it. She told me she didn't think I had the language skills to succeed. That didn't mean that she didn't believe in me, but it is a mother's job to worry about her children. She had looked after me through so many hard times in the Killing Fields and the refugee camps. Even though she was in her eighties and I was in my mid-thirties, she still saw me as her little boy who needed her help. She didn't want me to fail and be hurt. I know she prayed for me to do well.

The first time I took the tests, I did not pass. I was so upset. I had scores in the 70 percent range, but recruits were required to score 80 percent. Fortunately, I was allowed to study more and take the tests again. I told several of my friends in the class about my trouble, and they kindly helped me study in the dorm. I was so stressed, and I valued their support. I studied for a week and took the tests again. This time I passed! The entire class cheered for me when it was announced.

Those tests meant that I had successfully completed the first half of my training period. I was on my way to Washington to protect the president and his administration.

OUR TRAINING PROGRAM moved to the Secret Service James J. Rowley Training Center in Maryland, commonly known as the RTC. I was thrilled to be back on the East Coast because I could go see my family in Philadelphia on weekends. I had missed them tremendously.

At the training center, I ran into many of the officers I had known years before at the Tenley Mini Market. It was a thrill to see them. They were amazed that I once had been serving them coffee and donuts and making them sandwiches, and here I was about to become one of them. They were helpful and encouraged me in the training on law enforcement procedures.

Two weeks before I was set to graduate, I got a call from a hiring officer at the DEA—the federal Drug Enforcement Administration—who said they liked my application and wanted to interview me. They were hoping to hire more officers who spoke Khmer. I thanked them, but said I was about to graduate from Secret Service training. They said they would keep my application open and to contact them if I changed my mind.

That phone call made me think about what a funny thing fate can be. If the DEA had called me before the Secret Service, I would have gone down the path to becoming a DEA agent. The simple fact that one person got to my application and called before the other determined the fate of my career. How different my life could have been! I always say that everything happens for a reason, and I believe this was one of those times. I'm glad it worked out the way it did.

Other twists of fate in my life have dramatically changed its course. During the immigration process in the refugee camps, what if my mom had not spoken up about our aunt and uncle who lived in Maryland? Immigration officials had planned to send us to California. We would have been resettled there, and our lives would have been dramatically different. I would not have married Sophy, and we would not have had Timmy and Jenny. I would have gone to different schools and had entirely different influences. I would not have ended up as a Secret Service officer.

I'll say it again—everything happens for a reason. I do believe the gods have been looking out for me.

MY FIRST ASSIGNMENT as a Secret Service officer was at the vice president's residence at One Observatory Circle, on the grounds of the U.S. Naval Observatory. I started in 2003 during George W. Bush's administration, so we were protecting Vice President Dick Cheney and his family.

It was such an awesome feeling to put on that uniform and step onto the grounds each day. We had posts around the house where we stood guard, and we drove a few patrol cars to watch the grounds. I remember thinking on that first day, *Look at me, a kid from Cambodia who barely survived the Killing Fields, and here I am protecting one of America's leaders.*

I worked a lot of hours, usually twelve-hour shifts, and if there was ever a call for someone to step up and take extra hours, I did it. The work was not physically taxing. I was making more money than I ever could have imagined, and I loved being there. Although standing guard in the middle of the night can be boring, I thought back to all the hard labor I had done in my life. I'd spent endless days in rice paddies with the fear of being killed or dying hanging over my head every minute; I'd put in twelve hours straight washing dishes; I'd worked sixteen hours straight behind the counter of a convenience store; and I had often worked sixteen hours watching jail cells.

So, standing guard at the vice president's residence was a breeze. Not to mention, Lynne Cheney—we all called her Mrs. Cheney—was very kind to the Secret Service officers and occasionally would bring lemonade and cookies out to us at our posts. I was astounded by her generosity. I couldn't believe that the Second Lady, as the vice president's wife is known, would bring me—a Cambodian refugee—cookies and lemonade. Cookies and lemonade! I could not believe it. I said over and over to myself, *This is such a great country!* I couldn't believe that I got to do this job every day.

SOPHY, TIMMY, JENNY, MY MOM, AND I moved to Maryland in the summer, and we bought a four-bedroom house in Gaithersburg with more space than we'd had in our row house in Philadelphia. My mom and Sophy made the house a home. Mom, who was in her mid-eighties by this time, missed the Cambodian community in Philadelphia, but we visited often, and Sophy occasionally would take her back there when I was working. We've made that drive back and forth on I-95 so many times over the years, I can't even begin to guess how many thousands of miles we've put on our cars. Even though my mom was getting up in years, her health and mind were in great shape. She spent a lot of time working in our yard, growing flowers and vegetables. She loved to cook too.

All in all, I was loving my life. In late 2003, I was chosen to join the Secret Service Trek Team, which patrolled the White House area and the vice president's residence on mountain bikes. It involved a training class and a riding test, which included many difficult maneuvers and ramps. I passed easily the first time. The bikes they gave us were so nice! We were given high-end mountain bikes with twenty-one speeds—I had been used to cheap bikes, which were all I could afford in Cambodia and later when I commuted to my jobs in Maryland. I couldn't believe my job was to ride around on a bike and get paid for it.

In 2004, I also began to get called to do protection on campaign trips. President Bush and Vice President Cheney were flying all over the country, as were the other presidential candidates who were given Secret Service protection. This opportunity was exciting for me, as I had traveled little. Even though we had no time for sightseeing, the campaign events were held in interesting parts of American cities. One day we might start in Chicago, fly to Houston, and end the day in Orlando. I stood guard in so many cities I had never dreamed I would see. I was getting a better education about America than most Americans had.

I was traveling for free and getting paid to do it. The overtime money on the campaigns was great. I don't want to brag about the money, but I had worked all day in rice paddies for nothing and chopped wood in refugee camps for fifty cents a week. When I bought my first pair of tennis shoes at the age of sixteen in the Philippines, the $15 I had paid was almost every penny I had. I had washed dishes for $3.15 an hour. These Secret Service paychecks seemed like lottery winnings. I knew this money would help my family, friends, and others.

EACH DECEMBER the vice president holds a holiday party for Secret Service officers at his residence. I had gone in 2003 by myself and had my picture taken in my uniform with Dick and Lynne Cheney in front of the Christmas tree. The three of us fit easily into the frame. I had not taken my family because I didn't know what to expect at the party and didn't know the protocol. I didn't want to overstep the bounds on my first year. But I saw that most officers brought their wives and children and other relatives.

In 2004, I made up for going alone the previous year—I took Sophy, Timmy, Jenny, Sophy's sister, her sister-in-law, and our niece. All seven

At my first Secret Service holiday party in 2003
with Vice President Dick Cheney and his wife, Lynne.

of us crowded into the photo with Lynne Cheney on the left side and Dick Cheney on the right. I relished this opportunity, going from once being homeless and almost killed so many times to standing with my family between the vice president and his wife. Even though that year I might have overdone it with guests, the Cheneys were kind to us. My kids were so happy, and they stuffed themselves with delicious food. I wished that my mom had gone with us, but she was shy and refused to go, even though we had encouraged her. She loved hearing our stories about it and seeing the photos afterward.

IN LATE 2004, I was called in one day to meet with my lieutenant in his office. That was not good news. I thought that I must have done something wrong. I racked my brain trying to think over every moment of the previous few weeks to figure out which regulation I must have violated. I was nervous when I went in and sat down, expecting to be chewed out and possibly put on warning. I had seen other officers get into trouble for various infractions. The Secret Service is very strict—as it should be, considering the critical nature of our jobs.

He was friendly and told me to sit down at the table in his office. I steeled myself for whatever was about to come.

He took a seat and smiled. "Officer Oun, you're always happy coming to work," he said. "You work hard and really seem to enjoy what you do."

I nodded and smiled. The lieutenant continued, "I have a question I'd like to ask you. Do you like dogs?"

I could not believe my ears. "I love dogs," I said. "I have one now. Buddy, a German shepherd. I've had two German shepherds in America. Before I came to this country, back in Cambodia, I grew up with a dog. We went through a lot together. He was the best little dog."

"Would you want to join the K-9 team and handle a protection dog?"

"Yes sir. I would love that. But—I have not been here that long." I had seen the officers handling protection dogs, and I had thought that it was a job I would like to do one day. However, other officers told me that to get onto the K-9 team, you had to be in the Secret Service at least five to ten years. Even then, few were selected.

"It's OK," the lieutenant said. "I've seen your work ethic, and we need more officers for K-9. You will be fine."

To join the K-9 team required another physical test, similar to what I had passed in my initial training, which I passed easily. Not everyone, especially the older officers who had been in the Secret Service for many years, could do the pull-ups, sit-ups, and push-ups required, nor could they run a mile-and-a-half in the allotted ten minutes. I had gotten into the habit of driving to Washington early each morning and exercising before starting work. Also, being on the Trek team kept me on a bike for hours at a time, so I was in great shape.

The other requirement for joining the K-9 team was that you had to own your home and have space for a large kennel for the dog. When you are on K-9, you are with the dog twenty-four hours, seven days a week. You care for the dog on and off the job. We had plenty of space in the backyard to build the kennel, which would be six feet high and cover eighty square feet in a rectangle. The Secret Service paid for the kennel and required each dog handler to have one, even though I knew that I would keep the dog in the house with me.

A dog in my family is one of the family.

A few weeks after I had completed my paperwork for the transfer and passed the physical test, a sergeant named Eddie called me. I got off to a bad start with him because I thought he said his name was "Edith," and that's what I called him. He didn't like that at all. I apologized profusely. I felt like an idiot and hoped that I hadn't hurt my chances.

He visited my home and met my family. Our dog Buddy was in a bad mood that day and barked ferociously at Sergeant Eddie. I had to lock him in another room, and the sergeant looked concerned. "What will you do if the dogs don't get along?" he asked. "That German shepherd is much bigger than most of the protection dogs."

"Buddy is a good dog," I said. "He's just protective. I will introduce them slowly, and they will get used to each other. The Secret Service dog will always be my first priority."

He warmed up to me after a while. "Where will you put the kennel?" he asked.

I showed him the backyard, which was already fenced in for Buddy. "The kennel can go here, but the dog can have the whole backyard if he wants it."

To BECOME A HANDLER, you take a dog that is new to the Secret Service and guide it through a seventeen-week training period led by K-9 trainers. I started with a dog named Ben, a German shepherd, but the trainer leading the class thought that he was not healthy enough. They then gave me a beautiful dog named Danja, a Belgian Malinois, but he did not respond well to training.

The third dog they assigned to me was a Dutch shepherd named Bo. She was fierce and often barked at everyone. I took her to our house, and she got along well with Buddy and my family, but in training, she was a nightmare. She was completely unpredictable. She obeyed me, and often she was friendly with others, but many other times she would snap at strangers for no reason at all. The trainers and I did everything we could to calm her down, but she never would. After she bit an agent on the knee, they decided to remove her from the pool of protection dogs.

Because Bo's training had taken six weeks, I went back to working at the vice president's residence to wait for another K-9 class later in the year. I was disappointed because it delayed my dream of working with a dog, but I was willing to put in my time.

When another class was getting ready to start, I had to take the physical test again and redo the paperwork. I thought they might give me credit and use my results and paperwork from the previous class, but that's not how the Secret Service works. It is by the book. I didn't think requiring me to start over was fair, but I did not complain. I would do whatever they wanted me to do to handle a dog.

This time, they assigned me a wonderful Belgian Malinois. His name was Reik, a name he had been given in Europe, where the Secret Service acquires most of its protection dogs. He had been trained earlier by another Secret Service officer, so the instructors asked the higher-ranking K-9 officers if I could complete five weeks of training with Reik and then go operational. The trainers thought Reik and I were ready. The request, however, was denied, so Reik and I were required to complete the full seventeen weeks. I held my head high and said, "Yes, Sir."

I loved Reik from the beginning. I felt so comfortable with him that I started speaking Khmer to him on the first ride home. His ears perked up and his eyes glistened, and later I taught him the commands he knew in English in my native language. He was a fast learner, and soon I could command him in Khmer and English. I didn't speak to him in Khmer during the training sessions in Maryland because I knew that would raise eyebrows, but when he was at my house and in my yard, he was a Cambodian dog. He came to me with the name Reik, but I started calling him *kaan dao*, which means "fast rat."

My family loved him too, especially my mother. It was amazing how they hit it off. She spoke to him in Khmer, which is the only language she knew. It is what she and I and Sophy communicated with at home, although I spoke to my children in a combination of English and Khmer. Timmy and Jenny speak perfect English, as it is their primary language as native-born Americans, but their Khmer is pretty good.

Reik was skinny when I inherited him. He weighed about forty-eight pounds, and the K-9 team veterinarian said he could stand to gain about ten to twelve pounds to get up to sixty pounds overall. I made sure he ate well, mixing wet food and dry food. He ate dinner when we did, and I always made sure he was served first. I also would give him treats and healthy snacks. Once a week, I would stop at McDonald's and buy him an order of pancakes and a sausage. He loved that so much and would get excited in the car when he saw the Golden Arches as I pulled into the drive-through. I didn't do it more than once a week because I wanted to make sure he ate mostly healthy food, but a trip to McDonald's was a special treat that he loved.

He also got his own bedroom in our house—the large closet in our master bedroom. He had a bed in there, and that's where he slept. When he didn't sleep, he liked to look out the bedroom window at our front yard. He was such a great guard dog that I never had any fear. He also got along well with Buddy, and they often played together.

Reik was a perfect dog on the job. He was so talented, more so than most of the other protection dogs, all of whom are exceptional animals and among the best trained and skilled in the world. The Belgian Malinois breed's sense of smell is amazing—it is about a hundred thousand times stronger than a human's. They can distinguish between many kinds of smells. For example, his sense of smell was so strong that if he got near the kitchen, his nose could distinguish every single spice in the spice rack.

But not every dog can use that sense of smell in an effective way. That's where the training comes in—we have to teach the dogs to let us know when explosives might be present. That is done by presenting smells and then rewarding the dog with a treat when they detect it. That's why they get excited—they know something good to eat or a favorite toy is coming.

Our training consisted of numerous drills for dogs to detect explosives, and Reik was perfect every time. It is important for the handler to listen to clues from the dog—and this is something many handlers fail at doing. The dog and the handler must have a special connection. The dog can't speak, so the handler must know the clues the dog is communicating and understand. Even though the handler has the leash, the dog is in control. I understood that as a handler, I had to let Reik do his job and not pull him away or in another direction.

Reik and I had a deep bond, and we excelled in the training. He reacted more quickly to detecting explosives than other dogs and never fell for the decoys that trainers put out. We were the perfect team. After the seventeen-week training ended, Reik and I graduated with six other classmates, and he and I won the top award for detection. He was flawless in the detection tests and never once came up with a false response, which is rare.

With my beloved Reik, a Belgian Malinois, at Widener University in 2014. (Photo by Melanie Franz.)

On patrol in Washington with Reik in 2011.

Once we completed K-9 training, we had to do two more weeks of on-the-job training before we went fully operational. We have a critically important mission, and we undergo significant amounts of training with great seriousness. Failure is not an option, we often say.

When we went operational, we were assigned to patrol the White House, what in the Secret Service we jokingly call "the Rock," a play on the nickname for Alcatraz. It's the home and office of one the most powerful leaders in the world, and its security is treated as such. I would walk in there every day amazed at how far I—a refugee who had once been homeless—had come.

I had gone from no house to the White House.

Reik and I were given assignments at the entrances, sniffing every visitor who came into the compound for any reason—I mean *everyone*, from senators, to kings and queens and presidents of foreign nations, to movie stars. Nobody gets a free pass into the White House. If a vehicle of any kind came through the gate, Reik and I would sweep it, looking for any possible explosive or chemical that a terrorist might have planted there. We trusted no one and thoroughly vetted every vehicle.

When parts of the film *National Treasure: Book of Secrets* were filmed at the White House, Reik and I screened the movie star Nicolas Cage as well as every single piece of equipment the crew brought with them for filming. There were many transfer trucks full of lights and cameras, but none could go inside until Reik had done a sweep and sniffed it to deem it safe.

We had not been on the job in the White House long when a high-ranking officer asked how I would feel about working the overnight shift. I was glad to do it because it would give me time at home with my mother, who was in her late eighties. Her health was good, and her mind was sharp, but she was slowing down and I wanted to be there for her the way that she had been there for me for so many years. Sophy worked regular business hours, and my kids were off at school, so my mom was home alone for long stretches.

The overnight schedule was great. I arrived home in the morning about breakfast time and was able to see the kids off to school and visit with my mom, and then I'd sleep some during the day. I've never slept much, maybe three or four hours at a time, so when I awoke, I could spend more time with my mom. I know many Americans often put their parents into nursing homes when they get old, but I would never do that. I could have afforded the very best nursing home, but I wanted my mom to be where she wanted to be—with us.

She also loved spending time with Reik and would pet him and walk him and talk to him. He was such a sweet dog, and he loved her too. She would sneak him so many extra treats that I worried he would get fat. He had reached the ideal weight of sixty pounds in the first year I handled him, so I had started feeding him mostly healthy, organic food to maintain that weight. I kept a close eye on what my mom was feeding him and scolded her when I caught her slipping him table scraps and other goodies. But I also liked to spoil him with some limits, so I took him to McDonald's once a week for pancakes and once a month I fed him a piece of steak. On his birthday, recorded as January 2, we cooked a steak for him and sang "Happy Birthday."

Reik was such a beautiful dog. He had a light, cream-colored coat that had tints of gold in it when the sun hit him. He had perky ears and a touch of gray on his face. His eyes were expressive—as expressive as any human's. I could look at him and read his mind, and I felt like he could do the same to me. I've always had a special bond with dogs—it was like that with my first dog, Dino, the French bulldog in Cambodia. It was the same with my second Dino, the German shepherd in Maryland, and our second German shepherd, Buddy, who shared the house with Reik. They were all special, but Reik and I were together twenty-four hours a day, seven days a week.

We worked twelve-hour shifts patrolling the grounds of the White House in the middle of the night, always alert for trouble while President George W. Bush and later President Barack Obama and the first families slept. I appreciated this special duty that we were assigned and knew that a terrorist could try to attack the White House at any minute. In my childhood, I had seen cruelty and depravity. I knew that some men were willing to kill the innocent and had no regard for human decency, so I stayed alert and on my toes at all times. Even when it was four o'clock in the morning and all was quiet in Washington, I was ready. Reik was ready too. He sensed my every thought, and he was loyal. Even though I was speaking to him quietly in Khmer, we were Americans and we were assigned one of the most important jobs in all the world—keeping our leaders safe.

AFTER WE HAD PROVEN OURSELVES at the White House, we began to be assigned to travel with the president and the vice president on many trips. In the years we worked together, Reik and I visited forty-nine states—every state but Maine. We traveled to Texas with President Bush and later to Hawaii with President Obama. We did sweeps at campaign stops everywhere from California to New England and all points in between.

Reik traveled in a large kennel on the military planes we flew in ahead of the president, and he was the most patient traveler you can ever imagine. He never barked. He would sleep during the flight, but when it was time to work, he knew it. He would come to life and eagerly sniff whatever it was we had to sweep. The work was hard and important—bombs could be anywhere, so we screened big arenas, stages in public parks, and thousands of conference and meeting rooms. We would also check out hotel and conference rooms before the president and vice president could enter.

We stayed in nearby hotels when we traveled with the president and his team. When I could, I would get a room with two beds—one for me and one for Reik. If we couldn't, I would get a room with a king- or queen-sized bed so Reik and I would have plenty of room.

In addition to the frequent trips in the United States, Reik and I were assigned to travel on many overseas trips. I have been to almost every country in Europe, throughout the Middle East, to the Philippines, Japan, South Korea, and Vietnam. Reik and I fulfilled our duty to keep the president and vice president safe in more than a dozen countries.

I've seen temples and palaces around the world and had a front-row seat to many significant events in American history. I've worked security details at so many significant Washington events it would take too long for me to list them.

I CAN'T TELL YOU DETAILS about some of the things Reik and I found, due to the confidential nature of our jobs, but there were many times we helped avert possible disasters. I would never divulge any of the secrets that my commanding officers, all the way up to the president, expect me to conceal. I have had this successful career not only because I work hard and am committed to doing an excellent job but also because I am a team player and loyal to the Secret Service and the office. It is called the *Secret* Service for a reason. I hope you are not looking for an exposé here, because you won't get that from me.

But I can tell you a few vague details about one incident I'll always remember. Because of operational security reasons, I cannot divulge the specific location or exact year this happened, other than to say that we were traveling ahead of the vice president in a foreign country. Reik and I were assigned to do an advance sweep in the airport before the vice president arrived. Usually, we didn't find anything, but we were always diligent and thorough. Reik was so trustworthy that I let him off the leash to walk with me as we checked the terminal. He and I would walk through every inch of the space, and he would sniff anything that could possibly be a bomb or weapon of some sort.

We had been scanning the airport for more than an hour when we came upon an unattended backpack tucked away in a corner behind some empty seats. It was close to the gate where the vice president would get off the plane. Reik went straight for the backpack, put his nose on it, and then went back to it again. He looked at me and raised his nose, and then he sat and stared intently at the bag. This was his signal for explosives. I knew right away it was what we call a "hot bag."

I immediately called out, "My dog found explosives." Our officers and the local police who were working with us rapidly cleared the area, sending passengers and airport staff running away. Reik and I got out of there too. It's our job to find the explosives, but once we do, other experts are brought in. Local hazmat experts came in with special protective suits and a bomb-handling robot, seized the bag, and carried it away to examine and diffuse it, if necessary.

I often wonder—what if Reik and I had not found that backpack? What might have happened? Can you imagine the repercussions of a bomb attack on the vice president? It could have had global implications, but because Reik and I were good at our jobs and did what we were supposed to, nothing happened. We didn't make history, but we helped prevent an act that could have made for a terrible history. Our role was silent and didn't make the news. That's life for a Secret Service officer. When we do our job well, no one notices, and that's how it should be.

Although there was no fanfare, I made sure Reik knew he had done something special. That night, I ordered two steaks from room service—one for me and one for him—and we celebrated in our own way.

Home

[2005–2012]

I N **2007,** after I'd been with the Secret Service for five years, Sophy and I built a new house in northern Maryland, close to the town of Frederick, where Sophy had found a good job working with technology. It was our dream home. We chose a vacant lot and met with the builder. It was an amazing experience to design our own home. It featured three floors—four if you count the large, finished basement—and a living room with a high ceiling next to a spacious gourmet kitchen.

The house was a long drive from the White House, especially during traffic, but it was worth it, and it was close to Sophy's job. The home in total measured more than five thousand square feet of living space, with eight bedrooms. It offered plenty of room for my kids, my mom, and relatives who often visited and stayed with us. We hung a large painting of the temple of Angkor Wat over the fireplace.

I often would walk into the living room after a long day at work and look around in awe. It was so different from the places I had lived in the past: a one-room shack with a tin roof and a curtain for a door when I was a young child; the horrid conditions of the Killing Fields, which included some time sleeping outdoors on the ground; the shacks of the refugee camps; and even the cramped apartments in Maryland when we first arrived.

I could never forget those places.

IN 2005, two years before we had moved into the new house, we had made an amazing discovery. Sophy got a phone call one evening from her father, who had remained in Cambodia. He lived in a small town outside Battambang City. She had stayed in touch with him and talked to him often. I had never met him in person, but we communicated frequently and sent him money and long-distance telephone cards so he could call us.

Sophy spoke to him for a minute, and then her eyes got wide.

"He wants to tell you something," Sophy said, handing me the phone.

I took it from her and said hello.

"I met your sister," he said. "At the market. She said her name is Poch. She knew a lot about your family."

I could barely speak. My mother and I had tried to locate Poch years before, but with no luck. We had help from the Buddhist temples who had contacts in Cambodia, and my mother wrote to the few relatives she could find who had remained, but we could not find any record of Poch or my grandmother. The chaos of the Killing Fields had disrupted everything in the country. After trying for a number of years, we gave up and assumed the worst. So many had died in Cambodia of starvation and disease that we feared they were lost and we might never know what happened to them. It was a sadness we had learned to live with.

My mind raced back more than twenty-five years before, when I was only twelve and Poch was five. I had seen her a few times at my grandmother's rural shack, after the Vietnamese pushed the Khmer Rouge out of the cities and before we had gone to the camps at the Thai border. That was in 1979, but it seemed like a million years ago.

I thought about destiny and how what seem like little things make such big differences in a person's life. All those hard years and horrible fates that befell so many of my people rushed up in my mind.

I had to take some deep breaths and compose myself.

"Are you there?" Sophy's father asked.

"Yes, I'm here," I said. "It's hard to believe. How did you meet her?"

"I met her at the market. She works there. I told her that my daughter Sophy was doing well in America. She said she thought her brother and mother were in America, but she could not find them. When I told her your mother's name and your name, she started to cry. She said, 'That's my mother and my brother.'"

I was speechless. After a long pause, he said, "I have her phone number."

I wrote the number down and thanked him. I did not tell my mother right away because I was suspicious. We had been contacted before by Cambodians who had claimed they were related to us, but when my mom and I investigated, we found the claims were false.

I worried that if I told my mom I had found my sister—my mom's youngest daughter, her baby—and then it turned out not to be true, it would break her heart. She was eighty-eight, and she had had her heart broken enough in her long life. She was strong physically and mentally sharp for her age, but I wanted to protect her as much as I could. She had protected me for so many years.

I went up to the bedroom and closed the door while my mom was watching TV downstairs. I took a deep breath and dialed the number. If it was not true, I wouldn't bring up my sister's memory with my mom, because I knew it was painful for her. I nervously listened to the distant rings of the call trying to reach the other side of the world.

"*Soo-sdey*," my sister Poch answered, a Khmer phrase for "hello." The moment I heard her voice, I knew she was telling the truth. I didn't let on right away, but how she talked reminded me of my grandmother's and my mother's voices. She was family. I introduced myself and asked her questions about my grandmother and other relatives who had stayed behind. She knew the family names and history well. She knew all about what had happened to our father. She said that our paternal grandmother, Oun Sum, had died years before.

After a few minutes, I could contain my emotions no longer. "*Pa oun srey*," I said, the Khmer word for "younger sister," and I began to cry. I tried to compose myself and said, "It is so good to talk to you again. To know that you are OK. We thought you had not survived."

"How is my mother?"

"Hold on," I said.

I carried the portable phone downstairs and went to where my mom was sitting with Reik. She was petting him and watching a gardening show. I found the remote and turned off the TV and sat down next to her.

She looked angry that I had turned off the television while she was watching, but then she turned and saw the tears in my eyes and became alarmed. "What is it, Son? What's wrong?"

"It's OK, Mom. It's good news. Sophy's dad found Poch. She's alive."

My mom's jaw dropped, and her eyes opened wide and immediately teared up. "Poch? I don't believe it."

"I am talking to her now." I handed her the phone. She looked at it for a moment and then put the receiver to her ear. "Hello?" she said.

I watched as she listened. Soon the tears began to flow and she cried aloud, but they were tears of joy.

WE BEGAN MAKING regular phone calls to Poch and sent her long-distance calling cards so she could call us, as well as some money to help support her. She was thirty years old, single, and did not have children.

Reestablishing this connection to Poch brought up my intense memories of Cambodia, many of which were painful. For twenty-two years, I had worked hard in America to learn English and get an education and build a career, allowing me to distract myself from the brutal life I had lived in the Killing Fields followed by the uncertainty and squalor of the refugee camps. I love my native country, but I wanted to succeed in my new country, which I also love. I couldn't live in the past and the present at the same time, so I had chosen the present.

My past, those years in the Killing Fields, were imprinted on me in a way that would never leave. I thought back to April 1975 and how my mom hired a motorcycle taxi to take Poch, who was one year old, out into the country to my grandmother's only days before the Khmer Rouge invaded. That was a stroke of good fortune for Poch, as she did not have to endure the Killing Fields. As young as she was, she might not have survived had my mom not made that decision.

Talking with Poch also brought up memories of my pa. She was too young to have memories of him, but she knew his story well because she had grown up with his mother. My pa's memory was always with me. I often thought of what he would have thought if he could see me armed and in uniform, reporting for duty at the White House.

When Sophy's father died in 2006, the year after we met Poch,

Sophy returned to Cambodia to attend his funeral and see her family. She also visited with Poch, and they became close through that visit.

Poch wanted to emigrate to the United States, so I completed the paperwork and applied to bring her to this country. However, it was much harder for immigrants from Cambodia to win entry to the United States in 2006 than it had been in the early 1980s when we received political refugee status. (Even then, we were lucky. Again, here is fate at play. What if we had not won the lottery? We could have become French citizens, Canadians, or Australians. Some Cambodians were sent from the refugee camps in Thailand back to Cambodia to live. What if that had been us? Why were we so fortunate while others were not? I believe everything happens for a reason, but the gods don't explain the reasons to us.)

Although I knew the number of Cambodians who could emigrate each year was limited, I hoped that my position with the Secret Service might influence her case and that she would be welcomed as a citizen. I put in an application with the Immigration and Naturalization Service, but we had no luck.

She was denied, and there was nothing I could do.

We were disappointed, but we continued our long-distance relationship with Poch by phone. I sent money for her to help support herself. When social media and video chat technology came along and she got a smartphone, we began to chat with her that way. It was so great to see her face and hear her voice.

IN SEPTEMBER 2012, my sister Poch called me early one morning. "President Obama is coming to Cambodia!" she said.

She had heard this news before I had. President Obama was scheduled to attend a meeting of the Association of Southeast Asian Nations in Phnom Penh in November. A sitting American president had never visited Cambodia. It would be a historic moment, the first time the leaders of the two countries would meet on Cambodian soil.

I had to go on this trip. I spoke to my commanding officer that day and asked to be assigned to the Cambodian security detail. It was something I had never done—officers don't choose the trips, the higher-ups choose whom they want to take and where they go. But this trip was different. "I don't care what you want me to do, I want to go on that trip," I said. "I'll do anything you need. You don't have to pay me over-time. I can be very helpful. I know the country. I know the language. I know what it's like there."

He nodded, and I continued, "I'm the first and only native-born Cambodian to work for the Secret Service. I speak the Khmer language. It was my first language. I grew up there, and my dog Reik understands Khmer too."

He smiled at this. "Write a memo to me making the request, and I'll do what I can," he said. "It should be fine. We'll need protection dogs to do the sweeps beforehand."

The point I made about Reik speaking Khmer was a sore point for some of the dog handlers. A few believed I had taught Reik the language so no other handler could take him from me. No handlers commanded their dogs in a language other than English. But that wasn't why. I did it because Reik responded well to it, and Khmer is the language he heard in my home. My mom talked to him more than anybody. I did like that the commands in Khmer gave an air of secrecy to our work. No one knew what I was telling Reik to do, and that worked well for us.

I wrote my memo requesting to go on the trip to Cambodia, and, thankfully, my participation was approved.

I BEGAN TO GET READY for the trip. I was so excited to return and to see my sister Poch for the first time in thirty-two years, but I also was apprehensive. This would force me to even more directly confront the memories of my childhood: seeing my father for the last time before he was executed; my dog Dino being killed; witnessing numerous deaths; almost starving and being worked to death; being tortured; and seeing thousands upon thousands of corpses stacked and strewn throughout the landscape.

I had tried to put all those nightmarish memories out of my mind, but they will always be with me. This trip would bring them up even more than reconnecting with Poch had. My emotions were so strong, and I thought about how great it could be if my father were alive and could greet me at the airport. We had never found his remains, so perhaps it could be possible. I was extremely proud to be going home as an officer in the U.S. Secret Service, one of the most elite agencies in the world. My dog Reik and I would protect President Obama and his staff there, ensuring that no attacks would threaten him or the United States. I imagined what a moment that would be if my pa could see me get off the plane. But I knew he would not be there to greet me. I knew that he had been killed by the Khmer Rouge.

THE TRIP GENERATED a great deal of advance news coverage in Cambodia. The Voice of America Khmer Service, which has an office in Washington, learned about me. They interviewed me and broadcast a story about my life leading up to the trip.

When the C-17 I traveled on in advance of President Obama arrived in Phnom Penh, I was shaking with nerves when it came time to get off the plane. That feeling passed quickly when Reik and I walked out and were treated like celebrities. Everyone there knew who I was—not just the Cambodians, but also American military who were stationed there. They had all seen me on TV.

A Cambodian general approached me on the tarmac and shook my hand. "Welcome home, Officer Oun," he said. Soldiers, police officers, security guards, airline and airport employees, and even passengers in the terminal watched me through the windows. Many more followed the general and shook my hand and welcomed me, including many Cambodians who seemed thrilled to speak to me in Khmer and hear me respond in their language.

It was the closest I've ever been to being famous.

I could see my fellow Secret Service officers watching me, and I noticed a new appreciation in their looks. They were seeing the full picture of who I was and where I had come from. They were learning about Cambodia, and they were learning more about me. Some of them had known me for ten years, but they hadn't considered my past.

After we finished our meetings and security work at the Phnom Penh airport, I took Reik to our hotel. We stayed in the center of the city, very close to the Royal Palace. It was the palace built in 1866 where Prince Sihanouk, who had died only a month before my visit, and many other Cambodian royalty had lived.

I checked into our room—one with two beds so Reik would have his own—and showered and put on my civilian clothes. A fellow dog handler agreed to watch Reik while I went to dinner with my sister.

I was so excited to see my sister Poch, but also nervous. Our separation had been so long. I had not spent much time in her presence—only that first year of her life—but I had thought about her so much. She and I had the same blood. For years I had thought she was gone, and here I was about to see her.

I went down a few minutes before I was supposed to meet her outside the hotel. Poch was already there, waiting for me on the sidewalk. She looked so much like my mother had when she was younger, but I also could see my father's face in her face. I could see my face in her face. "*Pa oun srey*," I said.

We ran to each other and hugged in a long embrace. Both of us cried, standing right there in front of the hotel. The tears were tears of joy—joy that we had survived the genocide and desperation of more than thirty years before—but also tears of sadness that we had been separated for so long.

I saw a few of my fellow Secret Service officers coming out of the hotel to go to dinner. One came over from the group and asked if I was OK. "Yes," I said, wiping tears from my face. "This is my sister Poch. We have not seen each other in many years."

Poch smiled, but she didn't understand. He nodded and told Poch it was nice to meet her, and then he politely excused himself.

She and I went to dinner, and it was so great to share a meal with her. I was thrilled to have so many Cambodian foods to choose from, including many dishes I hadn't eaten in years. In America, with the exception of Cambodian neighborhoods in Philadelphia and Long Beach, California, there are very few Cambodian restaurants. The closest thing in America is Thai or Vietnamese food, but Cambodian dishes are distinctive, using fermented fish paste and stronger flavors, both bitter and sour. Smelling the fresh scents of soups and shrimp and pork dishes carried me back to my childhood.

It also was wonderful to sit and talk with Poch. She lived near Battambang City and had come to Phnom Penh to see me. She worked as a housekeeper and a cook for a Cambodian general and his family.

During the meal, we talked about our current lives, but I knew the

In 2012 in Cambodia with my sister Poch, whom I had not seen since 1979.

discussion would turn to our childhoods. After the plates were cleared, I asked her what she knew about our pa. "Grandmother talked about our pa all the time," she said. "She told me about how he was a brave soldier and very loyal to Cambodia. It broke her heart so much when he was killed. She said he was such a good son and a good father. The tragedy of the Khmer Rouge murdering him was so sad for her. I don't remember him, but I feel like I know him through Grandmother's memories. I am so glad I have gotten to know you. You were his only son. You look like the photograph Grandmother had of him."

I started crying again, and she did too. We talked more about our family and the hardships that had befallen us. I told her about our mother and how she had done the right thing in taking Poch to the country before the Khmer Rouge invasion. I told her about my other mothers— Oum Sakum, who, along with her husband and my uncle, Ho Kim Ban, had been killed by the Khmer Rouge; and Ath Yonn, who had immigrated to America and remained close to us still.

I talked, often through tears, about the hardships of the Killing Fields and the year that followed, when we made many treacherous trips back and forth to the Thai border. "It was so hard when we decided to stay at the border," I said. "We wanted to come back to get you, but then we were carried into the U.N. refugee camps in Thailand and couldn't come back. My mom tried writing to you, but there was no mail service to rural Cambodia then, and we had no way of communicating. It was so hard when we moved to various camps and then when we left for the United States. We had always hoped to find you and bring you with us, but we had no luck."

"That's OK, brother. I understand. You are here now. We are connected after all these years."

I was in Phnom Penh for three more days. When I wasn't working to protect President Obama, I was with Poch. We ate several more wonderful meals and toured Phnom Penh, and I took her shopping. I was thrilled to get to know her this way. She's very smart and kind, and I am proud to call her my sister. It was hard telling her goodbye, knowing how far away I would be from her again, but we vowed to stay in touch. I promised to return to Cambodia.

ON THE FLIGHT HOME, a number of officers asked me about my life. Several of them had visited the Tuol Sleng Genocide Museum, a Killing Fields memorial in a high school-turned-prison that the Khmer Rouge had named S-21. Thousands were tortured and executed there. The museum tells the story of the Khmer Rouge atrocities and remembers many victims in stark photographs taken before they were killed. I have read about this museum and am glad that people visit it to learn about this terrible moment in history, but I have no desire to go. I lived through it. I do not want to see the gruesome scenes in vivid detail ever again. It would be too sad and emotional for me.

A fellow officer sat next to me on the first leg of the flight and told me about his time in Phnom Penh, which included a visit to the Tuol Sleng Genocide Museum. After a while, he asked hesitantly, "Were you—were you there during the Killing Fields?"

"Yes," I said. "I lived through it. It was terrible." I told him some of my story—about working torturous days in rice paddies and almost starving, and that my father had been executed. I talked for a few minutes, but I barely scratched the surface. I could see in his face, however, that he couldn't comprehend what I had survived.

I'm not sure I can even comprehend it anymore.

He extended his hand and shook mine. "You've got an amazing story, Officer Oun. I admire your strength and courage."

I thanked him and turned to check on Reik, who was sleeping in his kennel.

Several other officers approached me to talk about my past on the long trip home. I gave them a few details, and they shook my hand and said kind words. I had talked to many of these officers about many topics—football games, our work, our families, and our lives in America. I had never told them that I had been a slave, a starved refugee, and a victim of torture. They seemed a little stunned to learn about my past, and part of me wishes I hadn't revealed the hardships I have overcome. I knew they saw me in a new light. Another part of me, however, decided that I wanted to write the story of my life to create a record of my experience. I knew it would be difficult to write such a book, but I thought it would be important to do so. We cannot forget our histories, but must tell these hard stories with the hope that younger generations will not allow such past mistakes to be repeated.

I NAPPED on long stretches of the flight. With stops for refueling, it took a full twenty-four hours. I had much from the trip to think about, but I also was looking forward to getting back to my home in Maryland and seeing Sophy, my kids, and my mom, who was eager to see photos of Poch and hear about my visit. I also had missed my dog Buddy, and Reik missed his canine friend too.

My family in 2015. Seated, from left, Ath Yonn,
my aunt who was one of my "other mothers" in Cambodia, and my mom;
standing, from left, Timmy, Jenny, Sophy, and me.

I got excited as I drove from the airport to our home in Maryland. I had been away for a week and had much to tell my family about my trip. I'm always glad to get home from traveling, but this time was even more special.

I smiled when I saw my house and pulled into the driveway. Buddy saw me from the front window and barked happily when I got out of the car. The front door opened, and he came running out of the house for me to pet him.

I let Reik out, and he barked happily back at Buddy. They ran to play in the backyard. Sophy and my mom and my kids came out to meet me, and we all hugged upon my return.

I held them close and thought, *Life is good, here in America.*

I'll never forget where I came from and what I endured—but this is my home now, my American dream.

I'm blessed to be here.

Epilogue

[2018–Present]

AWAKE at three in the morning, my usual time, on the third Saturday of August 2019. Sophy wakes up shortly after I do. I go downstairs to clean the house for expected guests and she starts working in the kitchen. She and my sister Dy and my cousin Lin Ban have been preparing a feast for several days.

About six o'clock, I wake up my son, Timmy, and he and I move all the furniture out of our spacious living room, crowding our large couches with built-in recliners and a large coffee table into the dining room. The furniture removed, we set up a shrine in front of the fireplace in the living room that includes photographs of my mother. We also place pillows for three Buddhist monks who will sit, chant, and pray.

A year earlier, on August 5, 2018, my mother passed away at the age of 101. On this Saturday, we are hosting the traditional Cambodian Buddhist ceremony that celebrates someone's memory one year after their death. Later this morning my family and friends will kneel on the floor before the monks to honor my mother's spirit and memory. It will mark the third of three ceremonies held in our faith to honor my mom.

She lived with us right up until the end of her life. In her last years, we had moved her bedroom to the first floor, next to the guest bathroom off the living room, so she would not have to climb stairs. She

My mother, Sin Chhoeum, at the age of 97.

filled it with photos of Cambodia and family and a few relics, including a Buddha statue. Her homeland was always in her heart.

My mother's mind was sharp and her health strong until her very last days, when she began to grow weak. She died at Frederick Memorial Hospital, where I took her when she began to be short of breath. She had not been sick, but simply passed due to old age.

She'd had such a long life. Fortunately, her death did not involve extended months of suffering, as it can for many elderly. She had suffered more than enough four decades before.

Even though my mother lived to be more than one hundred and I had known that she would not live forever, I was heartbroken. She meant everything to me. I had lived under the same roof with her all of my life except for two years during the Killing Fields. She had been through so much, and she had persevered and stayed strong for her family.

She is the reason I am where I am today

FIVE WEEKS after my mother passed away, Reik died. He was sixteen years old, the human equivalent of 112 years. He had been retired since

2013, when he had turned twelve. After his retirement, Reik became our full-time pet.

It took some time for him to adjust to retirement. He had been a working Secret Service protection dog for nine years, and that routine was ingrained in him. It took some adjustment for me too. I joined the ranks of the K-9 trainers, which was a very different daytime routine. In the mornings when I would get ready to leave for work, Reik would follow me to the door and sit there, expecting to go. He looked surprised when I did not take him with me. This went on for many months until he finally accepted the fact that he was retired.

He had it good, though. My mom spoiled him constantly, and I often took him for long walks. I continued to take him to McDonald's once a week for pancakes. He slept at the foot of our bed right up until the end, often jumping up between me and Sophy.

In 2015, he became our only pet when our German shepherd Buddy died. Reik missed his canine friend. When Reik was bored, I gave my daughter Jenny small samples of gunpowder to hide around the yard. He thrilled at the opportunity to sniff it out.

Reik breathed his last breath on September 11, 2018, the seventeenth anniversary of the terrorist attacks on the country he and I spent thousands of hours protecting. I do believe he sensed the significance and chose to depart on this hallowed date. He was as loyal, smart, and kind an animal as anyone has ever known.

I was heartbroken yet again, losing my dog that had been so close to me following the death of my dear, beloved mother. It was a very difficult couple of months to deal with their deaths so close together. I shed many tears.

To remember Reik on the day of my mom's one-year celebration, I designed and printed fifty T-shirts that I give to my guests as they arrive. The front of the shirt features my mother's image and the dates 10/11/1917–8/5/2018, which commemorate her life, beneath her photo. On the back, it includes a large photo of Reik in front of the White House's south portico with his dates, 1/3/2002–9/11/2018, beneath it. I know my mom would have loved those T-shirts. She would have been thrilled to know Reik was part of her memorial service.

My mother and Reik might be gone from this Earth, but their memories and spirits live forever in my heart.

IN MARCH 2015, I returned to Cambodia when Michelle Obama visited Siem Reap, where the temples of Angkor Wat are located. She was there to promote her Let Girls Learn initiative, established to give more girls around the world opportunities for education.

Just as Barack Obama had been the first American president to visit Cambodia, Michelle Obama was the first sitting First Lady to step foot in the country. Although she didn't visit Cambodia, First Lady Rosalynn Carter had visited Cambodian refugee camps near the border in Thailand in 1979 and was very sympathetic to the plight of Killing Fields survivors. She became very influential in encouraging the United States to accept refugees from Cambodia and other parts of Southeast Asia.

When Michelle Obama's visit was announced, I was working as a K-9 trainer, and I wrote a memo requesting to go. The Secret Service generously granted my request. I was thrilled to be there for another historic moment connecting my native homeland and my adopted country.

I received another hero's welcome, talking with many Cambodians in my native language who were amazed that an officer of the Secret Service came from their country. It was a thrill to visit Angkor Wat, which I had been to only once in my life. That first visit was when I was a toddler and too young to remember. My mother told me that I got bat poop in my eyes and cried for a long time. Needless to say, my second visit was much better! The grandeur of the great temples that date back nine hundred years is astounding. Angkor Wat, which is the world's largest religious site, is a World Heritage Site and truly one of the great wonders of the world. Its spires have served as a symbol of my homeland for centuries, and I'm proud to have a painting of it hanging prominently in our home.

While traveling with Michelle Obama, I spent time after my work shifts with my younger sister Poch. It was so good to see her in person again and share many meals with her.

By this time, Poch was helping me facilitate efforts I funded to support Cambodians in need. So many are poor in Cambodia, particularly in rural areas. Many don't have enough food to eat or fresh water to drink, and children lack educational opportunities.

Instead of donating money to organizations, which have administrative costs, I prefer to give directly to those who need it so all the proceeds help. I send funds to Poch, and she works with Buddhist temples to disburse the money to assist those in poverty.

One older couple we learned about who were friends of Sophy's late father illustrate the extreme hardships some Cambodians face. The man is blind and his wife is deaf. They can't work and have no one to support them. They also have a grandchild in their care. I've supported them by sending my sister money to buy them bags of rice and noodles. As little as $30 goes a long way, buying a one-hundred-pound bag of rice.

Another project I'm undertaking is to pay for wells in villages that need water. I send the money to my sister, and she goes into the villages without good sources of water and helps set up the wells. It costs $250 for a hand-drawn well and $1,000 for a well with an electric pump. She coordinates with Buddhist temples that help guide us to areas that need the most assistance. Before she passed, my mother helped identify villages that needed water and paid for a few wells. She, as I do, felt so fortunate that we found comfortable lives here in America, and she wanted to share our good fortune with those in Cambodia who need help.

If this book is successful and makes money, all proceeds due to me and my coauthor will go to Cambodia to support those in need. I also want to support education in Cambodia. My family and I have been blessed to have received help from so many—starting with the United Nations refugee camps in Thailand through the many assistance programs in the United States when we first arrived and were getting settled, all the way through financial aid I received in college. I want to return the many favors and generosity that I have received by paying it forward to help those in my home country who are very poor. I would not be where I am without the support that helped me when I needed it. I hope that some of the children we help can go on to live their own dreams as I have been able to do.

I recently have formalized my charitable efforts in Cambodia by creating the Leth Oun Cambodia Relief Fund. If you bought this book, you have already contributed. Thank you from the bottom of my heart. If you want to donate, we would greatly appreciate your gifts. You can give by visiting our website at LOCRF.org. As little as $30 can feed a family in Cambodia for a long time.

AFTER REIK RETIRED, I did not get assigned another protection dog but instead fulfilled a number of different duties for the Secret Service: K-9 trainer, bicycle patrol, and assignments protecting the White House and the vice president's residence. I've also worked protection on many trips, protecting the president and vice president on appearances in the States and around the world. Even after many years, I still am in awe of the job I get to do and the importance of my assignment. Throughout the coronavirus pandemic, I remained in service, working on the front lines to protect the leaders of this country.

In January 2020, I was recognized for twenty years of service to the federal government—two with the Department of Justice and eighteen with the Secret Service. That benchmark is significant because it will allow me to draw full federal retirement benefits. I'm not sure when I will retire, but retirement is mandatory at fifty-seven. I turned fifty-six in October 2022, so it will not be too long.

When I do retire, I hope to spend more of my time helping others and providing the kind of assistance that was shown to me when I needed it.

THE GODS SMILE on my mother's one-year memorial celebration, giving us a clear and beautiful sky with drier air and more pleasant temperatures than usual for a late August day. The weather could not be more perfect.

As family and friends begin to arrive throughout the morning, we smile and hug and are happy to see one another. Khmer greetings and laughter fill the house as older relatives and young children and all ages in between join us.

My brother-in-law and dear friend Yom Yong arrives in a van with three Buddhist monks from the Wat Khmer Palelai Buddhist Temple in Philadelphia, the wat where my mother's first memorial service had taken place after she died. During the service, the monks chant and pray, and my friends and family, many of us in the T-shirt with my mom on the front and Reik on the back, all kneel during the service and join in the prayers. We give thanks and pray for my mother's spirit and give our offerings to the gods.

While kneeling before the monks and praying to the gods, I close my eyes and think about my mother and how much she meant to me.

She went through so much to care for us after my pa was killed. She was willing to give up her life for us. When the Khmer Rouge wanted to take my older sister, who had a baby, my mom volunteered to be the one to go cook and clean for them when they hid in the jungles, sparing my sister. My mom did everything she could to protect us during the Killing Fields time.

I hope I was a good son to her and did my best to take care of her in her older years. I can never be thankful enough to my mother.

AFTER THE SERVICE in the morning, we eat and drink and eat some more on this glorious afternoon. Our tables inside the house and on the back patio are covered with seemingly endless amounts of food that we prepared and others brought. Waves of people pass through our house, most Cambodians speaking in Khmer, but also American friends whom we have come to know and love. The celebration stretches through the evening and into the night, with the charcoal grill outside continuing to turn out deliciously spiced pieces of steak on skewers and enough chicken wings to feed hundreds of people. Inside are more varieties of egg rolls, fish dishes, and types of noodles than I can list. We eat like kings and queens.

Many of my Cambodian cousins and aunts and uncles and other friends who have joined us survived the Killing Fields and lived in refugee camps. Had any of us seen a meal like this in the late 1970s or early 1980s, we would have thought we had died and gone to heaven.

We all had been starved and enslaved and some tortured. We had all lost so many loved ones to the Khmer Rouge. But none of us talk about that time on this afternoon. Instead, we drink beer and shots of cognac and laugh and tell stories of the good times, which we have been fortunate enough to experience often in our new lives.

I do not say it, but I think about how amazing it is that my mother and my sisters and I survived that awful period in human history. How did we make it? It's a miracle. I don't think I could survive it at my age, but my mother was older then than I am now. She was in her late fifties and early sixties when we lived as slaves and then refugees. They tried to work us to death. We almost starved to death. Diseases were rampant and we had no medical care. Every day brought the threat that we could be executed on the spot. But we survived. And my mom lived to be 101 years old.

At the Secret Service holiday party in 2014.
From left, my goddaughter Erika Smith, then–Vice President Joe Biden,
Sophy, my niece Jessica Yi, me, and Jill Biden.

Our will to live and our will to love are the strongest wills of all, stronger than anything else. We were scared and we were scarred, but we were not defeated. We loved one another and cared for one another and protected one another. We survived and recovered and made lives in America that make those miserable years seem like they were thousands of years ago, almost like they never happened.

But they did happen, and despite all the success and happiness I've found here in America, I will never forget that suffering. It is important to remember and do all we can to prevent it from happening again. I hope my story can inspire others who have suffered or are suffering. I plan for the rest of my life to try to do my part to help those in need.

I've always liked the quote, "Shoot for the moon. Even if you fail, you'll land among the stars." I was not sure what I was shooting for when I came to America, but I am happy where I landed. If I can survive the Killing Fields of Cambodia to become a protector of the president of the United States, nothing in this world is impossible.

I am living proof of that.

Acknowledgments

J OE SAMUEL STARNES AND I would like to extend heartfelt thanks to our many talented friends, family members, and associates who have offered us assistance, encouragement, and support in numerous ways throughout the journey of writing and publishing this book: Barbara Ryan, Sheryl Raskin, Shaun Vigil, Melanie Franz, Chris Decherd, Chris Hartlove, Maria Goodavage, Vernon Smith, Sophy Oun, Timmy Oun, Jenny Oun, Don Corrigan, Ed Tritt, Kosol Sek, Paul Lelii, Amy Woodworth, Diane Woodworth, Patrick Dolan, Dan Starnes, Summer Starnes, Jonathan Green, Ellen Geiger, Frank Weimann, Miles Orvell, Ashley Petrucci, Gary Kramer, Kate Nichols, Ann-Marie Anderson, Heather Wilcox, Barry Lefkowitz, Douglas Gordon (and everyone at New Door Books), Jessica Handler, William Hastings, Tony Knighton, Anthony Sergi, Elizabeth Adams, Glenn Griffith, Mickey Hess, Kevin Catalano, Karaamat Abdullah, and Dan Hanson. I also would like to extend special gratitude to His Excellency Keo Chhea, Cambodian Ambassador to the United States, for his enthusiasm and support of my book.

I would like to thank three brothers in law enforcement who have been dear friends: retired Capitol Police Lt. Dennis Kelly, DEA Special Agent Eric Duble, and DHS chemical security inspector Ed Barba. Finally, I'd like to thank from the bottom of my heart the men and women of the U.S. Secret Service Uniformed Division whom I have worked alongside for more than twenty years. We have protected campaigns on the hottest days of the year, inaugurations on the coldest days of the year, and America's leaders on extended trips across the country and around the world. You are my friends and family who I can always count on, no matter the day or time or wherever we might be.

—Leth Oun

Coauthor's Note

ETH OUN stepped into my office on a sleepy summer afternoon in 2011 when I was the editor of Widener University's alumni magazine. His story proved to be exceptional—so exceptional that more than a decade later, I am still deeply moved by his life's journey. That meeting eventually led to our close friendship and this book, which has proved to be the hardest yet most fulfilling writing project I've taken on, an experience that has changed me for the better.

Leth, who did not begin learning English until he was seventeen, wrote a much shorter first draft. Through almost five years of numerous interviews, additional writing, and revisions, which were assisted by Dr. Barbara Ryan, professor emerita of sociology who taught Leth at Widener, we completed the book you are holding.

Learning Leth's life story as intimately as I have has prompted me to appreciate with great gratitude the good fortune of the idyllic childhood I had growing up in rural Georgia and the comfortable existence I live today in southern New Jersey. I've been so fortunate compared to many around the world who live in fear of war, hunger, and poverty as Leth and his family did. His story for me is not just his American dream but a dream of America as a place that embraces immigrants of all races and religions and welcomes them into our family, a story that fulfills what the Statue of Liberty symbolizes.

Serving as coauthor for Leth—who introduced me to his fellow Secret Service officers as "my brother" when he took my family on a tour of the White House—is an honor that has been more rewarding than I could have ever imagined when I answered his knock on my office door.

—Joe Samuel Starnes

About the Authors

LETH OUN, a native of Cambodia who survived the Killing Fields, is a veteran U.S. Secret Service officer. He has protected presidents and vice presidents in four administrations in forty-nine states and more than a dozen countries. A political refugee who immigrated to Maryland in 1983, he became an American citizen in 1990. He is a 1998 graduate of Widener University, where he majored in sociology and minored in criminal justice. Before going to work for the federal government in 2000, he held numerous jobs that ranged from working as a bank teller to clerking at convenience stores to washing dishes for $3.15 an hour. He and his wife, Sophy, also a survivor of the Killing Fields, have been married since 1985 and have two grown children.

JOE SAMUEL STARNES has published three critically acclaimed novels, including *Fall Line* in 2011, which was included in the *Atlanta Journal-Constitution*'s "Best of the South" list. His most recent novel, *Red Dirt: A Tennis Novel*, was released in 2015. His first novel, *Calling*, was published in 2005 and reissued in 2014 as an e-book by Mysterious Press and Open Road Media. All three novels are highlighted in a critical essay in *Twenty-First-Century Southern Writers: New Voices, New Perspectives*, which was published by the University Press of Mississippi. He has had journalism appear in the *New York Times*, the *Washington Post*, the *Philadelphia Inquirer*, and various magazines, as well as essays, short stories, and poems in literary journals. He holds a bachelor's degree in journalism from the University of Georgia, an MA in English from Rutgers University–Newark, and an MFA in creative nonfiction from Goucher College.